Acclaim for
Stuff

"Fascinating."
— *People*

"*Stuff* is worth reading not only because of the authors' authority on the subject, but also because of its elegant prose, and its nuanced and well-researched take on the subject."
— *Salon*

"Amazing . . . The authors are refreshingly uncertain about what the causes of hoarding might be [and] rely upon a series of in-depth profiles of women and men, each of whom they treat with remarkable compassion and respect . . . [An] utterly engrossing book. Read it."
— *Washington Post Book World*

"Gripping . . . by turns fascinating and heartbreaking . . . *Stuff* invites readers to reevaluate their desire for things."
— *Boston Globe*

"To those who need to understand hoarders, perhaps in their own family, *Stuff* offers perspective. For general readers, it is likely to provide useful stimulus for examining how we form and justify our own attachments to objects."
— *New York Times Book Review*

"[Frost and Steketee's] examples are rich in storytelling and dialogue, and they admirably balance a fascination with the psychological profiles of their subject with a deep sympathy for their plights . . . The book is a valuable study of a poorly understood condition."
— *Minneapolis Star Tribune*

"Pioneering researchers offer a superb overview of a complex disorder that interferes with the lives of more than six million Americans . . . An absorbing, gripping, important report."
— *Kirkus Reviews,* starred review

"[An] eye-opening study . . . Frost and Steketee write with real sympathy and appreciation for hoarders . . . This succinct, illuminating book will prove helpful to hoarders, their families, and mental health professionals who work with them."
— *Publishers Weekly*

"Fascinating stuff."
— *Booklist*

"Randy Frost and Gail Steketee take a philosophical approach in their engaging and surprisingly cheerful study *Stuff.*"
— *Wilson Quarterly*

"An excellent starting point for family, friends, and neighbors of hoarders, but the vivid writing will attract readers who enjoy fiction or memoirs about extreme behavior."
— *Library Journal*

"Like those classics of psychological study, A. R. Luria's *The Mind of the Mnemonist* and Oliver Sacks's *The Man Who Mistook His Wife for a Hat, Stuff* is authoritative, haunting, and mysterious. It is also intensely, not to say compulsively, readable."
— Tracy Kidder

"A fascinating book — *Stuff* is the stuff of nightmares, of people living in a world subsumed by their obsession to collect and hoard things. You will surely recognize, to one degree or another, a part of yourself in these portraits."
— Jonathan Harr, author of *The Lost Painting* and
  A Civil Action

Other books on hoarding by

RANDY O. FROST AND GAIL STEKETEE

■

Treatment of Compulsive Hoarding: Therapist Guide

Treatment of Compulsive Hoarding: Client Workbook

*Buried in Treasures: Help for Compulsive Acquiring, Saving,
and Hoarding* (with David Tolin)

Stuff

COMPULSIVE HOARDING
AND THE
MEANING OF THINGS

. . .

Randy O. Frost
and Gail Steketee

MARINER BOOKS
HOUGHTON MIFFLIN HARCOURT
BOSTON   NEW YORK

First Mariner Books edition 2011

Copyright © 2010 by Randy O. Frost and Gail Steketee

www.hmhbooks.com

Library of Congress Cataloging-in-Publication Data
Frost, Randy O.
   Stuff : compulsive hoarding and the meaning of things / Randy O. Frost and Gail Steketee.
      p. cm.
   Includes bibliographical references.
   ISBN 978-0-15-101423-1   ISBN 978-0-547-42255-8 (pbk.)
   1. Obsessive-compulsive disorder. 2. Compulsive hoarding.
I. Steketee, Gail. II. Title.
   RC533.F76 2010
   616.85'227 — dc22   2009028273

The names of some of the people mentioned in this book have been changed.

Book design by Victoria Hartman

Printed in the United States of America

DOC 10 9 8 7 6 5 4

Our work on hoarding began more than fifteen years ago with our first study of people struggling with this problem. Work on this book began more than seven years ago when we met and gained the cooperation of the people portrayed here. We dedicate this book to all of these people for their willingness to open their lives to us. We remain in contact with many of them. We have changed identities and details not germane to their stories, while striving to represent their struggle with hoarding as we understand it from their narratives. It is ironic that those who struggle the most with hoarding and its sometimes severe consequences have helped us so much to comprehend their experience and record it as best we can. Our hats are off to all of them, whether their stories appear here or not. They have helped us more than they can know, and we hope that through this book others will understand their plight.

CONTENTS

Dead Body in the Collyer Mansion: *A Prologue to Hoarding*   1

1. Piles upon Piles: *The Story of Hoarding*   17

2. We Are What We Own: *Owning, Collecting, and Hoarding*   44

3. Amazing Junk: *The Pleasures of Hoarding*   63

4. Bunkers and Cocoons: *Playing It Safe*   83

5. A Fragment of Me: *Identity and Attachment*   99

6. Rescue: *Saving Animals from a Life on the Streets*   118

7. A River of Opportunities   134

8. Avoiding the Agony   152

9. You Haven't Got a Clue   169

10. A Tree with Too Many Branches: *Genetics and the Brain*   188

11. A Pack Rat in the Family   216

12. But It's Mine! *Hoarding in Children*   238

13. Having, Being, and Hoarding   262

    Reference List   281

    Acknowledgments   291

STUFF

DEAD BODY IN THE COLLYER MANSION
A Prologue to Hoarding

Here, too, I saw a nation of lost souls,
far more than were above: they strained their chests
against enormous weights, and with mad howls

rolled them at one another. Then in haste
they rolled them back, one party shouting out:
"Why do you hoard?" and the other: "Why do you waste?" . . .

Hoarding and squandering wasted all their light
and brought them screaming to this brawl of wraiths.
You need no words of mine to grasp their plight.

— Dante Alighieri, *The Inferno*

On Friday morning, March 21, 1947, the police in Harlem received a call. "There's a dead body in the Collyer mansion," reported a neighbor.

The call resembled many others the police had received over the years about the eccentric Collyer brothers, Langley and Homer, who lived in a three-story, twelve-room brownstone in a once fashionable section of Harlem. They dutifully checked it out.

The police arrived at the brownstone at 10:00 A.M. When they failed to get in through the front door, the crew used crowbars and axes to force open an iron grille door to the basement. Behind the door was a wall of newspapers, tightly wrapped in small packets and too thick to push through. The rear basement door was similarly blockaded with junk. A call to the fire department produced ladders, allowing the patrolmen to try windows on the second and third floors. Most were barricaded and impassable. By this time, the commotion had attracted hundreds of curious onlookers. Finally, two hours later, Patrolman William Barker squeezed through a front window on the second floor. What he found inside shocked him.

The house was packed with junk—newspapers, tin cans, magazines, umbrellas, old stoves, pipes, books, and much more. A labyrinth of tunnels snaked through each room, with papers, boxes, car parts, and antique buggies lining the sides of the tunnels all the way to the ceiling. Some of the tunnels appeared to be dead ends, although closer inspection revealed them to be secret passageways. Some of the tunnels were booby-trapped to make noise or, worse, to collapse on an unsuspecting intruder. A cardboard box hung low from the roof of one tunnel, and when disturbed it rained tin cans onto any trespasser. More serious were booby traps in which the overhanging boxes were connected to heavier objects such as rocks that could knock someone out.

Patrolman Barker had to push his way over an eight-foot-high wall of stuff in a room with a ten-foot ceiling. In a small clearing in the center of the room, he found the body of sixty-five-year-old Homer Collyer in a sitting position with his head on his knees. Barker leaned out the window and called out, "There's a dead man here!" The emaciated body was covered only in a tattered bathrobe. Homer had not been seen by anyone for several years, and over the past few decades there had been numerous reports of his death. Many of the neighbors believed he had been dead for years, but the autopsy revealed that it had been only about ten hours.

Homer had been blind since 1933 and was nearly paralyzed

with rheumatism. His brother, Langley, fed and cared for him. Langley once told the neighbors that since their father was a doctor and they had an extensive medical library, they had no need of doctors and could care for Homer's problems with a combination of diet (one hundred oranges each week) and rest (Homer kept his eyes closed at all times). The autopsy indicated that Homer died of a heart attack, probably brought on by starvation. Homer's body had to be lifted by stretcher down the fire ladder from the second-story window.

Despite the commotion, there was no sign of Langley. He'd last been seen several days earlier sitting on the steps of the run-down brownstone. Neighbors suspected he was still in the house, perhaps hiding. The Collyer brothers' lawyer, John McMullen, insisted that if Langley were in the house, he would come out. But by Saturday afternoon, there was sufficient concern over Langley's whereabouts that the police department issued a missing person alert. The hunt for Langley became so intense that on one occasion, after a sighting on the subway, the train was stopped just outside the station so that police could search all the cars. Several newspapers put up rewards for information on Langley's whereabouts. In the meantime, the police worried that Langley was indeed hiding somewhere inside the house.

In the days following the discovery of Homer's body, all the New York papers carried the story on the front page. "The Palace of Junk," read the *Daily News* on March 22. "'Ghost Mansion' Yields Body" read another headline. The Collyers quickly became household names.

When Langley failed to appear after three days, the police led an intensive search of the house. Thousands of spectators gathered to see what sort of mysteries would unfold. The house was in such deplorable condition that the Department of Housing and Buildings announced that it would have to be demolished or undergo extensive renovations to be habitable. Leaks from the roof had destroyed most of the upper floor. During inspection, the city building inspector fell through the third floor and was saved only by a conveniently placed beam.

The search and cleanout began in the basement, but after several days city engineers determined that without the tons of stuff supporting them, the walls of the building would not be able to sustain the weight of the contents of the upper floors. They insisted that the excavation begin on the top floor. Police had to force their way in through a skylight. The room was packed to within two feet of the ceiling, and workmen could only crawl in the narrow space. They began emptying the room by throwing things out the window into the rear courtyard. A gas chandelier, the top from a horse-drawn carriage, and a rusted bicycle were among the first things to come crashing down, along with an old set of bedsprings and a sawhorse. The crowds swelled to witness the spectacle and to see if the rumors of a house filled with treasures were true. In the first two days, workers removed nineteen tons of debris. All possessions deemed to have value were stored in a former schoolhouse nearby. Each day of cleaning brought new and strange discoveries: an early x-ray machine, an automobile, the remains of a two-headed fetus. For the police who were involved in the search, the whole affair was a nightmare. Roaches and rats thrived in the mess, alongside more than thirty feral cats that lived in the building.

After nearly three weeks, workmen in the room where Homer was found stumbled on Langley's body, not more than ten feet from where his brother died. While crawling through one of the tunnels to bring Homer some food, Langley's cape, a staple of his odd fashion, had accidentally triggered one of his own booby traps. He was crushed beneath the weight of bales of newspapers and suffocated, trapped between a chest of drawers and a rusty box spring. Rats had chewed away parts of his face, hands, and feet.

Langley apparently died first, and Homer, unable to see or move, died sometime later, perhaps knowing what had happened to his brother. At this point in the cleaning, workers had removed 120 tons of debris, including fourteen grand pianos and a Model T Ford. In the end, they removed more than 170 tons of stuff from the house. In all of the searching and clearing of the house, they never found where Langley slept. There appeared to be no place other than the tunnels for him to lie down.

Langley and Homer Collyer had not always lived this way. They came from a distinguished and wealthy New York family. The brothers' great-grandfather, William Collyer, built one of the largest shipyards on the East River waterfront. A great-uncle, Thomas Collyer, ran the first steamboat line on the Hudson River. Homer and Langley's mother was a Livingston, a member of another esteemed clan. They once received the gift of a piano from Queen Victoria—one of the fourteen found among the hoard. Dr. Herman Collyer, Homer and Langley's father, became a noted obstetrician-gynecologist, and their mother, Susie Gage Frost Collyer, was an opera singer and a renowned beauty. But the pair were first cousins, and their marriage scandalized the socially conscious Collyer and Livingston clans. Most of the family ostracized them.

Herman and his wife moved to the Harlem brownstone in 1909. Dr. Collyer used to paddle a canoe down the East River to Blackwell's Island (now Roosevelt Island), where he worked at City Hospital, and carry it back to the brownstone every night. Like so much other family memorabilia, the canoe was among the debris found in the Collyer mansion.

Susie Collyer insisted that her sons receive the finest education and helped assemble their library of more than twenty-five thousand books. Both studied at Columbia, where Homer was elected to Phi Beta Kappa. He went on to obtain several law degrees and become an admiralty lawyer, but he practiced law only for a short time. Langley studied engineering and graduated from Columbia but never worked as an engineer, though by all accounts he was gifted: he built a generator out of parts of an automobile kept in the basement, and his elaborate tunnels were no doubt a reflection of his engineering skills. He did, however, become a concert pianist of some renown, playing professionally until his debut in Carnegie Hall. Langley would play Chopin for Homer after he went blind and also read the classics to him.

Even before their parents' deaths in the 1920s, the brothers began having less and less contact with the outside world. In 1917, they disconnected their telephone. In 1928, they shut off their gas. Sometime in the 1930s, they had their electricity turned off. Langley told Claremont Morris, a real estate agent who worked with him, that they had simplified their lives by getting rid of those things: "You can't imagine how free we feel." They never opened their mail, and their only contact with the outside world was a crystal radio set that Langley built himself.

The last time Homer was seen outside the house was in early 1940, when Police Sergeant John Collins saw the brothers carrying a tree limb into their basement. Langley did not deny the clutter. Despite the appearance of slovenliness or laziness created by the condition of the house, Langley was always busy and often complained of not having enough time to do the things he needed to do. One of those things, Langley told the police on several occasions, was clearing and organizing his home. He claimed to be saving things so that he and his brother could be self-sufficient.

The Collyers were frequently at odds with the courts for exercising their "freedom." Their failure to pay taxes, mortgage bills, and utilities, as well as neglected bank accounts, brought on injunctions, evictions, and foreclosures. In 1939, after repeated failure to get a response at the door, Consolidated Edison got a court order to break in and remove the company's unused electric meters. When they broke down the door, they found a wall of newspapers and boxes, sacks of rocks, logs, and rubbish blocking their way. An irate Langley, his long white hair partially covered by a bicycle cap, called angrily from a second-floor window that they had no right to break into his home. Reluctantly, however, he allowed the men to take the meters.

In 1942, the bank foreclosed on their house for failure to pay a mortgage note of $6,700. No payments of any kind had been made on the mortgage for eleven years, since shortly after Susie Collyer's death. Because it now legally owned the house, the bank was ordered by the health department to make repairs to the crumbling façade. When the workmen arrived, Langley appeared and ordered them off. A few months later, the bank and city officials appeared at the house to take possession of the property and evict the brothers. They broke down the door with hatchets, but a solid wall of papers stopped their progress. A large crowd gathered, as it always did when things happened at the "Ghost House." The bank officials decided to enter through a second-floor window. After three hours of work, they were only two feet into the house. The sounds of the excavation finally alerted Langley, who demanded to see his lawyer. John McMullen had been the brothers' lawyer for some time and knew of their peculiarities. He was quite frail and elderly; nonetheless, he crawled up the fire ladder and through a tunnel in the parlor to find Langley hiding behind a piano. When McMullen told him that the only way they could avoid eviction was to pay the $6,700, Langley handed him a wad of cash, borrowed a pen, and signed the papers saving his house.

In the fall of 1942, a rumor began spreading through the neighborhood that Homer was dead. It finally reached Sergeant Collins of the 123rd Street Station, who knew the brothers well. The sergeant went to the Collyer house and persuaded Langley to allow him inside to verify that Homer was alive. It took them thirty minutes to traverse the sea of possessions and avoid the booby traps. Finally, they emerged into a small, dark clearing. When Collins turned on his flashlight, he saw Homer, a gaunt figure sitting on a cot and covered by an old overcoat. Homer spoke, "I am Homer L. Collyer, lawyer. I am not dead. I am paralyzed and blind." That was the last time Homer spoke to anyone other than Langley. The next day, Langley lodged a complaint with the police about the incident.

THE COLLYER BROTHERS' house was demolished in July 1947. The salvaged belongings were sold at auction but netted less than $2,000. The lot on which the house stood was sold in 1951, and in 1965 a small park was fashioned there. Parks commissioner Henry Stern named it the Collyer Brothers Park. In 2002, the Harlem Fifth Avenue Block Association took on the challenge of increasing the use of the park. The first order of business, they decided, was to change its name. The president of the association argued that the Collyers "did nothing positive in the area, they're not a positive image." She wanted the name changed to Reading Tree Park. The board turned down her request. Parks commissioner Adrian Benepe commented, "Sometimes history is written by accident. Not all history is pretty, but it's history nonetheless — and many New York children were admonished by their parents to clean their room 'or else you'll end up like the Collyer brothers.'"

The Collyer brothers' behavior was bizarre and mysterious, but not unusual. It is now known as hoarding, and it is remarkably common. Although few cases are as severe as the Collyers', for a surprising number of people the attachments they form to the things in their lives interfere with their ability to live. Since we began our research on hoarding, we've received thousands of e-mails, letters, and phone calls from relatives and friends of hoarders, public officials grappling with the public health and safety aspects of hoarding, and hoarders themselves. When we speak to professional audiences including psychiatrists, psychologists, social workers, and other human service workers about hoarding, as we often do, we usually ask for a show of hands in response to the following question: "How many of you know personally of a case of significant hoarding—yourself, a family member, a friend, or someone who is not one of your professional clients?" Over and over again, at least two-thirds of the people in the room raise their hands. All are a bit shocked by the numbers. Afterward, many come up to admit that the topic attracted them because they have begun to realize they have a problem that is out of control and not going away soon.

Chances are you know someone with a hoarding problem. Recent studies of hoarding put the prevalence rate at somewhere between 2 and 5 percent of the population. That means that six million to fifteen million Americans suffer from hoarding that causes them distress or interferes with their ability to live. You may have noticed some of the signs but have never thought of it as hoarding. As you meet the people in this book, you will begin to see hoarding where you did not recognize it before. And while hoarding stories like the Collyers' may sound unusual, the attachments to objects among people who hoard are not much different from the attachments all of us form to our things. You will undoubtedly recognize some of your own feelings about your stuff in these pages, even if you do not have a hoarding problem.

The Collyers' story may have been front-page news in the 1940s, but the intense media interest did not carry over to the psychiatric community. Until we began our research, the scientific literature contained few studies and scant mention of hoarding. I (Randy Frost) began that research almost by accident. In the early 1990s, I was teaching a senior seminar at Smith College on obsessive-compulsive disorder (OCD), as I had for many years. OCD has become a relatively high-profile disorder, experienced by an estimated six million people in the United States, perhaps most famously by the late industrialist Howard Hughes, and depicted in movies such as *As Good as It Gets* and the TV show *Monk*. In this particular class, I had an unusually inquisitive student named Rachel Gross. Early in the semester, Rachel asked why there were so many studies on contamination fears and compulsive cleaning and checking rituals, but virtually none on hoarding. She brought up a famous hoarding case that had fascinated her since her childhood—that of the Collyer brothers.

Rachel's question evolved into a term paper, a summer project, and then a senior honors thesis. As part of the research, I suggested placing an ad in the local newspaper looking for "pack rats" or "chronic savers." Hoping to get a few responses, we were amazed to receive more than one hundred calls—so many, in fact, that we launched two separate studies. We visited the homes of several of our volunteers and discovered a wide range of clutter, some relatively mild and some quite severe. Our research culminated in the 1993 publication of the first systematic study of hoarding in the journal *Behaviour Research and Therapy*. The findings from these studies helped shape much of the research to come. The chronic savers we studied were highly perfectionistic and indecisive, having trouble processing information quickly enough to feel comfortable making decisions. They acquired things wherever they went, and every day they carried lots of things with them—"just in case" items they couldn't be without. Surprisingly, they were not alone in their peculiar behavior; most had family members who hoarded as well.

Rachel went on to graduate school to study public health, heading in a new direction. I developed an enduring fascination with this neglected subset of what many consider obsessive-compulsive behavior, and with the people who can't part with the objects they've so avidly gathered.

Up to this time, my research had focused on OCD and the trait of perfectionism. As part of that work, I came to know Dr. Gail Steketee, a well-established scholar of OCD at Boston University. We were already collaborating on several OCD projects when hoarding began to capture my interest. Her reaction mirrored my early response to Rachel's queries: hoarding seemed to be a narrow, fringe aspect of OCD and a dubious area of research. Why study something so rare and esoteric — who would care? But gradually, as I had before her, Gail came to appreciate that hoarding was a substantial and intriguing phenomenon, far more widespread and problematic from a public health perspective than she or I had ever imagined. In our collaboration for this book, I've done the bulk of the fieldwork, investigating and interviewing cases. Hence, the interviews and cases herein are mainly mine, recounted in the first person. The conceptual work, however, has been fully collaborative, and both of us have spoken to and seen more people who compulsively hoard than we could possibly recount. We have experienced awe, the excitement of discovery, and empathy for those caught in the web of hoarding.

The Hoarding Syndrome

In the past decade, we've learned that hoarding seems to be such a marginal affliction in part because it's carried on largely in secret: we think of it as an "underground" psychopathology, occurring most often behind closed doors. Hoarders tend to be ashamed of their disorder and unwelcoming to those who would interfere with their activities. Yet hoarding is far from rare, and Collyer-like cases appear with regularity, so that references to the Collyer brothers can be found in emergency services and legal arenas. Even now in New York City, firefighters talk about a "Collyer house." In New

York City housing law, tenants who fill their apartments with clutter and fail to maintain sanitary conditions are called "Collyer tenants." Collyer tenancy in New York and many other cities across the country has become a significant problem.

Most cases of hoarding are not life threatening, and for those who can afford lots of space or help to manage a hoard, collecting may never reach a crisis level. Most with this problem, however, are left depressed and discouraged by the overwhelming effects hoarding has on their lives. For them, hoarding is certainly pathological. In our work, and indeed in most mental health research, distress and dysfunction are the determining factors as to whether hoarding constitutes a disorder in a particular case. If clutter prevents the person from using his or her living space, and if acquiring and saving cause substantial distress or interference in everyday living, the hoarding is pathological. But exactly what kind of pathology is not clear.

Hoarding has been widely considered to be a subtype of OCD, occurring among one-third of the people diagnosed with that disorder. Interestingly, when we flip it around and study only those who complain of hoarding, only just under one-quarter of them report having OCD symptoms. Recent findings have begun to challenge the view that hoarding is a part of OCD and suggest that hoarding may be a disorder all its own, quite separate from OCD, though sharing some of its characteristics. Classic OCD symptoms are associated with anxiety. The sequence begins with an unwanted intrusive thought (e.g., "My hands are contaminated from touching the doorknob"), followed by a compulsive behavior designed to relieve the distress created by the intrusive thought (e.g., extensive hand washing or cleaning). Positive emotions are not part of this OCD picture; compulsive behavior is driven by the need to reduce distress or discomfort. In hoarding, however, we frequently see *positive* emotions propelling acquisition and saving. We see negative emotions in hoarding as well—anxiety, guilt, shame, regret—but these arise almost exclusively from attempts to get rid of possessions and to avoid acquiring new ones.

Other evidence suggests crucial differences between hoarders and people with classic OCD. The genetic linkage studies show a different pattern of heritability for OCD than for hoarding. Likewise, brain scans reveal a different pattern of cerebral activation for hoarders. Hoarders don't seem to respond to the same treatments as people with classic OCD symptoms, and they show more severe family and social disability, as well as less insight into the nature of the problem.

In fact, the mixture of pleasure and pain hoarding provides distinguishes it from all of the anxiety and mood disorders. In many ways, hoarding looks like an impulse control disorder (ICD). ICDs are characterized by the inability to resist an urge or impulse even though the behavior is dangerous or harmful. In fact, compulsive buying, a major component of hoarding, is considered to be an ICD, as is kleptomania. Because pathological gambling, like compulsive buying, is classified as an ICD, we wondered whether it, too, would be related to hoarding. To find out, we put an ad in the newspaper looking for people with gambling problems. We found that people with serious gambling problems reported problems with clutter, excessive buying, and difficulty discarding things at much higher rates than people without gambling problems. What may unite these disorders, besides a lack of impulse control, is a psychology of opportunity. One gambler from our study described his experience to me: "Seeing the scratch tickets over the counter at the convenience store leads me to think, *One of those tickets is surely a winner, maybe a million-dollar winner. How can I walk away when the opportunity is there?*" Our hoarders have said similar things about items they've wanted to acquire.

Although the acquisitive features of hoarding look like an ICD, the difficulty discarding and the disorganization do not. The emotional reactions to discarding are more reminiscent of anxiety disorders and depression. At present, there is a growing consensus that hoarding should be included as a separate disorder in the next version of the *Diagnostic and Statistical Manual of Mental Disorders*. Intensive study and decisions about this plan will take place over the next few years.

The boundaries between normal and abnormal blur when it comes to hoarding. We all become attached to our possessions and save things other people wouldn't. So we all share some of the hoarding orientation. The passion of a collector, the procrastination of someone who hasn't taken the time to put things away, the sentimentality of one who saves reminders of important personal events—all these are part of the hoarding story. How, when, and why do these otherwise commonplace and normal experiences develop into hoarding? What compels these compulsive collectors to create unlivable conditions for themselves and often for others? Why do they go too far? This is what we seek to explain in this book.

About fifteen years ago, I received a desperate phone call from a woman named Irene. She'd found me by contacting the Obsessive Compulsive Foundation (OCF) and asking for someone who might help her with her hoarding problem. (In recent years, the OCF has experienced a dramatic increase in requests for information about hoarding.) When she learned that I was researching the problem, she literally begged to be included in our study. Irene was fifty-three and had just separated from her husband. She had two children, a thirteen-year-old daughter who was away at boarding school and a nine-year-old son who lived at home. Irene worked part-time as a sales associate for a real estate company. She had lived in her house for more than twenty years. Her husband, an engineer, had been after her for years to get rid of the clutter, which waxed and waned but never went away. Finally, he told her to clean it up or he would leave. She couldn't, so he did. Now she was worried that she would lose her children in the upcoming divorce.

Many people with hoarding problems have a predominant theme to their hoarding, such as fear of waste, the allure of opportunity, or the comfort and safety provided by objects. Irene possessed all of these traits. She is the first of many hoarders you will meet in this book (see chapter 1), all of whom helped us better understand the forces that drive them—and us.

It is no coincidence that most of the people described in this book are highly intelligent. Although hoarding is considered a mental disorder, it may stem from an extraordinary ability. For hoarders, every object is rich with detail. We disregard the color and hue of a magazine cover as we search for the article inside. But if we paid attention, we might notice the soothing effect of the colors, and the meaning of the object would expand in the process. In this way, the physical world of hoarders is different and much more expansive than that of the rest of us. Whether we look at them and see limitless potential, limitless information, limitless utility, or limitless waste, the people in this book are undeniably free of the usual rules that affect how we view and treat our stuff.

HOARDING CARRIES WITH IT an agonizing stigma. We thank the people who so courageously shared their lives with us for this book. We have changed their names and other identifying details that were not germane to their stories in order to protect their anonymity and privacy.

1

PILES UPON PILES
The Story of Hoarding

I attach meaning to things that don't need it.

—Irene

I spotted Irene's home immediately. Despite its commanding view of the countryside from atop a hill, it was dark and gloomy. Overgrown trees and bushes hid much of the house from the street. The paint was peeling, and the fence needed mending. A car parked in the driveway was packed with papers and clothes. I had brought along my student assistant, Tamara Hartl, and as we walked toward the house, we could see boxes, newspapers, clothes, and an assortment of unidentifiable objects pressed against the windows.

We knocked on the front door but got no answer. We found a side door and knocked. Something stirred inside the house. Behind us, a door to the garage opened, and out stepped Irene, slightly overweight and rumpled, with straight brown hair and a friendly smile. She introduced herself with a nervous laugh and invited us in: "You can't get in that way. You'll have to come through the garage." A sea of boxes, bags, ski poles, tools, everything imaginable—all in a jumble, chest-high—covered the entire length and width of the garage. Along the wall was a narrow pathway to the only door to her house that was not blocked by debris.

The foreboding exterior of the house belied Irene's personality. She was friendly, bright, and engaging and very curious about our research. Like others we've interviewed, she was tormented by her situation and demoralized by her inability to do anything about it. Though happy to see us, she worried that she was wasting our time, since her problems were of "no consequence to anyone but me."

In Irene I'd found an extraordinarily articulate and insightful subject. I agreed to work with her as she tried to clear her home. In exchange, she agreed to describe everything she felt and thought during the process and not to filter out any reactions, positive or negative.

Irene lived about ninety miles from my college in Northampton, Massachusetts, which meant a long drive for each visit with her (forty-five visits over eighteen months). Each visit lasted about two hours. Tamara accompanied me on most of the trips. On our way to Irene's home, we'd review what we had learned the week before, and on the way back we'd discuss the visit as Tamara made notes on a laptop. By the last of our sessions with Irene, we had generated a theory for hoarding—a framework for future research and a major breakthrough in understanding the phenomenon.

Some theorists have posited that people with hoarding tendencies form attachments to possessions instead of people. Erich Fromm claimed that a "hoarding orientation" leads to social withdrawal. Hoarders, he suggested, are remote and suspicious, preferring the company of objects to that of people. Indeed, for some people prone to acute social discomfort, possessions can be stable and comfortable companions. Irene, however, defied this categorization. She had a wide circle of friends, some of whom I met in the course of my work with her. They displayed a great deal of affection for her, and she for them. She had a quick wit and a well-developed sense of humor. It was easy to see why people liked her. She laughed readily and was often amused by the ironies of her plight. One day, as she pondered why she had saved a newspaper ad for new tires, she fell into gales of laughter when she noticed the headline: SAVE THIS AD. She was also quick to shed tears when she encountered something sentimental, such as a picture drawn by her son when he was a toddler.

With Irene as a model, the classic definition of hoarding as a socially isolating syndrome appeared to be flawed. One of Irene's favorite things, she said, was to make connections between people with mutual interests. She would frequently give me the names of people she thought would click with me. She planned to give many of the things she saved to friends and acquaintances for whom they seemed suited. Unfortunately, her gift of seeing these connections was a factor in her keeping virtually everything she acquired.

Irene was intelligent and well educated. She seemed to know something about almost every subject and displayed curiosity and a wide range of interests. She had a story to tell about each possession—most of them remarkably detailed and engaging. For instance, one day she found a piece of paper with a name and phone number on it among the pile of things on her kitchen table and excitedly recounted its history. "This is a young girl I met at a store about a year ago. She's Hawaiian and had such wonderful stories about Hawaii that I thought Julia [Irene's daughter] would like to write to her. They are about the same age. She was such an interesting person, I was sure Julia would enjoy getting to know her."

Her face lit up at the prospect of making this connection.

"But Julia wasn't interested. I thought about writing her myself, but I never did. Still, I don't want to get rid of the contact. Julia might change her mind."

I have met few people who are as interested in the world around them as Irene, though I later learned that this attribute is fairly common in people with hoarding problems. As she talked, I could see the way each of her things was connected to her and how they formed the fabric of her life. The advertisement for the tires led to a story about her car, which led to a story about her daughter wanting to drive, and so on. A piece of the hoarding puzzle seemed to be falling into place. Instead of replacing people with possessions, Irene was using possessions to make connections between people and to the world at large.

As we were soon to learn, the hoarding phenomenon is composed of a number of discrete factors, some well hidden and unexpected. But the most obvious factor was the simple problem of accumulation: from a scrap of paper with an unidentified and long-forgotten phone number on it to a broken vase purchased at a tag sale, Irene had great difficulty getting rid of things. The value she assigned to objects and the reasons she had for saving them were many and varied. Irene's beliefs about what should be saved seemed isolated from everything going on around her. She was truly baffled that her son and daughter didn't share her penchant for keeping things. One day, as she went through the mound on her kitchen table, she found instructions for one of her son's toys. "I'll put it here in this pile of your stuff, Eric," she told him when he got home from school. Eric immediately picked up the instructions, walked to the wastebasket, and threw them away. She stopped what she was doing, looking surprised. Eric saw her and responded angrily, "I don't need it. I know how it works." She didn't say anything. A few minutes later, she found a bookmark. "Oh, this has all the book award people on it. Do you want it, Eric? I'll put it in your pile."

"No," he responded before she'd finished her sentence.

"Don't you even want to look at it?" she asked incredulously.

A few minutes after that, she found an old birthday card some-one had sent Eric. She put it on top of the pile of things she was saving for him without saying anything. Almost as if on cue, he walked by, picked it up, and threw it out. Irene stared at him in disbelief. She simply could not comprehend his lack of interest in things she considered full of significance.

The sense of emotional attachment that Irene felt for her pos-sessions has been shared with us over and over by people seeking help with their hoarding problems. These sentiments are really not that different from what most of us feel about keepsakes or souve-nirs—the abnormality lies not in the nature of the attachments, but in their intensity and extremely broad scope. I find many arti-cles of interest in the newspaper, but their value to me is reduced when piles of newspapers begin to impinge on my living space and overwhelm my ability to read what I have collected. For Irene, the value of these things seemed unaffected by the trouble they caused.

Hoarding involves not only difficulty with getting rid of things but also excessive acquisition of them. Irene's upstairs hallway con-tained hundreds of shopping bags filled with what she described as gifts for other people. Whenever she saw something that she thought might make a great gift, she purchased it, even though she had no particular recipient in mind. The items were all still in their original wrappings. Many people shop ahead to have gifts on hand when the need arises, but Irene and many like her cannot control their urge to buy when they see something they fancy. In addition to buying excessively, Irene collected things that could be had for free. She had an agreement with the postmaster of her town: he placed any newspapers or magazines that were undeliverable in a box, and on Saturday morning he put the box in the foyer of the post office, where Irene picked it up. Her home was stuffed with these free newspapers and magazines.

The Tour: "Homogenized" Clutter

On our first visit, Irene gave us a tour of her house. Hustling through each room, she held her arms up in front of her bent at the wrists with her hands drooping down, like a surgeon who had just scrubbed for an operation. Her small steps propelled her deftly through the maze in each room. She insisted that we not touch anything, and she watched us carefully as we negotiated the space. It was hard to avoid touching things in some places because there was so little room to move; the stacks rose to the ceiling. Several things struck me about her hoard. She saved pretty typical stuff, the sorts of things we'd seen in other homes: stacks of newspapers going back years, newspaper clippings of interesting articles, thousands of books, mountains of clothes, containers of various sorts from previous attempts to organize. And also as we'd seen with other hoarders, the piles had no apparent organizational scheme.

We moved through each room on "goat paths" (a phrase well-known in the hoarding self-help world), narrow trails not more than a foot wide where the floor was occasionally visible. My hand brushed the top of a chair back in the dining room. She saw it and immediately rushed over with a moist towelette to wipe off the chair. This curious behavior and the way she held her hands, as if to shield them from germs, led me to wonder whether she also suffered from more classic OCD contamination and washing symptoms. At this point in our research, we had seen few houses in worse shape than Irene's. (Since then, we have seen many homes more extreme.)

Irene was apologetic to the point of tears about her situation. Her husband had just left her because of the clutter. She had no money. She was afraid her children would be taken away because of the condition of her home if her husband were to petition for custody. Her daughter had developed severe dust allergies, making it difficult for her to stay in the house. Irene recognized that she had a problem and needed to do something about it. Some people who hoard never have lucid moments about their habits, so Irene was fortunate in this respect. She at least had what psychiatrists and psychologists call "insight" into the irrationality of her hoarding behavior. Yet despite having insight when talking generally about her problem, when trying to decide whether to discard a five-year-old newspaper, she could not see the absurdity of keeping it.

Our first stop, the kitchen, showed the enormity of her predicament. A two-foot pile of stuff covered her kitchen table. The pile contained a wide assortment of things—old newspapers, books, pieces of children's games, cereal boxes, coupons, the everyday bric-a-brac of family life. Only a small corner of the table's surface was visible, about the size of a dinner plate. The table had been cleared once, according to Irene. Five years earlier, she'd removed everything to the floor so that her son could have a birthday party. After the party, the stuff went back on the table. Four chairs were covered with clothes, boxes filled with long-forgotten things, and more. It was possible to walk around the table, but the floor under the table and chairs was packed with boxes and paper bags. The kitchen counters were completely covered, their surfaces obviously long buried in the mess. A pile of unwashed dishes balanced precariously in the sink. Bottles of pills and piles of pens and pencils were strewn among the dishes, utensils, and containers covering the countertops. As Irene was going through each of the items in her kitchen, it became clear to me that there was something peculiar about the clutter. Most descriptions of hoards include piles of worthless and worn-out things. Initially, the clutter in Irene's kitchen seemed consistent with this model—empty cereal boxes, expired coupons, old newspapers, plastic forks and spoons from fast-food shops. But mixed among the empty boxes and old newspapers were pictures of her children when they were young, the title to her car, her tax returns, a few checks. Once when I had convinced her to experiment with getting rid of an old Sunday *New York Times* without first looking through it for interesting or important information, she agreed but said, "Let me just shake it to make sure there is nothing important here." As she did so, an ATM envelope with $100 in cash fell out. This wasn't exactly the outcome I'd expected from this experiment, but it did illustrate something important. Irene's clutter contained a mixture of what seemed to me both worthless and valuable things but what was to her a collection of equally valuable items. She described it herself one day as we worked through one of her many piles: "It's like this newspaper advertisement is as important to me as a picture of my daughter. Everything seems equally important; it's all homogenized."

As we learned more about her and her home, Irene's contamination fears became more apparent. On the counter next to the kitchen stove was a relatively neat pile of newspapers, magazines, and mail, grown into a leaning tower that threatened to cascade onto the burners. This, Irene explained, was her "clean" stuff. No one could touch it, nor could it come into contact with anything else in the room, because everything else was "dirty" (contaminated). She kept her purse next to the stack and took it out only if she felt clean. If she didn't feel clean, she covered her purse with plastic wrap before she picked it up so that she wouldn't contaminate it.

The dining room was clearly the worst room in the house. Every surface was covered. The piles of clothes, containers, books, and newspapers climbed above my head. One skinny path led from the kitchen along the side of the room to the door of the TV room. Another path, even narrower, ran along the adjacent wall to the front hallway. Again, the array of things was impressive: magazines, baskets, clothes, papers, boxes, even three or four books about organizing. But still Irene had a strategy to separate the clean from the dirty. On the dining room table were layers of items separated by blankets or towels. Irene explained that the towels and blankets were clean and that laying them over dirty objects protected the clean ones on top.

Soon it became clear that Irene had different degrees of clean. Some objects had to be kept apart from all the others because they were "pure" and uncontaminated. The pure state was only nominal, however. In fact, making things clean often resulted in their deterioration. Once when we were helping her clear a pile of papers from her couch, an envelope from the clean pile fell onto the floor, rendering it contaminated. Irene stopped her work and rushed the envelope to the kitchen, where she ran it under the faucet. She carried the soggy letter back to the couch and propped it up to dry on top of the pile. The letter had already begun to dissolve into the envelope.

As Irene walked us through the house that first day, she pointed out the piles of things that were clean and the piles that were dirty. This distinction was hard to grasp because everything in her house had a thick layer of dust, but gradually we gathered that everything on the floor was dirty and most things on the furniture were clean. We were dirty. Touching me or shaking my hand, or even hugging her children, left Irene dirty. Some days she strived to maintain a clean state, and some days she decided to be dirty. If she was dirty, she avoided touching anything in the house that was clean. Of course, she preferred to stay clean, but getting dirty allowed her to carry on a relatively normal life. In fact, her dirty state was what most of us consider normal.

Irene developed unusual ways to clean herself when she became contaminated. She always kept a Wash'n Dri towelette tucked into her blouse, even when she was dirty. When something got contaminated, she pulled out the towelette and wiped the item off, thereby decontaminating it, as she had done when I'd touched the chair in the dining room. Caught without a towelette, she would put her fingers in her mouth to decontaminate them, as if she were licking off sticky food. Putting her fingers in her mouth looked like a normal behavior, as did wiping something with a wet cloth. I wouldn't have noticed except that she reacted the moment I touched the chair. Only by watching closely could I tell that these behaviors were compulsions, designed to prevent the ill effects of contamination. But exactly what these effects were was unclear.

For many people with OCD, obsessive fears and compulsive actions are tied to feeling responsible for some sort of harm that might possibly befall them or others. But Irene's cleaning behavior was not exactly a fear of dirt or germs. She was not worried about getting ill or making others ill. She was, however, plagued by intense feelings of discomfort if certain things were not clean, including herself, but her clean was different from everyone else's. She described it as a "pure" state, a way of being separate from everything, a state of perfection—pristine and unpolluted. She created her own world—a comfortable and safe one. Such desires play prominent roles in hoarding, as we would find out later.

Frank Tallis, a British psychologist, has suggested that this type of washing compulsion is attributable to perfectionism rather than to a fear of harm. Indeed, our research has shown that most people who hoard are perfectionists and that the perfectionism plays a major role in their hoarding. Irene often spoke of having a place that was truly hers and things no one else could touch, as if yearning to achieve some type of ideal state. She longed for a place of retreat when she was stressed, a place where she was clean and secure, undisturbed by outside concerns. She had several such safe havens in her home where no one, including her children, was allowed. Her bedroom was one of them. Here she collected her most cherished possessions and kept them solely to herself. Her "treasure books" were there—books that had special meaning because she had once enjoyed reading them or she simply liked the way they looked. Magazines with pictures she liked were part of the hoard, as well as other things she wanted to keep her children from contaminating.

Despite the complications it created, Irene's cleaning compulsion was not as serious as her hoarding. She could function quite effectively despite her contamination fears by dabbing at dirty objects with her towelette whenever she felt she must. She seldom had to thoroughly wash contaminated items. Her rituals did not, as is sometimes the case, take up enormous amounts of time, and she could go for long periods in a dirty state. The biggest problem her cleaning compulsion created was the effort required to maintain the distinction between clean and dirty objects.

"Churning"

Irene's TV room, where she and her children spent most of their time, was just off the dining room. One chair was completely clear; no other sitting space was apparent. Videotapes were scattered about—hundreds of them. Most of them were recordings of TV specials Irene had taped so that she wouldn't lose the information they presented, but none of the tapes were labeled. She lamented that there were so many, but she had no plans to reduce her collection. On one side of the room was what appeared to be a couch, completely engulfed in papers. In fact, all that was visible was a pile of papers four feet high, extending about five feet out from the wall and running the length of the couch. A coffee table was also submerged beneath the pile. One small corner of the couch, about six inches wide, was clear. This was Irene's sorting spot. She reported that she sat there for at least three hours every day trying to sort through her papers, but the pile was growing steadily despite her efforts. We asked her if she would show us how she worked.

Irene began by picking out a newspaper clipping from the pile. It concerned drug use among teenagers and the importance of communication between parents and teens on this issue. The clipping was several months old. She said she intended to give it to her daughter as a way of initiating a conversation about drug use. However, since her daughter was away at school, she would have to wait until she got home. She said she would put it "here, on top of the pile, so I can see it and remember where it is." She then picked up a mailing from the telephone company offering a deal on long distance. She said she needed to read it to tell whether she could get a better price on her long-distance plan. She put it on top of the pile so that she could see it and wouldn't forget it.

She followed a similar logic with the third item, which also went on top of the pile. This process continued with a dozen more objects. The clipping about drug use was soon buried. For each item, she articulated a reason to save it and a justification for why it should go on top of the pile. Most of her reasons had to do with the intention to use the object. Her rationale was that if she put it away in a file or anywhere else, she would lose it and never find it again. The result of all this effort was that the papers in the pile got shuffled and those on the bottom moved to the top, but nothing was actually thrown away or moved to a more suitable location. We have seen this process so often among people who hoard that we have come to call it "churning."

The churning we saw in Irene's TV room was driven in part by something we'd found in our earlier studies of hoarding—a problem with making decisions. With each item Irene picked up, she failed to figure out which features were important and which were not, in the same way that she struggled to distinguish important from unimportant objects. Moreover, she thought of features and uses most of us wouldn't. When she picked up a cap to a pen, she reasoned that the cap could be used as a piece in a board game.

She couldn't throw it out until we had talked through whether this was a reasonable and important purpose for the object. The same problem arose with a piece of junk mail from a mortgage company. She couldn't get rid of it until she figured out what was really important (or unimportant) about it. Sometimes she could decide to throw things away, but the effort it took was enormous. Often the effort was simply too much, and things went back on the pile.

As with other hoarders, her indecisiveness was not limited to possessions. One day her daughter, Julia, asked for some money to go to the mall with a friend to buy some shoes. Irene pulled a wad of cash from her purse and started to hand it to her daughter. As the money was about to change hands, she wondered aloud if it would be enough. She took the money back and pulled out her credit cards, but now she wasn't sure whether to give Julia the Master-Card or Diners Club card. "Which should I give you?" she asked. Before Julia answered, she said, "I don't know, maybe I should give you both," and she handed both of them to her. "No," she said, "I might need one to get groceries." She took both of them back and handed Julia the MasterCard, but again took it back, adding, "I'll probably need the MasterCard for the groceries." She gave Julia the Diners Club card, but just a second later she said, "Is Diners Club accepted everywhere?" Before Julia could respond, she took back the card and said, angrily, "Oh, just take this one," and handed Julia the MasterCard, obviously frustrated and flustered by the process. Her indecision seemed to stem from a flood of ideas about what might happen if she chose one action over another.

Irene's churning revealed another facet of her disorder besides her trouble with decisions: she wanted to keep objects in sight in order to remember them. When we toured her bedroom, this became even clearer. Stacked on her dresser, all the way to the ceiling, were clothes—while her dresser drawers were empty. When I asked about this, she replied, "If I put my clothes in the drawers,

I won't be able to see them, and I'll forget I have them." On another occasion, she was going through pamphlets advertising various home care products. She remarked, "I want to remember these things. If I throw them out, I'll never remember them. I have such a terrible memory."

Irene frequently complained about her poor memory. This contradicted our observations of her elaborate stories about so many of the objects she found in her hoard. She remembered details about where and when she got things, whom she was with, and even what she was wearing that day. It wasn't that she had a poor memory; she just didn't trust it. Her organizing style may have played a role here as she tried to remember exactly where things were in space. With thousands of objects in her home, this was an impossible task. She was asking too much of her memory, and not surprisingly, she lacked confidence in her recall. We got a further sense of this one day as she was trying to get rid of a pile of newspapers she'd already read. She said she wasn't comfortable discarding them because she couldn't remember the articles she'd read in them. Saving them would be a good substitute for her memory. Her belief that she *should* remember all this information, much of it unimportant for her daily life, led her to save the newspapers. It also explained why she felt that her memory was poor.

Another apparent problem had to do with the ability to categorize, to group like objects together. Most of us live our lives categorically—at least the part of our lives dealing with objects. Tools are kept in the toolbox; bills to be paid are kept in a special place in the office area and then filed after payment; kitchen utensils go in a drawer. But Irene organized her world visually and spatially, not by category. When I asked her where her electric bill was, she said, "It's on the left side of the pile about a foot down. I remember seeing it at that spot last week, and I think I've piled about that much stuff on top of it." Many of us do this on a smaller scale. I have faculty colleagues whose offices are populated by piles of paper, and although they get a bit nervous that I'll label them hoarders, most actually know what each pile contains and can readily find what they need. Others, who are less sure of the content, remain confident that their piles have only low-priority, unimportant stuff. In short, they are unconcerned about their memories.

Although a visual/spatial organizing scheme might work on a modest scale, it's not an efficient way to deal with a large volume of possessions. In fact, Irene frequently did lose things in the piles and found herself buying replacements for items she knew she had but couldn't locate. After we set up a filing system for her important papers, she reported being able to find things much more easily. But because she couldn't see the papers, she felt uncomfortable, as if she had lost them. This dependence on the visual connection with objects is a common trait among hoarders.

As Irene worked her way through the pile on her couch, something else struck me. She often picked up an item from the pile, looked at it for a second, and caught sight of something else. She then picked up the new item, putting down the first one. This happened often enough that it seemed like a pattern. She simply couldn't keep her attention on things that posed a decision-making challenge or seemed boring. She preferred to focus on objects that had positive connotations or evoked a story. As she drifted into an anecdote, she lost track of the sorting she was supposed to be doing. Not maintaining our attention while performing tedious tasks is certainly common, but it seemed to be especially pronounced in Irene's case.

Thanks to our close observation of Irene, the first piece of our theory for understanding hoarding was taking shape. Hoarding appeared to result, at least in part, from deficits in processing information. Making decisions about whether to keep and how to organize objects requires categorization skills, confidence in one's ability to remember, and sustained attention. To maintain order, one also needs the ability to efficiently assess the value or utility of an object. These mental processes seemed particularly challenging for Irene. As we shall see later, these dysfunctions may reflect problems with how the brain operates in people who hoard.

Irene's History

After Irene gave me the tour of her home, she asked, "How did I get this way?" It completely baffled her that her home was nearly unlivable. "I know I am smart and capable, so why can't I manage my stuff? I see other people doing it. Why can't I?" I had no answer for her.

When we began studying hoarding, we were told by other mental health experts that it was a response to deprivation. Living through a period of deprivation, such as the Great Depression of the 1930s or the Holocaust, might cause people to stock up on whatever they can find to prevent such an experience from occurring in the future. Indeed, in our first study of hoarding, we found that many people described much of what they collected as "just in case" items. But when we asked our hoarding research participants if they had ever experienced periods of deprivation, by and large they said no. In fact, many of them grew up quite wealthy and never faced any shortage of food, money, or luxuries. Irene's experience was typical: She grew up in a middle-class family. Her father was a high school accreditor, and her mother taught typing and shorthand at the local high school. They had enough money and never experienced any material deprivation.

Irene could not remember exactly when her hoarding began. She remembered saving her schoolwork from elementary school, much of which she still had. But when she was young, her room was not cluttered, and she had little trouble managing the things she owned.

Her father traveled a lot for his job. She remembered being spellbound by his descriptions of the places he visited and the things he saw, and his stories left her with a lifelong interest in travel. Although she traveled very little herself, travel sections of newspapers and travel brochures could be found throughout her house. They were among the most difficult things for her to discard. Perhaps they represented a bond with her father that she cherished. The rest of her relationship with him was not so warm.

Outside of his travel stories, Irene remembered him as distant and cold. Irene recalled her father's terrible temper when she was growing up. Although he never hit her, she remembered being afraid of him. That dynamic continued into her adulthood. One day she showed me a letter he had written to her several years earlier. It was formal and criticized the way she cared for her house. "You have failed in your obligation to properly maintain the house and grounds," he complained. He had helped them buy the house but now threatened to cut her off if things didn't improve.

On another occasion, not long after she got married, Irene went looking for a pair of gray wool slacks some friends had given to her husband. She recalled putting them in a box in the barn behind her house with some of her many "lists," but the box was nowhere to be found. Her father had been in the barn, so she asked if he had moved it. He admitted to having thrown the slacks away, trying to secretly rid his daughter of stuff. Irene drove to the town dump and spent several hours searching through the trash. She never found the slacks.

More recently, she saw her father tear up and throw away some of her late mother's handwritten lesson plans. Irene was incensed that he would do this and rescued them. The shredded papers now rested in her living room. After her mother died, Irene stopped receiving birthday or holiday cards from her father, though she knew that he wrote to other people. Perhaps he feared contributing to her clutter, or perhaps out of frustration he'd lost interest in communicating with her, so different were they in their views of the world. We have often wondered whether cold and distant parenting may be a contributing factor in the development of hoarding. In several recent studies, people with hoarding problems recalled disconnected relationships with their parents, particularly their fathers.

In contrast, Irene was extremely close to her mother. Whenever she faced a crisis, she turned to her mother for advice and comfort. She came to value anything connected with her mother, especially after her death.

Irene's earliest memories were of a very happy childhood, filled with lots of children and activities. She walked to school with the neighborhood kids. They all gathered together after school and on weekends, and there was always someone around to play with. When she was in the second grade, however, her family moved to the suburbs. With only one other child in the new neighborhood, Irene felt isolated and alone. She rode the bus to school by herself and found the bus driver loud and menacing. He frequently yelled at the kids. She was frightened of him and avoided speaking to anyone on the bus. Her teacher seemed no better. Irene was so scared, she seldom spoke in class and began to dread going to school. "I was scared all the time," she told me. "It was horrible."

Under these conditions, she began to devise strategies to manage her emotions. She recalled getting wrapped up in objects as a child. "Things were fun, interesting, and different," she said. "They were removed from emotional life — soothing. All my fears were gone." She elaborated: "Things were less complex than people, less moody. People either leave or hurt you." Ironically, it was her things that eventually caused her husband to leave.

Fear still permeated Irene's life nearly fifty years later. During one of our sessions, she admitted, "Every day, I wake up in fear," although she couldn't articulate exactly what she was afraid of. She coped with her fear by surrounding herself with things, just as she had as a child. One day she told me, "You know, yesterday, without thinking about it, I sat down and built a little fortress around myself. It felt nice, comfortable." She made a number of such comments during the time we worked together.

Around the age of seven or eight, Irene began ordering and arranging her possessions in peculiar ways. She arranged her books and papers so they were perpendicular and perfectly aligned with the edge of the desk. At first this compulsion was mild and did not interfere with her life. But over time the feeling got stronger, and she began to spend hours arranging and rearranging things. She had trouble getting her homework done, doing her chores, and even getting ready for school on time. If she was prevented from doing her arranging or interrupted in the middle, she felt uncomfortable and anxious. This was the first hint for Irene of problems related to possessions, and it is consistent with research finding symmetry obsessions and arranging compulsions in children who also have hoarding problems. Since symmetry, arranging, and hoarding all have to do with physical objects, the connection may suggest a deeper problem with how people interact with the physical world or separate themselves from it. Luckily for Irene, the symmetry obsessions and arranging compulsions eventually disappeared.

During those early school years, Irene began to gain weight and had struggled with her weight ever since. At one point in high school, her eating habits became rigid and unusual. In retrospect, she thought that she may have been anorexic at the time. Now she believed that her weight and hoarding were connected: "My body and my house are kind of the same thing. I take things into them for solace." We've had a number of other hoarding clients who believed that their weight problems were related to their hoarding, and in one study we found that people with hoarding problems had higher than average body mass indexes.

When Irene was nine years old, her grandparents moved in with the family. They were elderly immigrants from Europe, and their grooming habits were at odds with Irene's. They seldom bathed or used deodorant, and they seemed to Irene to leave an odor wherever they went. She would not sit in a chair that one of her grandparents had recently used; it disgusted her. Before long, she stopped sitting in any chair her grandparents had once occupied. Still, there was no cleaning compulsion, just a sense of disgust. In all likelihood, this was a precursor of her contamination fears.

Objects seemed to have a special significance for Irene as a child. Although she was not deprived, she had relatively few toys and cherished the ones she had. She recalled never taking a number of them out of the package, perhaps foreshadowing her tendency to value mere possession over use of an object. She remembered one treasure, a cylindrical paisley pocketbook with a mirror on top, that her parents threw away when she was about ten. By this time, they had become annoyed with the number of things she was saving and occasionally took matters into their own hands. Perhaps this shaped her response, years later, to a friend who agreed to help her clean up but was dismissed for throwing away a gum wrapper. Irene developed elaborate strategies to foil those who insisted that she get rid of her stuff. When her husband threw out her piles of newspapers, she sneaked them back into the house by using them to line the bottoms of boxes she brought in to help her organize.

Even losses that were not emotional were troubling, particularly the loss of a potential opportunity. I got a sense of this one day as we excavated in Irene's TV room. She came across a piece of paper with a telephone number written on it. Judging from its depth in the pile and the fact that it was yellowing, it had been there for quite some time, possibly years. Clearly, she had written it in haste on whatever she could find. As was the case for most of the information in the pile from which it came, she had not taken the time to identify it or put it in a phone or address book—it was just a number on a piece of paper. When she picked it up, she exclaimed, "Oh, a phone number! I'll put it here on the pile where I can see it and deal with it later."

"Why do you think it is worth keeping that number?" I asked. She said, "Well, I made an effort to write it down, so clearly it was important to me. And it will just take a minute to call and find out what it is. I don't want to do it now, though, because it will interrupt us." She hadn't made the call in all the years the paper had sat in the pile. Whether making the call would have helped her make a decision about keeping the number is uncertain. Perhaps the idea of a potential opportunity that the number provided was better than the reality provided by making the call.

In high school, Irene's behavioral oddities became more rigid and extreme. She felt compelled to do things in a certain way, particularly her schoolwork. Irene was an exceptional student, but at some cost. She insisted on using a #3 pencil sharpened to a very fine point so that she could write precisely. She printed everything in very tiny letters, and the formation of the letters had to be perfect. If she did not form a letter just right, she would start over and rewrite the entire page.

In college, her room was not cluttered, though she remembers having lots of stuff packed in boxes. But other peculiarities caused her considerable discomfort. She recalled feeling tormented when other students came into her room and sat on her bed. It reminded her of her grandparents sitting on chairs and leaving an odor. Still, this torment was private. By all outward appearances, she was functioning extremely well. She had friends and was getting straight A's. As her senior year progressed, however, her tightly controlled world began to unravel.

Irene majored in art history and decided to write a senior thesis on Iranian art and architecture. As she collected and read book after book on the subject, she began to see connections everywhere. One obscure fact led to another, and when she saw these connections, she felt compelled to pursue them. To keep track of it all, she kept copious notes on each book she read. Sometimes her notes approached the length of the book itself. She felt the need to collect information until she had a "complete" picture before sitting down to write. For the perfectionist Irene, anything less than perfect meant disgrace. As the end of the term approached, she had written very little, and for the first time in her life, she faced the prospect of failure. Still, she couldn't quite see how to limit her material, and she went on collecting.

When she realized that she didn't have time to complete her thesis, she became suicidal. It began as a thought that gave her some respite from her terror about the upcoming deadline. Soon she found herself thinking about how to kill herself every day. Instead of writing, she made plans to drive her car into a nearby lake. Death seemed like a better alternative than failure. In the end, she put all her notes and the few pages of her thesis she had been able to squeak out in a manila envelope and gave them to her professor with an explanation of her problem. He took pity on her and gave her a C–, her only grade below an A in college.

She had struggled with depression since then, though she had never again been suicidal. Irene's depression impeded her ability to deal with her clutter. During her depressive episodes, no sorting or discarding occurred, and one of the few things that made her feel better, shopping, only added to the problem. Depression is a common affliction among hoarders. In fact, nearly 60 percent of the participants in our research meet diagnostic criteria for major depression—much of which results from the hoarding itself. People draw conclusions about their worth and competence based on their inability to control their living space, and not being able to entertain people in their homes isolates them and limits their social lives.

On my first visit to Irene's house, she said something unusual. When I asked her if she would agree to be studied while we tried to help her manage her stuff, she said, "Why would you want to waste your time on someone like me?" When I asked her more about what she meant, it became clear that her low opinion of herself reflected ambivalence or uncertainty rather than pure low self-esteem. When she was at work, talking to other people, or shopping, she did not have the same feelings. But when she was at home, her unworthiness was more apparent to her, mostly when she focused on the clutter. When she focused on individual items, however, her possessions seemed more comforting than threatening. The irony that her hoard could be comforting and tormenting at the same time was clear to her.

After college, Irene lived at home with her parents for a year and took some additional courses at a local college. She planned to start graduate school the following year. This was the first time she remembered living in a messy room. She saved all her college books and notes and packed them in "clean" paper bags that nearly filled her room. The room had two twin beds, but only one was visible. She recalled someone looking into her room and not being able to tell there were two beds there. Thirty years later, she still had those books, papers, and clothes.

The following year, Irene entered graduate school in library science. She had no problem categorizing, cataloging, and organizing library materials, as long as they did not belong to her. If they were hers, she struggled and failed to keep things organized. She lived in an upstairs apartment filled with books and papers. She described the room as very messy, but her landlady was blind and did not know. Her hoarding behavior became noticeable when she began carrying large paper bags wherever she went. The bags contained books, papers, and anything else she thought she might need — her "just in case" items. They became such a part of her image that the other students jokingly called her "the bag lady."

Her concerns about contamination also became stronger during this time. When teachers gave handouts in class, Irene licked her fingers before and after she touched them to neutralize the germs. This ritual became one of her primary "decontamination" strategies later when her OCD became severe.

At the end of graduate school, Irene married her boyfriend, and they moved into an apartment together. Clutter was a feature of their household from the beginning, although it didn't seem to affect their relationship until much later. Most of the clutter was in the form of boxes filled with books and papers. Irene began work at the college library and was put in charge of "weeding" the vertical files, a job that involved discarding newspapers, magazines, and books. Many of them came home with her and greatly expanded her developing hoard.

Just how much of Irene's history is relevant to her hoarding is uncertain, but particular features appear again and again in the histories of hoarders. From an early age, she was sensitive, anxious, and perfectionistic. Though highly intelligent, she felt afraid of adults and disgusted by physical contact. She found stability and comfort in her possessions. Perhaps these features led her to use things to give her life meaning and connect her to the larger world. Her hoarding took years to develop; getting rid of it would be hard.

Recovery

Plastic bins, most stacked and empty, littered Irene's home. The containers were clear so she could see what was inside. Lids for the containers had migrated elsewhere. Irene had purchased the materials over the years with the intention of using them but had been unable to do so. Instead, they only added to the clutter, as did numerous books on how to organize. Invariably, people who suffer from hoarding problems fail to maintain even the most rudimentary organization of their stuff—but not from lack of effort. Like Irene, most have spent countless hours trying to organize their possessions, with little success. Deficits in executive functions such as planning, categorization, organization, and attention leave them lost amid a sea of things, unable to figure out what to do next.

Irene and I worked to create a filing system for her papers. Despite the fact that she was a librarian and could do this easily with things that didn't belong to her, the work was difficult. Each possession had too many meanings to be categorized in only one way, and cross-referencing everything was exhausting. But before long, her new filing system began to pay off. The week after we finished it, she excitedly told me, "You know, I had to find the letter from my insurance company about my car accident last year. I went to the insurance file and found it right away. It would have taken me weeks to find it before."

Still, her lifelong pattern of organizing by piles was hard to break. She complained that when she needed something, she pictured the item in its last location. Even though the item had likely migrated elsewhere, the mental picture gave her the sense that she knew where things were. Now, with a filing system in which she put things out of sight, she couldn't do that, and she felt lost. We had to help her not only to develop a filing system but also to use it enough to create a feeling of comfort and confidence.

Much of the work we did involved conducting experiments to test the nature and strength of Irene's attachments to her things. When she had difficulty discarding the scrap of paper containing an unidentified phone number, I suggested an experiment to clarify how important this was to her. "Why don't we throw it away just to see how it feels," I said. She agreed and threw the paper into the recycling box. "I feel somehow incomplete," she said. "It's not earthshattering, but just nagging. I'm sure I'll get over it." She paused and then added, "But I could rectify it with a brief phone call." She looked at me pleadingly. I suggested that we continue with the experiment just to see what would happen, and she reluctantly agreed. She resumed her excavation, but just a few minutes later she stopped and said, "You know, it would only take a few minutes to make the call. It may be important." At this, she reached in and pulled the paper out of the box.

Most hoarders are capable of discarding things if they can convince themselves that the object will not be wasted, that it will go to a good home, or, as in this case, that the opportunity it presented is no longer available. But the amount of time and effort involved in attaining this certainty makes it impossible to keep up with the volume of stuff entering the home. Eventually, most hoarders give up and simply let the piles accumulate again. Irene could have called the number and perhaps realized the opportunity it presented was lost. Then she may have felt comfortable discarding the number, but she would have learned nothing about how to give up on opportunities that have passed her by. One goal of the experiment was to teach her how to tolerate uncertainty regarding unrealized opportunities. We talked some more about this, and she agreed to keep going with the experiment. She put the paper back in the recycling box but couldn't keep from glancing at it every few minutes. Each time she did, she reiterated her urge to make the call and how it would make her feel so much better. Finally, she said, "Having the paper in sight, it's like a beacon. It pulls my eyes and then my thoughts. I'm going to cover it up so I can't see it." She covered the paper and never brought it up again.

The more experiments like this she did, the more her thinking about things changed and her ability to make decisions improved. In the beginning, Irene could tolerate very little of the work I asked her to do. "Can we stop now?" she asked just five minutes into our first treatment session after she had discarded one scrap of paper. But Irene persevered and worked very hard for a year and a half to clear out her home. Each step brought her more of a normal life. When her kitchen table was cleared, she and her children started sitting down to eat together. When her whole kitchen was cleared, she resumed cooking, and it began to feel normal to be in an uncluttered room. By the time we stopped working with her, the majority of her home was virtually clutter-free.

As I got to know Irene, it became clear that she was a prototype. She possessed all the characteristics we had been observing in other hoarders: perfectionism, indecision, and powerful beliefs about and attachments to objects. Possessions played a role in her identity, leading her to preserve her history in things. She felt responsible for the well-being of objects, and they gave her a sense of comfort and safety. In addition, things represented opportunity and a chance to experience all that life had to offer.

Irene's recovery taught us a great deal about how these behaviors can change. Most significant was the fact that she made every decision about what to keep and what to discard. Such freedom might have been a license to do little. Yet Irene willingly challenged herself to experience the distress of discarding cherished possessions. Had she not done so, she would not have succeeded. Each possession held a story. Often just telling that story loosened her connection to it and allowed her to let it go.

2

WE ARE WHAT WE OWN
Owning, Collecting, and Hoarding

> It is clear that between what a man calls *me* and what he simply calls *mine* the line is difficult to draw. We feel and act about certain things that are ours very much as we feel and act about ourselves.
>
> —William James

Recently, I asked the students in my seminar what things they owned that they considered meaningful. One young woman sheepishly admitted that she owned a shirt once worn by Jerry Seinfeld, which she had bought on eBay. All the students agreed that Seinfeld once having worn the shirt gave it value and meaning. Exactly what meaning they couldn't articulate. "But it was worn by Jerry Seinfeld!" was the best they could do.

"But if you didn't know it had been worn by Jerry Seinfeld," I asked, "would it have any special value?"

"No, absolutely not" was the reply.

"So the value is in your head and not really in the shirt?"

The students objected, saying that something of the essence of Seinfeld was connected to the shirt, as if he had left some part of himself there, even though the shirt had been laundered.

"Even if this was true, so what? Why would that give it value?" I asked.

"Because then you would be connected to Jerry Seinfeld" was the response.

After class, I thought, *Wasn't this what Irene was doing?* Perhaps she was trying to get connected to the world through her things—and to her, each one of those things was just like Jerry Seinfeld's shirt. They connected her to something bigger than herself. They gave her an expanded identity, a more meaningful life. It wasn't the objects themselves that she valued, but the connections they symbolized. And it's the same whether we collect celebrities' clothing, a piece of the Berlin Wall, a deck chair off the *Titanic,* or five tons of old newspapers. We can't help but imagine that some essence of the person or the event symbolized by the objects will magically rub off and become part of us.

At the end of the nineteenth century, a Scottish anthropologist named Sir James Frazer wrote an influential treatise on "magical thinking" and religion called *The Golden Bough* that shed some light on the lure of possessions. He described two forms of what he called sympathetic magic. According to this thinking, objects are in sympathy if they have properties that resemble each other (similarity) or if they were at one time touching or physically near each other (contagion). If two things are in sympathy, they have a continued and mutual influence on each other. The second definition of sympathy, contagion, seems to be at the core of our tendency to see magic in objects such as Jerry Seinfeld's shirt. One study, for example, found that children judged an object that had been touched by the queen of England to be more important than an identical object that had not been touched by her. The first object contained an essence not apparent from its physical characteristics.

Another way contagion may influence hoarding has to do not with the desire to be connected to someone or something else, but rather with the fear of being disconnected from a part of oneself. In many early civilizations, people took great pains to make sure that no one gained access to discarded parts of their bodies (e.g., fingernails, hair, teeth) or even pieces of their clothing. According to the laws of sympathetic magic, these items could be used to influence or control the person who lost them. For instance, someone who obtains another person's hair may be able to use it in a magical ceremony to make that person fall in (or out of) love. In some severe cases of hoarding, people show a seemingly irrational fear of discarding anything associated with their bodies, including nail clippings, used tampons, and even feces and urine (see chapter 11). This apparently delusional behavior may reflect magical contagion. Anthropologists consider this kind of thinking a precursor to scientific thought.

Owning

Irene loved only the things she owned or was about to own. Other people's stuff carried no such allure. She liked having her own "treasures" around her, preferably untouched by anyone else. Time and again, we have been struck by the idea that hoarding is not about the objects themselves but about ownership.

To understand hoarding, we must first ask a simple question. What does it mean to own something? It turns out that the answer to this question is not so simple. Philosophers have debated the nature of ownership as far back as Plato in the fourth century B.C.E. Plato was convinced that owning things was a vice to be avoided. He even argued that private ownership should be banned and that all property should be held in common. Aristotle, his stu-

dent, held the opposite view: he believed that individual ownership was essential for the development of moral character. However, he thought that ownership should be reserved only for those
who knew how to use the possession. In the thirteenth century,
Saint Thomas Aquinas took a middle path and spoke of "steward-
ship" rather than ownership, whereby people are merely the temporary guardians of God's possessions. In the seventeenth century,
John Locke suggested that things should belong only to those who
work for them, while a century later David Hume theorized that
when we see an object in someone's possession and accept that object as part of that person, we are conveying ownership to the pos-
sessor—so ownership is in part defined by social consensus. These
philosophers' interest in ownership stemmed from their interest in
how society should be structured and economies should be run.
It was left to more recent philosophers and social scientists to explore the meaning of ownership from an individual's perspective.

Jean-Paul Sartre insisted that we learn who we are by observing
what we own. He argued that ownership of most tangible objects
occurs with their acquisition or creation. Actively creating or acquiring the object is key. If something is passively acquired, ownership has to come from mastery over it or intimate knowledge of
it. He suggested that ownership extends beyond objects to include
intangible things as well. For instance, mastering a skill conveys
an ownership of sorts. Also, by knowing something intimately, we
come to own it, like a hiker who "knows" every inch of a mountain
trail and comes to feel as if he or she "owns" the trail. Reflecting
on the meaning of existence, Sartre wrote that "to have" is one of
three basic forms of human experience, the other two being "to do"
and "to be."

Apart from Sartre, most of the writings about ownership in the
twentieth century came from the social and biological sciences.
In 1918, psychologist William James described "appropriation" or

"acquisitiveness" as an instinct, something that is part of human nature, present at birth and with us throughout life. This instinct contributes to our sense of self. What is "me" fuses with what is "mine," and our "self" consists of what we possess. The use of instincts to explain behavior was in vogue in the late nineteenth and early twentieth centuries but fell out of fashion for several decades, only to revive again in the past few years thanks to increasingly sophisticated neuroscience research.

It is unclear whether the acquisition of possessions is instinctually or culturally driven, or both. What is clear is that notions of ownership vary widely across cultures, and acquisitive tendencies vary widely within cultures. In some early civilizations, possessions were seen as part of an individual's "life spirit" or self. Anthropologists have proposed this as the basic psychological process for ownership, which can be refined by cultural factors. Among the Manusians, an island tribe in Papua New Guinea described by Margaret Mead in 1930, this belief was readily apparent. They held possessions to be sacred and grieved for things lost as they would for lost loved ones. In contrast, the Tasaday of the Philippines, an isolated culture first discovered in the early 1970s, placed little value on possessions, perhaps because they needed few of them to survive.

By the middle of the twentieth century, psychoanalyst Erich Fromm had developed a theory of character in which he suggested that acquiring things is one way that people relate to the world around them. He believed that acquisition forms a "core" aspect of character. Excessive acquisition, or what Fromm called a "hoarding orientation," is one of four types of "nonproductive" character. People with a hoarding orientation, he thought, gain their sense of security from collecting and saving things. Fromm described people with this orientation as withdrawn, compulsive, suspicious, remote from others, orderly, and overly concerned with cleanliness and punctuality. In his later writings, Fromm posited two contrasting aspects of existence: having and being. Having, or the state of avarice, he claimed, is the most destructive feature of humanity.

Classical psychoanalysts such as Karl Abraham viewed possessions as socially acceptable alternatives to saving excrement — parts of the self these analysts believed every child has the impulse to retain. According to Abraham, the child replaces the desire to retain feces with a more acceptable impulse — to acquire possessions. The more recent object relations school of psychoanalytic thought describes the situation slightly differently. Donald Winnicott introduced the phrase "transitional object" to refer to physical objects to which children form intense attachments as they develop autonomy from their parents. These objects (e.g., blankets, soft toys) are replacements for the mother and form a transition from mother to independence. Early on, the mother is able to soothe the child. At some point, the transitional object takes over that role until the child is old enough to soothe himself or herself. (My own daughter became attached to a blanket she named Mana. Though now in her twenties, she still takes Mana with her whenever she travels.)

Sigmund Freud said little about hoarding, but he did describe a trio of traits he believed result from an anal fixation: orderliness, parsimony, and obstinacy. The parsimony component of the anal triad includes the hoarding of money: miserliness, or stinginess. Langley Collyer seemed to fit at least two of these traits, parsimony and obstinacy, although there is little evidence of his orderliness. Freud saw the hoarding of money as symbolic of fecal retention. Remnants of the "anal triad" can be seen in the current diagnostic criteria for obsessive-compulsive personality disorder (OCPD). This disorder, which is distinct from obsessive-compulsive disorder (OCD), also closely fits Fromm's description of people with a "hoarding orientation." For example, one of the eight criteria for OCPD is a preoccupation with details, rules, order, and organization; another is being stingy with money; and a third is being rigid and stubborn. Included among the eight is "the inability to discard worn-out or worthless objects even when they have no sentimental value." Objects in a hoard may appear to be without value to an observer, but someone with a hoarding problem would hardly describe them as worthless.

Only in the past three decades have scientists begun testing these theories with empirical research. Lita Furby, a pioneer researcher in the field of ownership and possessions, studied explanations for the things people own. She found three major themes among people of all ages. The first and most frequent was that possessions allow the owner to do or accomplish something. In other words, possessions provide a sense of personal power or efficacy. Possessions have instrumental value; they are tools to perform tasks. We need things to do things, to exert some control over our environment. This mirrors findings from our earliest study of hoarding, in which both our hoarding and non-hoarding participants said that they owned things because they had uses for them. Virtually all of our hoarding clients make this claim for things they save, but so do people who don't have hoarding problems. The difference between people who hoard and those who don't is in the volume and variety of things they view as "useful." For example, one elderly hoarder saved the labels from cans and jars of food to use as stationery.

Furby's second theme was that possessions provide a sense of security, reminiscent of Winnicott's transitional objects. This theme was also emphasized by Alfred Adler, an analyst who broke with classical psychoanalysis in suggesting that acquiring possessions is one way people compensate for a sense of inferiority created at birth. That inanimate objects can provide comfort was demonstrated by Harry Harlow's classic experiments with infant monkeys, who showed an innate preference for a soft, cloth surrogate mother over a wire-mesh one, even though the wire-mesh surrogate provided them with food and the cloth one didn't. When frightened, the monkeys ran to the soft surrogate, demonstrating that the texture of objects can provide comfort and security. Such comfort in objects led Irene to build a fortress of stuff and many of our clients to describe their homes as "cocoons" or "bunkers." One recent theory about hoarding by Stephen Kellett suggests that it evolved from attempts to create and maintain secure living sites, similar to nesting behaviors in animals.

The third major theme identified by Furby was that possessions become part of an individual's sense of self, just as Sartre believed. This kind of attachment can be subtle yet powerful. Objects can increase one's sense of status or power and expand one's potential: my purchase of a piano provides me with the potential to become a pianist, thereby expanding my identity. Objects can also maintain identity by preserving personal history. Most people save mementos of their personal past. These mementos become repositories for the sensations, thoughts, and emotions present during earlier experiences, promoting sensations such as the rush of nostalgia that can accompany hearing a song or smelling a scent from the past.

Collecting

People collect and save objects as a hobby in virtually all cultures. The earliest documented evidence of collecting comes from excavations of the Persian tombs at Ur in what is now Iraq. A collection of eleven hundred seal impressions on lumps of clay found there date to the fifth century B.C.E. In contemporary society, of course, many people collect objects of various types, from antique cars to matchboxes. By one estimate, one-third of adults in the United States collect something, and two-thirds of all households have at least one collector in residence. Some people collect odd items, such as empty cigarette packs or coffee cans, and people join together as societies dedicated to certain kinds of collecting, from the American Philatelic Society (stamps) to the more unusual Victorian Button Collectors Club. In contrast to the very limited science about hoarding, research on collecting has a long history, mostly from the perspective of sociology, anthropology, and the economics of consumer behavior.

Exactly what makes something a collection or someone a collector is elusive. Virtually anything can be and has been collected, from stamps to swizzle sticks. But just how many swizzle sticks does it take to make a collection? Most scholars who study collecting seem to agree that a collection must be a set of objects, meaning more than one, and that the items must be related in some way—they must have some kind of cohesive theme. They also must be actively acquired, meaning there must be some kind of passion or fire to seek out and obtain them. Someone who simply receives gifts that otherwise fit the definition is not a collector.

The process of collecting can be quite elaborate. Some sociologists liken it to a courtship in which the collector spends considerable time planning the hunt for an object and anticipating the moment of acquisition. The objects in the collection, once acquired, must be removed from their typical use. This feature was made abundantly clear to me in college when I visited a friend's dorm room and sat down next to a pile of Marvel Comics still in their wrappers. I pulled one out and started reading it, only to be physically assaulted when my friend's roommate arrived and saw what I was doing. They were, he informed me in no uncertain terms, not meant to be read! Another feature of collecting is that the objects are organized in some way. In one of our first studies, we visited a woman who described herself as a pack rat, but most of her home was spotless and not only uncluttered but almost empty. In her basement, however, she had every newspaper clipping about the British royal family from every major newspaper in the United States. Boxes of these clippings were stacked to the ceiling and arranged in rows by year and family member.

The key features that define a collection seem to be that it involves more than one thing, the things have to be related somehow, and the things have to be acquired and organized in a certain way. That means the dozen pens and pencils in my desk drawer are not a collection because I simply dump them there whenever I find myself with another writing implement, and when I need to, I use them. But if I actively sought them out and acquired them, carefully organized them, and never or rarely used them (and didn't allow anyone else to use them either), they could be a collection. A collector, then, is anyone who has a collection.

Collectors come in all types and ages. Researchers in the field say that nearly all children collect things, sometimes beginning as early as age three. Not coincidentally, it is at that time that children begin to understand possessive pronouns such as "mine" and "yours." Interestingly, children's use of the word "mine" seems to occur before their use of the word "yours," usually between the ages of two and two and a half. When "yours" first enters the vocabulary, it is often in an attempt to convince someone that they already have something and should not pursue "mine."

In general, the knowledge that someone can own something reflects a sophisticated self-understanding. Children's first use of "mine" is frequently associated with physical aggression to get or retain a possession, but early use of possessive pronouns is also associated with more sharing behavior later on. Most children younger than two don't have a clear understanding of ownership.*

---

*Interestingly, Margaret Mead observed that about the time children are developing an understanding of the word "mine," they are able to walk and thus pose a menace to other people's things. In that context, they may be more likely to be punished for possession-related transgressions and as a result learn the meaning of ownership.

Passionate collectors spend a great deal of time doing things related to their collections. Exactly what they do has been a subject of interest to scholars studying collecting. According to some scholars, collectors follow a series of steps in collecting. The first of these is setting a goal of what to collect. Once this decision has been made, planning for the acquisition begins. A byproduct of the planning process is fantasizing about the object. The fantasies increase the object's subjective value and give it a magical quality, and soon the value of the object outstrips and becomes disconnected from any functional utility it may have. Next comes the hunt, frequently the most pleasurable part of collecting. Many collectors shift from a self-focused state to what some have described as a "flow state," a mental state in which the person is so absorbed in the activity that he or she is unaware of his or her surroundings — commonly experienced by an athlete at the height of physical exertion or by someone immersed in a game or project.

Watching a passionate collector at a flea market makes it clear that his or her state of consciousness is altered during "the hunt." The person has little appreciation for anything going on around him or her; only the pursuit matters. When the acquisition occurs, it is accompanied by a wave of euphoria and appreciation of the object's features, which become part of the "story" of the acquisition. Finally, the excited collector catalogs the object and adds it to the collection, arranging for its display. Often subtle rituals accompany newly acquired objects. For instance, Freud used to place new acquisitions on his dining room table so that he could admire them while he ate.

Some people collect out of a desire for an aesthetic, others for prestige, and still others for a sense of mastery. But most theories of collecting elaborate on attempts to define, protect, or enhance the self. This is borne out by people's reactions to losing things to natural disasters or thievery. Most burglary victims feel that they have been violated, and many women liken it to being raped.

Anthropologists have described cultural practices in which people connect themselves to objects by licking or touching them. Likewise, the grieving in some cultures over the possessions of a deceased loved one demonstrates the extent to which a possession can be considered an extension of personal identity. This is the same phenomenon we observed with my students and Jerry Seinfeld's shirt. The connection between the object and its former owner transcends rationality. It is symbolic and magical.

Many collectors think of their collections as a legacy to pass on to their heirs or even the world. Some, especially art collectors and collectors of historical artifacts, donate their collections to museums or create their own museums for posterity. This has led some scholars to suggest that collecting is a way of managing fears about death by creating a form of immortality. This is consistent with a popular theory in social psychology called the terror management theory (TMT). TMT grows out of an existential predicament—that people, like animals, are mortal. But unlike animals, we are aware of our own mortality. Knowledge of the inevitability of death and its unpredictability can produce paralyzing fear. To cope with this potential terror, cultures provide beliefs, rituals, and sanctioned strategies for managing it. One of these strategies is the belief that some part of ourselves can live on after we die. Producing or amassing something of value is one way to accomplish this. Thus a collection offers the potential for immortality.

Quite a different theory of collecting relates to how people evaluate their self-worth. The compensation theory suggests that people who question their self-worth need evidence to reassure themselves of their value and importance. Physical objects provide clear and tangible verification of mastery over the world. The feedback boosts the collector's self-esteem and contributes to a positive self-image. William Randolph Hearst, founder of the Hearst publishing empire (and the model for the title character in the movie *Citizen Kane*), accumulated a vast collection of tapestries, paintings, sculptures, furniture, coins, and much more. He used some of the items to furnish his palatial home, but the majority filled warehouses throughout the country. Perhaps his collecting provided him with much-needed evidence of his mastery over the world. (Many of these collections are now on display at the Hearst Castle in San Simeon, California.)

Some collectors show extreme behaviors that straddle the border between eccentricity and pathology. Andy Warhol, an artist, filmmaker, photographer, and celebrity, is credited with the development of pop art, a movement in which art reflected the popular culture of the time. Warhol's paintings of brand-name products such as Campbell's soup and Coca-Cola were re-creations of the culture, ways of preserving not the exceptional but the mundane. He was also an avid collector and spent part of every day shopping at flea markets, antique stores, auction houses, and galleries—anywhere he might find something of interest. He collected not only fine art of every style and period but also what many considered junk. Like other famous collectors, Warhol displayed little of what he bought and tucked most of it away in warehouses. Still, his five-story house in New York City was so crammed that he could live in only two of the rooms. According to Stuart Pivar, a frequent shopping companion, Warhol had a plan to sell at least part of his collection, but he was still in the acquiring phase of this plan when he died at age fifty-eight. Whether he would ever have gotten past this phase is questionable. He once gave an antique shop a Mexican ceremonial mask to sell but then retrieved it out of fear that it would in fact be sold.

One of the most unusual aspects of Warhol's collecting became apparent shortly before his death. During the 1970s and 1980s, Warhol preserved nearly every bit of ephemera that came into his possession. He kept a cardboard box beside his desk, and when the impulse struck him, he cleared everything off his desk and into the box, no exceptions. Valuable prints, cash, and apple cores all went into what he described as his "time capsule." He dated it and stored it along with more than six hundred others. About one hundred of his time capsules have been opened so far. There seems no discrimination regarding what went into each one—an electric bill, silverware from a trip on an airplane, telephone messages, large sums of cash; whatever was in his life at that moment was swept into the box. Warhol's time capsules have become a pop culture archaeologist's dream. They are a record of Warhol's life in all its detail and triviality—as perfect a record as could be had. Material from the time capsules has been displayed in museums around the world. In this way, Warhol has become immortal.

Warhol was not the first to collect such seemingly unrelated objects in one container. Common in Europe during the sixteenth century were "cabinets of curiosities," or German *Wunderkammers*—jumbled collections of strange, wonderful, rare, and curious objects designed to create a picture, if not a wholly representative one, of the world at the time. Cabinets of curiosities were the precursors of early museums, filled with whatever the collector found interesting. Warhol certainly followed in this tradition, but he found *everything* interesting. His definition of art was all-encompassing, from the Jasper Johns painting he found at a flea market to the plastic trinket he bought at the same time. For Warhol, even the process of collecting seemed to be a form of art. Judging by the interest generated by his time capsules, many share this view.

Hoarding

Is such a passion for collecting pathological? It hardly matters how much stuff anyone owns as long as it doesn't interfere with his or her health or happiness or that of others. But when it does, the result can be dramatic, as was the case with the Collyer brothers and with Irene. Distress or impairment constitutes the boundary between normal collecting and hoarding. Many of the people we see experience great distress because of their hoarding. Acquiring and saving things has wrecked them financially and socially, driven their families away, and impaired their ability to carry out basic activities of living. In some cases, neighbors' and family members' lives have been impaired as well. Hoarding is not defined by the number of possessions, but by how the acquisition and management of those possessions affects their owner. When hoarding causes distress or impairs one's ability to perform basic functions, it has crossed the line into pathology.

Defining hoarding this way means that people with smaller living spaces and those without the resources to rent storage space may be at greater risk for developing a hoarding problem. In our experience, however, people with hoarding problems fill the space they are living in regardless of the size or number of storage units they have. We have seen clients who own four or five houses. When they fill one house, they move to another and fill it in short order. Then they move on to the next one. The more space they have available, the more space they fill. Perhaps this is actually the goal—to fill space.

The edges of hoarding are not always clear. Excessive clutter is the hallmark of hoarding and the feature most likely to cause distress and interference. But definitions of what constitutes clutter vary widely. We once received a referral from a psychiatrist shortly after he read a newspaper story about our research. He was treating someone with a severe hoarding problem and thought the man would be a good candidate for our research. When the patient called us, he complained that his hoarding was so bad that his wife had left him. We braced ourselves when we approached his house, but when we got inside, it was as neat as a pin except for two piles—one under the dining room table and one behind a chair in the living room. We assumed that he had miraculously cleared his home, but he said that this was as bad as it had ever been. He complained bitterly about the clutter, insisting that it had resulted in his wife's departure. Apparently, he had convinced his psychiatrist, who had never been to his home, that hoarding was his problem. It was clear to us that he had no hoarding problem, but rather needed an explanation for why his wife had left. After a few minutes with him, it became apparent that his temper, rigidity, and controlling behavior were more likely explanations for his wife's departure. Clearly, his understanding of the word "clutter" differed from ours, a common occurrence when we talk with people about what we study.

To make sure we had an accurate way to assess clutter, we set out to develop a nonverbal measure that did not rely on the word. We tried photographing my lab filled with stuff, but it just didn't look right. Piles of newspapers, clothes, boxes, bags, and other things I had brought from home looked out of place in the laboratory. I asked the students in my senior seminar if they would help. As a class project and with money from Gail's university, we rented a college-owned apartment and set about filling it with stuff. We planned to take pictures of each room at various levels of clutter. The students enjoyed filling the apartment with newspapers, magazines, clothes, and things otherwise destined for the dumpster.

We got permission to borrow couches and chairs from the psychology department lounge to furnish the apartment. Unfortunately, word of that permission did not reach campus security. The class met in the evening, and after class one night, we removed the lounge furniture and put it on top of my car. It was nearly midnight by the time we got it to the apartment and unloaded. When I got home, my telephone was ringing. It was a campus security officer informing me that security had had a report that my students had stolen furniture out of the psychology lounge. I explained that I had orchestrated the removal, not my students, and that we had permission from the department chair. He did not accept my explanation, nor did he see the humor in the situation. He informed me that I would have to return the furniture immediately, or he would file charges against me and the students. One of the benefits of working at a small college is that you get to know most of the people working there. Campus security reported to the director of facilities, who happened to be a friend of mine. Luckily, he had a sense of humor when I called him at 1:00 A.M. and explained my problem. He made a phone call, and we didn't get arrested.

We focused on three rooms—the kitchen, the living room, and the bedroom. Our plan was to fill each room nearly to the ceiling and take photographs as we uncluttered the space. To make the job easier, we started with several layers of empty copy paper boxes. On top of these we put the stuff accumulated by the students. As we removed the boxes, the top layer remained roughly the same for each photo. This allowed us to create a series of photographs from Collyer-like to clutter-free for each room. We ran into a problem trying to remove boxes from the room, so we "buried" a student in the midst of the clutter near the back of the room. When we were ready to set up the next picture, she popped up and took out some of the boxes from underneath the clutter. I wondered whether her parents would have thought her tuition was well spent on a class in which the professor buried her under a mountain of clutter.

The result of the project was a series of nine photographs depicting clutter in each room. People can simply point to the picture that looks most like their bedroom, living room, or kitchen, and we don't have to rely on their interpretation of the word "clutter." We use the "Clutter Image Rating," as we now call it, in most of our ongoing research. It gives us an unambiguous marker of the seriousness of the problem and clarifies the word "clutter" in the world of hoarding.

Hoarding in Literature

Hoarding has a distinguished literary history. Literature from as far back as the fourteenth century makes reference to hoarding. Dante reserved the fourth circle of hell for "hoarders" and "wasters" in his *Inferno.* Charles Dickens created several hoarders, including Krook, a *Bleak House* (1852–1853) character whom Dickens described as "possessed of documents" in a shop where "everything seemed to be bought and nothing to be sold." Honoré de Balzac's *Cousin Pons* (1847), a collector of "bric-a-brac," was thought to be loosely based on Balzac himself. Sir Arthur Conan Doyle's Sherlock Holmes was described by his accomplice Watson as having "a horror of destroying documents," to the extent that "every corner of the room was stacked with bundles of manuscript." The Russian novelist Nikolai Gogol described a classic hoarding case in *Dead Souls,* written in 1842. Plyushkin was a wealthy landowner whose peasants took to calling him "the fisherman" for his habit of "fishing" the neighborhood for "an old sole, a bit of a peasant woman's rag, an iron nail, a piece of broken earthenware," all of which he piled into his already packed manor. Since *Dead Souls,* the word "Plyushkin" has been used in Russian slang to describe someone who collects discarded, useless, or broken objects. In Russian psychiatry, the Plyushkin syndrome is a disorder in which someone collects and saves useless objects, usually trash.

Hoarding is not just a Western phenomenon. In 2005, the *Mainichi Shimbun*, an English-language newspaper in Japan, ran a story describing a fifty-six-year-old man whose apartment floor collapsed from the weight of twenty years' worth of magazines and newspapers. The term for such cases in Japan is *Gomi yashiki*, or "garbage houses," the subject of research by Fabio Gygi, a British anthropologist. Hoarding has been reported throughout the world on every continent but Antarctica. Although its severity may vary and the nature of the items hoarded may be different in Egypt than in China, the behavior of excessive collecting and storing of objects does not appear to be an exclusively culture-bound syndrome.

3

AMAZING JUNK
The Pleasures of Hoarding

Tag sales. That's my thing. It's what gives me joy. I get a
real high from finding a bargain. Every Saturday morning,
I'm supposed to work, but I go tag-saling instead. They
dock my pay, but I don't care. This is what I love to do. I'm
in a much better mood when I get to work.

—Irene

If she hadn't gotten onto the highway, it might not have happened.
If she had turned north instead of south, things might have been
different. But she went south, a direction that took her past the
entrance to the mall. The Target billboard hooked her. Before she
had time to think about it, she was in the parking lot and out of the
car. At this point, it didn't matter which way she turned. Shopping
cues surrounded her, and favorite stores stretched out in all direc-
tions. The pleasure of buying—of acquiring stuff—was at her fin-
gertips, and she was powerless to resist.

Janet came to us not long after that binge. Her home was seriously cluttered, but more problematic for her was her excessive
buying. Although she had a successful professional career with a
good income, her family was always short of money. Her credit
cards were maxed out, and she owed more than $25,000. She had

tried but failed to pay off any of the debt in three years. In fact, the total was growing rather than shrinking.

Her financial problems were the source of serious arguments with her husband. The week before she came in for treatment, her husband had criticized her for her spending and refused to help her with cooking or cleaning at home. She was angry and upset. She felt unappreciated by him and complained that he had made her "slave of the year." Depressed about her circumstances and anxious to avoid further conflict with him, she got into the car to go for a drive.

Her drive led her to the mall, and before she knew it, she was standing in a clothing store, still brooding over the fight at home. Even at this point, however, a shopping episode was not inevitable. She had not yet thought much about what she was doing. When she did, however, her thoughts betrayed her. Her first thought was not of shopping, but of her husband: *What right does he have to tell me how to spend my money? I work hard and make a good salary. I deserve nice things!* These thoughts wiped away any chance she had of resisting the urge to buy. Despite the fact that she understood the seriousness of her addiction to shopping, the thoughts made it seem to her that she had a *duty* to shop just to prove her worth. The combination of her emotional state and the rack of dresses in front of her strengthened her rationalizations, and they in turn kept her from thinking rationally about her plight.

She tried on a dress. The clerk commented on how nice it looked. Janet's mood brightened. She forgot about the argument with her husband. The attentiveness of the clerk pleased her. She felt respected, important, worthy—things she didn't feel at home. She found shoes and a belt to match the dress. She was happy. She found a card that wasn't maxed out and bought more than $500 worth of stuff. Her euphoria was palpable as she headed out of the store.

But even before she got to her car, her thoughts changed. How much had she spent? Was it really more than $500? She had hoped to reduce her credit card debt by that much this month; now she had increased it by that. How could she tell her husband about this? She couldn't very well hide it from him. He saw all her credit card bills. How mad would he be?

As she pondered these questions, the implications of her purchases sank in. She sat in the parking lot and cried. Regret and worry engulfed her. Worse, she began to draw damaging conclusions about herself that usually surfaced only during her occasional bouts of depression: *What is wrong with me? I must be a terrible person to put my husband and children under such financial strain for things I don't even want. Anyone who does this must be totally worthless.*

Janet's depressed feelings persisted after the episode, and little in her life seemed to alleviate them. Shopping helped, but only temporarily. It was the only time she felt important and respected, but afterward she felt even more depressed and worthless. Postbinge, the conflict at home intensified, making it that much harder for her to resist her shopping urges: a vicious cycle.

One feature of hoarding that sets it apart from disorders such as OCD is that it can be intensely pleasurable. For most people who hoard, the experience of shopping or acquiring is so overwhelmingly rewarding that it erases all thoughts of consequences. Recently, we surveyed nearly a thousand people with hoarding problems. More than two-thirds of them bought or shopped excessively, and just over half had problems with the acquisition of free things. Both Gail and I speak frequently to self-help groups about hoarding. On these occasions, we avoid bringing handouts, as experience has taught us that many in our audience will collect multiple copies, adding to their clutter.

People who hoard also derive intense pleasure from the things they own. During one of my visits with Irene, she got very excited and said, "I have to show you something." She scurried to the next room and returned with a large plastic bag filled with bottle caps. "Look at these bottle caps—aren't they beautiful? Look at the shape and the color," she said. Much as I tried, I couldn't muster much enthusiasm for this collection. Old bottle caps? What in the world did she see in them? She seemed hurt when I didn't share her appreciation. It is possible that people who hoard see and appreciate features of objects that others overlook, perhaps because of their emphasis on visual and spatial qualities. Irene put pieces of broken toys, packing material, and the like in a box she labeled AMAZING JUNK. When her kids were young, they played with it. When they lost interest, she hauled the box out occasionally to admire the features of these treasures. Might this reflect a different way of perceiving the world, one focused on aesthetic pleasures that the rest of us overlook? If so, is this a gift or a curse?

The pleasure extends beyond aesthetics. Much of Irene's hoard consisted of newspapers, magazines, and books. She described herself as an information junkie: notes to herself, names of restaurants recommended by people at work, lists of places to see, TV specials to watch, and various bits of wisdom all found a place in her home. On the pile in her TV room, a page torn out of a magazine article read, "When your cat won't take his medicine, spill some on his fur; he'll instinctively lick it off." Although she had no cat, she saved it in case one of her friends ever needed such advice. She loved knowing details like this and doubted her ability to remember them, so saving seemed a good idea. Gradually, her collection got out of hand.

"I used to go through the newspaper, page by page, looking for interesting articles," she told me. "When I found one, I would read it and then cut it out and throw away the rest. Before long, to save time, I looked through the paper and cut out the interesting articles, but I didn't read them. After a while it was easier to look through the paper and just keep the whole thing if it contained an interesting article. Finally, I stopped even looking through the paper and just saved the whole thing. I plan to read them when I have time." Over time, simply having the papers substituted for reading them. Just to know she had them was almost as pleasurable as actually reading them. Even after reading them, she was reluctant to get rid of them because she might forget what she read.

The pleasurable aspects of hoarding are even more apparent during the process of acquiring things. Despite the fact that Irene was in very poor financial shape after her husband left her, she couldn't stop herself from buying more things: "That's my thing. It's what gives me joy. I get a real high from finding a bargain."

Irene's high from shopping echoes the experience of most compulsive buyers and resembles that of people addicted to drugs or alcohol. Some researchers have suggested that compulsive buying is a form of behavioral addiction similar to drug dependence. If so, processes in the brain that control pleasure and reinforcement may be involved. Addiction researchers have identified the ways in which certain substances such as cocaine, heroin, and alcohol influence the brain's reward system. Cocaine prevents the neurotransmitter dopamine from escaping the synapse, the area between brain cells where communication occurs. The dopamine that builds up stimulates the pleasure center, not only producing the high that addicts feel but also interfering with normal judgment and memory, making it that much harder to resist the drug. Heroin causes the same flooding of the pleasure center by blocking the neurotransmitters that inhibit the effects of dopamine.

So far, no studies have shown disrupted neurochemical transmission in compulsive buyers. However, it is theoretically possible that behavioral addictions such as compulsive buying or even compulsive gambling might begin as habits and gradually evolve into addictions that are controlled by disruption of neurochemical transmission.

Aside from the high of shopping, resisting the impulse carries costs that make buying easier than not buying. I asked Irene what would happen if she resisted the urge to go to a tag sale. She replied, "I would feel like I'd lost out on something. There's something out there that I might need or want, and I'll lose it."

Irene's upstairs hallway was crowded with shopping bags containing her purchases—things she justified buying by telling herself she would use them as gifts. In her mind, the fact that these were destined to be given away put them outside the realm of her hoarding problem, despite the fact that they had cluttered her hallway for years. Irene's decision to buy these gifts was influenced by a variety of beliefs. Chief among them was the belief that she needed to be prepared for a situation in which she might need to give someone a gift and not have time to shop for it. In our first study, we found that hoarders reported more buying of extra items "just in case" they might be needed than did non-hoarders. One of our first participants showed us her stash of thirty-four shampoo bottles and said that if she used one bottle, she felt compelled to replace it so that she always had thirty-four bottles available. She did the same with bars of soap. She said, "It's nice to know that when the bar of soap gets this big," and she moved her thumb and forefinger just a few millimeters apart, "I have fifteen more bars." Her sense of how many extras she needed "just in case" was obviously considerably higher than most people's.

Also affecting Irene's buying was her addiction to the idea of opportunity. This was so powerful that she avoided going to any large city because, inevitably, she would pass a newsstand. Newsstands drew her like a moth to a light. The number and variety of newspapers and magazines left her giddy at the thought of all they contained. She described her thought process: "When I gaze at all the riches, I say to myself, 'Look at all those newspapers and magazines. Somewhere in the midst of all of that there may be a piece of information that could change my life; that could make me into the person I want to be. How can I walk away and let that opportunity pass?'" Not pursuing that elusive but all-important piece of information would torture her. The only way she could tolerate a trip to the city was to cross to the opposite side of the street and look the other way whenever she saw a newsstand. Curiously, Irene actually spent very little time reading. The idea of reading or the image of herself reading was what motivated her, not the reading itself.

For Janet, buying served many functions. When she was dwelling on her problems at home, she never felt worthwhile or appreciated. In contrast, the store clerks treated her with respect, especially those who had waited on her in the past. She described a sense of control while shopping that was missing elsewhere in her life. Shopping distracted her from family conflict and worries about her debt, and even served as an indirect way of communicating displeasure with her husband for his criticism of her. But perhaps most of all, it offered her a brief respite from her worries and frustrations. For a short time, she could dream of all that her new clothes and sports equipment promised. During each shopping episode, these dreams swamped the memory of what came after—guilt, conflict, and depression.

Janet seldom used the things she bought. Her home was full of clothes with the tags still attached. As with other of our clients, many things never left the original box or packing material. For those who suffer from compulsive buying but not hoarding, the purchased items are frequently returned, sold, or given away. For people who hoard, boxes pile up and gobble up living space.

Although most compulsive shopping episodes begin with a bad mood that the shopping temporarily alleviates, occasionally a good mood sets them off. After one therapy session in which Janet described being able to resist the urge to shop for the entire week, she left the clinic feeling pleased with herself. She was proud of her progress and could see some light at the end of the tunnel. But on the way home, the traffic slowed just before the exit to the mall. She was inside a store in minutes, celebrating her success in therapy with more buying. Predictably, the result was more regret, depression, and self-blame.

Although it is hard for most of us to imagine, the urge to buy can completely obliterate compulsive shoppers' knowledge of themselves and their circumstances. Several years ago, I worked with *Dateline NBC* on a TV special about hoarding. The show featured Phil, a man whose buying and collecting had already cost him his job and his house and threatened to break up his marriage. Yet when the camera crew accompanied him to a thrift store, he could not resist the urge to buy a set of left-handed golf clubs. Phil already had multiple sets of left-handed clubs, despite the fact that he was right-handed and seldom golfed. From his point of view, they were rare and special and called to him. During the episode, Phil described himself as being "in the zone." During intense shopping episodes like this, our clients often describe dissociative-like states, periods of time where they are so focused on the item they want to buy that they forget about the context of their lives—such as whether they have the money, space, or need for the item. Some people may have a tendency to experience this "flow state" more readily than others, making them vulnerable to becoming compulsive buyers or hoarders. Breaking out of this state and thinking about whether the purchase makes sense is terribly difficult.

Early in the twentieth century, Emil Kraepelin, the German psychiatrist widely considered the founder of scientific psychiatry, proposed a disorder he called "oniomania." From the Greek *onios,* meaning "for sale," oniomania is a pathological and uncontrollable impulse to buy things despite harmful consequences. The Swiss psychiatrist Eugen Bleuler, another early pioneer in psychiatry, described it as "impulsive insanity." Both considered oniomania a serious disorder. Documented cases include such notables as Mary Todd Lincoln and Imelda Marcos. Despite its early recognition, oniomania was virtually ignored by psychiatry and psychology until the early 1990s. Renamed "compulsive buying," it has become the focus of a great deal of research in psychiatry, psychology, business, and even anthropology. Regardless of whether compulsive buying should be considered a disorder, it clearly creates enormous problems for many people. Financially, these buyers have been found to carry twice the debt load of noncompulsive buyers. They experience considerable marital and legal difficulties because of their excessive purchases, not to mention the emotional costs—shame, embarrassment, remorse, and depression. We are just now beginning to recognize how common compulsive buying is. A recent study by Lorrin Koran, a Stanford University psychiatrist, and his colleagues revealed that nearly 6 percent of adults in the United States suffer from it. Although it seems (and some studies suggest) that women are especially prone to having this problem, recent research indicates that as many men as women are afflicted.

Sometimes people can partially or temporarily control their compulsive buying urges by avoiding the triggers for buying. Like Irene dodging newsstands, Janet often averted her eyes when she neared the cosmetics aisle. Others avoid whole sections of town because of a store that is too hard to resist when they are in the vicinity. Invariably, avoidance of this sort fails; it is almost impossible to get away from buying signals in our increasingly consumer-driven world.

Dumpster Diving and Free Stuff

Even for those unwilling to spend like Janet, there are plenty of pitfalls. For example, Phil from the *Dateline* episode could not resist the urge to scavenge through the neighborhood trash. Even the teasing his children received from other kids in the neighborhood was not enough to get him to stop. One day the film crew worked with Phil to get him to throw away something from his storage unit. He settled on a pair of old ice cube trays. The crew filmed as he walked to the dumpster to throw the trays away, a triumph for a man who had been unable to let go of anything. As he tossed them into the dumpster, he spotted a camera bag in there. He couldn't believe someone would throw out a camera bag. Then something else caught his eye, and in a matter of seconds Phil was inside the dumpster tossing out treasures destined for his unit. The incident was captured on film, and later Phil was horrified at the spectacle of himself in a dumpster on national TV. For Phil and most other people who hoard, any unowned object that might have residual value or use can be irresistible.

Acquiring free things isn't limited to people who scavenge dumpsters or castoffs. Colin, a gay man in his mid-sixties, retired from a lucrative career as a gallery owner and arts producer, had a similar problem, though you'd never catch him in a dumpster. "I'm living in an earthquake—Bergdorf Goodman slammed into Saks Fifth Avenue. Clothes are just everywhere," he said. "I'm such a capable person, but I'm addicted to clothes. I constantly need a fix." When Colin refused to allow a visit to his home, Gail interviewed him at her office.

He arrived dressed to the nines in expensive leisure clothes: a well-draped and zippered dark shirt with fine white piping, matching sports pants, and soft leather shoes that cradled his feet. He lounged casually in the office chair, punctuating his responses to questions with gestures that embellished his words. He complained that his possessions "seem to be controlling me. It's getting a bit dangerous; they trip me and fall on me and make me late. I just can't get a grip." His grammar implied that the objects, not him, were in control. Colin said that he hadn't noticed a problem of accumulation and disorganization until two or three years earlier when he felt he couldn't find things he was looking for. He wondered with amusement if he needed glasses.

Colin owned hundreds of fine cotton and silk shirts, dozens of gold cuff links, and scores of expensive watches, designer suits, and wingtip shoes, his favorites. "I have all colors," he reported with some pride, "three dozen of each." Imported tweeds were a special pleasure—the feel of the fabric, the colors in the weave. When he was working, he used to change his clothes five or six times a day, but now in retirement he did so only twice or maybe three times. It was important, he noted, to wear the right clothes for each social occasion, day and night, and since he still had free dry cleaning from his arts producer days, there was no need to worry about cost. "But now I can't find what I'm looking for," he said, adding that it sometimes took him two hours to dress as he struggled to locate the right item in his mass of clothes and accessories. "I live as if it's a dressing room."

Colin acquired nearly all his clothes for free. His designer friends and former colleagues regularly sent him haute couture for his personal use. These gifts were intended to gain his approval and pay him back for favors in the past. If Colin merely mentioned to a friend that he might need something for his travels, it arrived on his doorstep from London, Moscow, or Paris. Because his income was now fixed, Colin relied on these former colleagues and friends to support his "habit." "When I travel, I go to boutiques and look at their stuff. But I'm not paying for any of this," he said. "I gave them their start. If I want something, I make it known, and it arrives." On his way to Europe to join some friends and hobnob with royalty, Colin found time to request cuff links, shirt collars, sock braces, studs, more wingtips, and flowers for various people, all to be delivered to his suite on his arrival.

But Colin confessed to scheduling fewer social events lately in case he was unable to get ready in time. Locating the right clothes and accessories was becoming harder and harder. He expressed concern that his friends were enabling his penchant for too many fine clothes, and he also wanted to reclaim more living space. Traveling now provoked mild panic, as he couldn't decide how much to take and what would fit in his oversize suitcase.

As for a number of other people we have interviewed, perfectionism made almost everything more difficult for Colin. "Don't tell me looks don't matter. Of course they do. Pullese!" He gesticulated with a flourish of his hand. While clothes may make the man in some situations, Colin carried this mantra to an extreme. "Everything has to match, including my underwear," he said. Getting dressed became a struggle as he sought to precisely match the belt to the shoe leather. He took pride in his fifty pinstripe suits, each a slightly different color of blue. From his point of view, color mattered, and it was important to have exactly the right combination—the perfect tie to match the suit and shirt, not to mention the shoes, belt, and cuff links. "I start at perfection and then make improvements," he declared proudly.

He acknowledged being "really tightfisted," and volunteered, "I hoard money, too." When he dined out, he made sure others picked up the check. Although he could be tight, he nonetheless took pleasure in helping others and found charity work interesting. He paid tuition anonymously to support children's education in a Third World country. On one trip to a poor country, he randomly selected several of the most unattractive men in a gay bar and handed each an iPod as a gift. "It really makes a difference in their lives," he pointed out.

But giving things away now seemed harder. "Objects now seem to matter more: they're accumulable," he observed. "I *am* older. I used to be considered very attractive, interesting, and desirable. Now experience and perceived wealth are the things I can trade on." Although he didn't say so, he seemed worried that the current source of his expensive apparel might dry up, built as it was on old obligations that would one day expire.

Concerns about his own personal value seemed to lie behind Colin's addiction. "I keep more of the things people give me [rather than those he himself acquires]. They make me feel more valuable." Colin acknowledged that sometimes he now felt invisible, whereas before he used to be the center of attention. "I'm crankier, more short-tempered; things annoy me more easily now. When did I go from being Dennis the Menace to Mr. Wilson?" The pathos of his words echoed that of many hoarders whose self-image has become dependent on the objects they believe represent them.

Stealing

Billie was a seventy-five-year-old grandmother of six. Because of a hip problem, she used a walker. She had been to a number of my talks and corresponded with me about her hoarding problem, but not until a friend called on her behalf did I learn that she also had a habit of stealing.

An exceptionally bright and active woman despite her mobility problems, Billie always seemed to be on the go and always had a project or activity that commanded her attention. Yet she'd had a lifelong struggle with hoarding, clutter, and compulsive buying.

The stealing began when she was struggling with a serious shopping problem that she couldn't afford. To control the problem, she invented excuses for not buying things. Her best one was "For the money this costs, it's not worth it." One day after making this excuse to herself, she thought, *But if I just take it, I wouldn't have to pay anything.* With her major defense gone, she started acquiring again. She knew how to shoplift: as a child, she had worked in her uncle's store watching for shoplifters. In no time, stealing gave her a thrill, a "high" she couldn't get from anything else. Could she outwit the store clerks and security? She pitted her cunning and grandmotherly charm against their vigilance. One day a few years earlier, while in a department store, Billie stuck a small book about golf in her pocket. She didn't play golf, but her son-in-law did, and this would be part of his birthday present. Unbeknownst to her, the book contained a code that set off a sensor when she left the store. The alarm sounded, and clerks came running. As she made her way back into the store, she acted as though she didn't understand what was happening. When they found the book, she coolly explained that she'd put it there because she was afraid it would fall out of her shopping cart. She must have forgotten she had it in her pocket. Though frightened inside, she acted calm and cool, pretending to be befuddled—just a confused granny. She convinced them it was not intentional and let them help her out to her car. She recounted the episode to me with some pride. She showed no shame or concern over the consequences.

Billie seemed to fit the profile for kleptomania: She never planned her stealing; it just happened. She no longer had financial problems and had ample resources to buy the things she stole. And most of her stealing involved things of little or no value. We suspect that disorders such as kleptomania are part of a cluster of problems including hoarding, compulsive buying, and even patho-logical gambling.* Certainly, kleptomania and compulsive buying are related to the acquisition we see in hoarding. What may unite these disorders is a psychology of opportunity. Walking away from something that could be acquired means walking away from the potential benefits of ownership. Most of us learn that any action we take means pursuing one opportunity at the expense of another. For people afflicted with this problem, the fear of losing an oppor-tunity is greater than the reward of taking advantage of one. Con-sequently, all opportunities are preserved, but none are pursued.

A few weeks later, Billie's friend called again. "You have to do something! It's like your conversation with Billie opened a Pan-dora's box. She's stealing everything." I called Billie. Although her friend had exaggerated, Billie had had several stealing episodes that were more serious than usual. Her favorite jewelry store had marked down a box of stuff—bracelets, rings, and necklaces. Normally, each was between $40 and $50, but they were on sale for $5 each. She bought two bracelets and pocketed eight more. She planned to keep the two she bought and give the rest to her daughter.

For Billie to get control of this behavior, she needed to exam-ine what her stealing meant to her sense of self, and she needed to experience the consequences of her actions. I asked Billie what she thought about herself when she reflected on her behavior. She said that basically she felt like an honest person, but not an honor-able one. She couldn't quite articulate the difference. I asked her what it would take for her to be an honorable person with respect to the items she had stolen from the jewelry store. At first she just said she should stop stealing, but I pressed her about this episode.

*In one of our studies, we found a significant correlation between problem gambling and hoarding (Frost, Meagher, & Riskind, 2001).

She said that perhaps she could send back the stuff she had stolen anonymously.

"Is that the honorable thing to do?" I asked.

"No," she said.

"What is?"

"Perhaps I could bring it back and say the extras got put in my bag by mistake or that I accidentally put them in my pocket and forgot to pay for them."

"Is that the *honorable* thing?"

"Maybe I could bring in one or two of them to the sister store in a different town. I know this is a chain."

"Is that the honorable thing to do here?"

"No, it's not."

"What would it be?"

"I should go in and confess to the store manager and tell him what I've done."

"And then what would happen?"

"I don't know."

"Perhaps we should talk that through. What is he likely to say?"

"Well, he'll be mad, I'm sure. And he'll probably call the police."

"So tell me what it will be like when the police show up."

"I guess they may arrest me."

"Put you in handcuffs maybe?"

"Yes."

"And what will you have to do?"

"I guess I would have to call my daughter to bail me out."

"So your daughter will have to come to the police station. Since she has young children, she may have to bring them along, right?"

"Yes."

"So you are at the police station, and your daughter and grand-children come in and the policeman explains to them what you did. Can you imagine what that will be like?"

Billie was crying at this point, but she continued to describe the scene, the disappointment on her daughter's face and the confused, worried looks on her grandchildren's.

I wanted her to follow through with the story so that she could experience something of the consequences that her behavior might set in motion. Her initial description of the stealing was colored by thrill and excitement, with no attention to the likely consequences and no sense of what it said about her as a person. Imagining consequences seemed to change how she felt about her behavior.

At the end of our conversation, she resigned herself to making things right and accepting the consequences of her behavior. A few weeks later, her friend called me again. "I don't know what you said to Billie, but she stopped cold turkey. She hasn't stolen anything in weeks and says she's got no desire to do so." I later heard from Billie, who said she had indeed stopped stealing. Whenever she had the urge, which was now seldom, she thought about her daughter's and grandchildren's faces at the police station. "It's just not worth it," she declared. But she never returned the bracelets, probably precisely because of these images.

Luckily, only a very small number of people with hoarding problems steal. However, the vast majority of hoarders have other problems controlling their acquisition. Research on compulsive buying gives us some clues as to why. As we've seen from the cases described here, the act of collecting is a central feature in the lives of many hoarders. Their sense of themselves and their self-worth seem to be tied to their possessions, but not in a simple way. Our recent studies show that rather than being associated with low self-worth, as is the case with depression, compulsive buying and hoarding seem to be related to people feeling ambivalent or uncertain about their worth. A question rather than a conclusion defines them: "Am I a worthwhile person?" The question provokes them to seek evidence regarding their worth. Our culture provides, and perhaps encourages, several tangible forms of evidence, such as accomplishments or material possessions. When self-worth depends on tangible markers such as these, emotional problems follow.

Being "in the zone" brings intense satisfaction and pleasure, but what follows can crush the self-esteem of even the most well-adjusted person. The catch-22 is clear: the taker is damned if she does and damned if she doesn't. Fixing this problem takes a heroic effort. It requires bringing the full context of one's life into focus during the decision-making process—something few of us do on a regular basis. It means relearning how to react to the sight of a desired possession. Instead of narrowing and focusing his attention, the person must learn to expand it to consider how this object fits into the fabric of his life.

Janet's therapist helped her understand how shopping functioned in her emotional life. Together they identified the different ways that shopping lifted her mood. Since she was "in the zone" during shopping episodes, Janet had never recognized any of her real reasons for buying. When she did, she began to see how her shopping fit into the bigger picture of her life. Answering a few subsequent questions had a big impact on Janet. Does buying really give you these things (resolution of family problems, self-worth, control, excitement, communication with your husband) in a satisfactory way? Is buying the way you want to achieve these things? Knowing that she used shopping as a way to manage her bad moods and that its long-term costs far outweighed the instant gratification, Janet had the motivation to work with her therapist to develop more appropriate ways of managing her moods.

Still, it was difficult to resist the urge when she experienced a buying trigger—such as driving near the mall. Clearly, it takes more than just understanding how buying occurs to control one's urges. Early in treatment, Janet found herself "in the zone" several times, unable to control her buying. Our approach to gaining control is much like a physical conditioning program, but instead of exercise, we gradually increase the intensity and duration of urges to acquire. To do this, Janet's therapist accompanied her on "non-shopping trips," or more accurately for those who also pick up free things, "non-acquiring trips." This meant exposing Janet to the very cues that enticed her to buy, in order to build up her resistance. This method is similar to those that have been used effectively to help people resist the urge to drink, use drugs, or gamble excessively. Rather than avoiding cues altogether (impractical in daily life), Janet needed to learn how to face her problems and the world without the pleasure and comfort of shopping. She began by simply driving past a store (what we call drive-by non-shopping) and worked her way up to handling an item in the store and then walking away without it.

This process sounds simple, but it can be painfully challenging for those who are unaccustomed to resisting their urges and have no emotional armor to protect them. On her first non-shopping trip alone, Janet had a difficult time. She wanted to buy a pair of jeans so badly that she felt sick while she was in the store. Despite her feeling, she persisted, and the urge to buy gradually declined. She went home empty-handed and proud of her accomplishment. Our work with compulsive hoarders shows that both the urge to acquire and the sense of distress at not doing so subside as the minutes pass during these non-shopping exposures. The more frequently our clients engage in non-shopping, the more quickly the urges subside and the less powerful they become. Understanding this is crucial for treatment; when one of our therapists met his client at a store for a non-shopping trip, the woman announced proudly that she had arrived thirty minutes early and shopped for items she was eager to show her therapist. Now, she asserted, she was ready to practice non-shopping. Clearly, she had missed the point. She couldn't properly engage in the treatment until she understood why she must endure the urge.

Our non-acquiring trips work in part because a therapist is available to help talk people through their urges and place them in context. Since therapists can't accompany people everywhere they go, we ask our clients to create a list of acquisition questions to carry with them. These are simple, commonsense considerations such as "Do I have anything like it already?" or "Do I have a place to keep it?" Janet found these questions particularly helpful. They seemed to work nearly as well as having her therapist present, although they will work only if they are used. On one occasion, I overheard a member of one of our treatment groups tell another member, "I went shopping last week, but I didn't bring my questions because I knew if I did, I wouldn't buy anything."

Our research indicates that most people who undergo this treatment learn to control their acquiring more easily than they manage to get rid of their clutter. For some the effect is financially rewarding. Janet, for instance, paid off her credit card debt and ended treatment with more than $10,000 in the bank. By the end of her treatment, Janet could look through clothes racks and walk away without buying. Whereas controlling acquisition is pretty straightforward, changing the meaning of one's possessions and ridding one's home of hoarded clutter is far more difficult.

4

BUNKERS AND COCOONS
Playing It Safe

I had such a terrible week that I just wanted to come home
and gather my treasures around me.

—Irene

Chris lived in a small bungalow on the edge of Berkeley, California. Overgrown trees and shrubs hid her house from the street. Potted plants covered most of her porch. She had an eye for Persian rugs and hung them from ceiling to floor along her hallway. There were eight or nine of them on top of one another, narrowing the hallway by at least a foot and giving her home a cavelike feel. Goat paths threaded through the waist-high piles of books, clothes, magazines, and other stuff filling the house—certainly enough clutter to impair her quality of life. She told us her refrigerator had broken recently, but she couldn't remove it through the maze of stuff, nor could she get the new one in. So the new refrigerator ended up in the basement, adding one more inconvenience to her already complicated life. Like so many of the people we've met, she was very intelligent. It was clear that she had read most of the hundreds of books that were strewn throughout her home. Chris was a nurse who had found me through an online hoarding support group, and we corresponded for quite a while before we met. Though she was a great resource for others, she had trouble controlling her own passion for collecting.

"I have pioneered a method of spotting hoarder houses from the street," she wrote to me once. "I just drive slow and look for front yards that look like mine, a jungle of hundreds of plants. Porches are often full too." She offered to make a study of it, taking pictures and sneaking by when a door or window opened to get confirmation. "I estimate the incidence of H-C [hoarding and cluttering] homes at about one household per block here in Berkeley," she claimed. Chris knew her neighborhood and the characters who lived in it. She accompanied us on a "hoarding tour of Berkeley" (see chapter 13), and she pointed out homes occupied by people she knew or suspected were afflicted with hoarding. "Like mine, complex and jungly" was how she described them. Pruning trees and shrubs was clearly a low priority. Permanently drawn shades pressed against the windows; apparently unsteady piles of stuff had fallen against them inside. Old and dented buckets, broken lawn mowers, paint containers, and piles of wood littered the yards, which were often obscured by tall grass and weeds.

Many of these homes needed repair and painting, but there is some variability on this point among hoarders. One of our most severe hoarding clients lived in a home whose exterior could be featured in *House & Garden* magazine, but whose interior was a horror. Our research has shown that only about half of identified hoarders live in dilapidated homes, so I guessed we were probably seeing only half of the hoarding population of Berkeley.

The darkness of the houses we drove by struck me: they were practically caves. To me they seemed dreary and menacing, but I came to understand that many hoarders, like Chris, view their homes very differently. It's possible that people who hoard prefer small, enclosed personal spaces — almost the opposite of claustrophobia. Perhaps they close in their living spaces to achieve a co-coon-like feeling of comfort and safety. I remembered how Irene, after a stressful day, wanted to come home and "gather my treasures around me." Irene's "treasures" helped her feel safe; when threatened, she wanted to surround herself with them. Investigators who study fear make a distinction between events that signal threat and events that signal safety. We commonly think of fear as occurring in the presence of threat signals. But fear can be activated by the absence or removal of safety signals as well. For many hoarders, the thought of losing possessions fills them with fear.

In many yards, we saw cars and trucks given over to storage. The truck beds, back seats, and even driver's seats were full of newspapers, clothing, and other overflow from the homes. Rusty charcoal grills, usually in multiples, peppered lawns, as did containers of various sorts, barrels, beat-up trash cans, and planting pots. The stuff the containers held looked disorganized and chaotic and had obviously been untouched for years. As we passed block after block, every street seemed to have two or three cocoon-like houses. It reminded me of the surprise I felt at the large number of phone calls we got when we placed our first ad looking for pack rats. Is it possible that so many of us have lost control of our stuff? Were all these houses just containers for the things that make us feel safe?

Walling off the Danger

Bernadette was a large, light-skinned black woman, attractive and stylishly clad when she first came to therapy. Her personality filled the room when she wasn't depressed. She dressed very well on some days, with matching shoes, purse, and scarf; she favored pink and patent leather. On other days, she dressed to match her depression, throwing on whatever she found in front of her—even pajamas with snow boots. She had been a schoolteacher for many years until the birth of her daughter when she was forty-four. Shortly thereafter, she and her husband adopted a little boy. Her daughter and son were now five and three, respectively. Her husband was a committed preacher, busy taking care of his flock in a largely African American community. Bernadette's and the children's lives revolved around her husband's church as well. She assisted her husband as a deacon, attended a Bible study group, and joined her fellow churchgoers to pray whenever anyone needed help. Now she was the one in need. Bernadette and her family lived amid mounds of clothes, shoes, kids' drawings, pet projects, and assorted everyday family paraphernalia. After years of struggle and conflict with her husband over her hoarding, which had taken over their three-story, fourteen-room Victorian home, she finally decided to seek treatment for her problem.

By then, her home was nearly uninhabitable. The entry hallway and first-floor landing were full of children's clothing and toys, shoes, decorations for various holidays, books, Sunday school papers, and lesson plans from her teaching years. Just as we've seen in so many homes, ineffective efforts to organize were evident in the innumerable empty plastic bins and lids stacked elsewhere. The living room and adjacent dining area were waist-high with clutter of a similar sort—lots of clothes and shoes, plus place mats and table decorations, random papers, and assorted knickknacks. The stairwell contained more plastic containers and covers, cascades of newspapers and magazines, and more clothes and shoes. The bedrooms ranged from waist- to ceiling-high mountains of mostly clothes and shoes. The children could still sleep in their beds, but barely.

Most of what filled Bernadette's home came from her daily shopping sprees. She was devoted to her kids and insisted that they should have the things she never had. She tried to be frugal, shopping primarily at discount stores, because the family had very little money. Nonetheless, her buying so taxed their finances that the electricity had been shut off for nonpayment, and the family was facing bankruptcy. To cope with the loss of electricity, they stretched extension cords up the cluttered stairwell from the single working outlet in the basement. Although this provided them with light, it increased the risk of fire in a home from which escape would have been difficult.

Child and Family Services had been inquiring about the conditions in the home, and the loss of her children was a possibility if Bernadette could not learn to stem the tide of clothing and toys. Still she shopped. Her husband was angry. The chaos at home prevented his finding important papers or inviting anyone from the church to their home, and it kept their kids from having friends over to play. He wanted to know how she had let this happen and why she kept bringing new stuff home.

From our earliest studies of hoarding, we've noticed a connection between possessions and security. Violations of ownership lead to extreme feelings of vulnerability. When describing their reactions to someone else discarding one of their belongings, a number of our clients have said, "It feels like I've been raped." It is possible that in some people, hoarding might develop as a response to severe trauma. Compared to people who do not suffer from hoarding problems, clutterers report a greater variety of traumatic events (an average of six versus three), as well as a greater frequency (an average of fourteen versus five) of such events. The types of trauma most often experienced by hoarders include having had something taken by threat or force, being forced into sexual activity, and being physically assaulted. Traumatic events often cause people to reach for things. A survey of survivors of the World Trade Center attack in 2001 found that nearly half spent time gathering possessions before evacuating, even as the building shook beneath them.* Hoarding may be an extreme version of this phenomenon in response to trauma.

Of course, not every case of hoarding stems from trauma. But in some cases, the connection is undeniable. One study showed that hoarders who experienced traumatic events had more severe hoarding problems than those who were not exposed to trauma. One unexpected finding in this study was that clutter, rather than difficulty discarding or excessive acquisition, was associated with trauma. For some hoarders, such as Irene and Bernadette, clutter helps them feel protected within their homes. In cases where a traumatic experience precedes the onset of hoarding, perhaps the trauma triggers a nesting instinct to protect the person from further harm.

Bernadette had coped with adversity most of her life. As a child, she saw more than her share of violence, both in her rough neighborhood and within her own family. Her father was a pathological liar and petty criminal, in and out of prison from the time she was born. Her mother criticized her mercilessly, demanding perfection of the sensitive young girl but spending little time attending to her needs. After her parents divorced when Bernadette was small, she and her siblings rotated among relatives. She formed the strongest bond with her great-aunt, the most stable figure in the large extended family.

When Bernadette was ten, she was sexually abused by her stepfather. The experience left her with doubts about her own basic

---

*Kiara Cromer and her colleagues at the National Institute of Mental Health followed up on this survey by comparing people with hoarding problems to people with OCD (but not hoarding). They theorized that since traumatic experiences have been associated with the development of several mental disorders, perhaps the association with hoarding is not specific. Among their hoarding group, 69 percent reported at least one traumatic life event, compared to 51 percent of the OCD group, although the events did not always coincide with the onset of hoarding.

safety and self-worth. As a teenager, she sought comfort in drugs and casual sex. About the time she went off to college, she began to shop. She bought mostly multiples of things, such as boxes of tampons, to avoid having to borrow them from others. But her excesses left her more than $10,000 in debt. Some "messy piles," as she described them, grew in her room, but at that point she had little trouble getting rid of things.

By her mid-twenties, Bernadette had found strength and solace in religion. She devoted herself to God and pulled her life together. She remembered the moment that God spoke to her, and she vowed to give up sex for God—to remain celibate until marriage. In the wake of her newfound faith, she encountered little difficulty with shopping or hoarding.

That changed when she was thirty. By that time, she was working as a teacher and had her own home. Late one night, a man broke into her second-floor bedroom by climbing up the rain gutter. He raped her at knifepoint. This horrifying assault—an unpredictable and uncontrollable event—was especially damaging to Bernadette, already cursed with a fragile sense of security from her earlier abuse. She found little help in her community. When she approached the minister of her church, he was too busy to talk to her and seemed to imply that she'd done something to invite the rape. She felt angry that God had seemingly abandoned her, and at the same time she felt ashamed, as if perhaps she *had* done something wrong.

Bernadette's family helped her pull down the gutter, but that wasn't enough to make her feel safe. She moved to a different room and locked the windows, but she couldn't shake the feeling of vulnerability and grew depressed. The world was not a safe place for her, and perhaps, she thought, she didn't deserve to be safe. A life of happiness must be reserved for those more worthy.

Despite her disillusionment, Bernadette did not abandon her

religious beliefs. She shut out all thoughts about the rape and got on with her life. She fulfilled her Christian responsibilities as best she could but found little comfort in them. She did, however, return to one activity that pleased her — shopping. She loved buying clothes. She bought more and more things, which she put in the now unused bedroom where the rape had occurred. Soon the room was full, and her things spilled out into the hallway and eventually down the stairs. The rest of the house began to fill up as well.

Almost ten years after the rape, Bernadette met and married the pastor of a nearby congregation, and he moved into her house. Their first few years were happy, and although their home was cluttered, it was still manageable. At age forty-two, Bernadette experienced another disaster. She had a miscarriage, but her body would not discharge the fetus. She was devastated. Three weeks later, she finally acceded to her midwife's insistence that the dead fetus be removed medically. Afterward, her shopping and saving grew worse, and the clutter took over her home. She soon became pregnant again and this time gave birth to a daughter. A year later, she and her husband adopted a son. Despite her improved fortune, Bernadette could not escape the effects of her earlier traumas. She felt guilty and depressed much of the time, convinced that something was fundamentally wrong with her.

She continued her shopping sprees. Buying lifted her spirits for a few hours, but then the disappointment and depression set in again. She tried establishing rules for acquiring, but she couldn't stick to them. The urge to buy had become too hard to resist. When she was shopping, her world felt safer and things seemed clearer to her. Her goal was to look "classy," and she prided herself on her taste in clothes, choosing brilliant colors and styles that looked good on her. She felt important when she dressed well. Soon she was able to wear only a fraction of the cartloads of clothing she bought, and so she then turned to her children's needs. She justified her purchases as a means to ensure that her children wanted for nothing, and her old habit of buying in multiples returned.

She described the typical shopping trip: "I'm out looking for white shirts for my son—he's hard to fit because he's a big boy. And there I am at Wal-Mart, and lo and behold, there are the white shirts in his size. So I start thinking about how many to buy. 'Course he'll mess up the shirts, so I gotta have at least five, and they are a really good price. It's a hard item to find, so I buy six of them, and I find sneakers for him, too."

Getting rid of her purchases, or for that matter anything in the house, was next to impossible. Bernadette spent little time organizing or sorting and wouldn't allow her husband or children to discard anything without her approval. Whenever she tried to get rid of something herself, she felt vaguely uneasy and afraid. Understandably, her husband was becoming frustrated, but his criticism of her excess strengthened her conviction that she was bad, inadequate, a failure. Her only respite from these feelings seemed to be shopping. Like Janet in chapter 3, Bernadette was caught in a vicious cycle.

Bernadette self-medicated with things the way other trauma survivors self-medicate with drugs or alcohol—but the cure was getting worse than the disease. Still, the pain she was treating was very real, and her methods had an immediate effect. Despite the high frequency of traumatic events in the lives of people who hoard, relatively few of them develop posttraumatic stress disorder (PTSD). Whereas other anxiety disorders and depression are often accompanied by PTSD, in a 2006 study we found that it afflicted only 6 percent of compulsive hoarders. A low frequency of PTSD among people with a high frequency of severe traumatic events suggests that something is operating to limit the development of

PTSD. Perhaps hoarding actually helps prevent the development of PTSD following a trauma.

To understand the reasons for hoarding, it's often necessary to examine what's going on in the lives of individuals at the time the hoarding develops. In our study of the onset of hoarding, we asked hoarders to describe their lives at around the time they first noticed the hoarding. More than half remembered some kind of important event, either positive or negative, many times associated with a loss or death. The hoarding problems of those who remembered such an event, like Bernadette, began later than the hoarding of those who did not identify a particular trauma. It appears that for some, a stressful life event precipitates hoarding, while for others hoarding begins early and continues on a steadily worsening course.

We knew that the common wisdom of hoarding being a response to deprivation was not the whole story. As we've already discussed, plenty of hoarders have lived comfortable lives. But deprivation is not always material, and emotional deprivation also can be devastating. To examine the relationship between emotional deprivation and hoarding, we compared people with hoarding problems to people with OCD and people without either problem (our control group), based on the nature of their attachments and recollections of their early family life. Both the hoarding group and the OCD group experienced more tenuous attachments to people than did the control group. They endorsed statements such as "I have always been 'hot and cold' with other people" and "I've not been sure how others feel about me" more frequently. We found no difference between hoarders and people with OCD, however, indicating that poor attachments may be a consequence of having significant emotional problems rather than anything specific about hoarding. On the second measure, recollections of early family life, people with hoarding problems were much less likely to report having been reared in a warm and supportive family than people in either of the other two groups. Hoarders were less likely to endorse statements such as "My childhood featured a constant sense of support" and "My family was always accepting of me." Perhaps the comfort provided by possessions developed during a childhood filled with inadequate protection.

The findings on trauma and attachment, together with the soothing effects possessions seem to have for people who hoard, suggest that part of this problem relates to feelings of vulnerability generated by difficult life circumstances. Hoarding affords many of its sufferers the illusion of control and replaces fear with a feeling of safety. For those for whom safety and control are a driving force, treatment necessarily requires exploration of a painful history. Resolution requires them to observe themselves closely so that they can fully grasp the causes of their hoarding. They must also shift their misguided thinking and beliefs along with their acquiring and hoarding behaviors. Put another way, they must "put their money where their mouth is," so that core values, such as Bernadette's commitment to her children and her religious beliefs, can translate to appropriate buying and saving behavior. Of course, as Bernadette's situation illustrates, this is easier said than done.

Bernadette's treatment progressed in fits and starts. Sometimes she could work on her clutter and clear space, and sometimes she couldn't. Her therapist noticed that whenever she encountered something reminding her of the rape, such as a picture of her room at the time or a fabric resembling the curtains, she shut down emotionally and couldn't go on. A similar thing happened whenever they got close to the point of sorting stuff from the bedroom where the rape had occurred. She had, in effect, walled off the still frightening bedroom, and indeed the entire third floor. Her therapist mentioned one day that she'd done an effective job of making sure no rapist could ever get into that bedroom again. She thought about this carefully. "I never realized what I was doing," she said.

To break this cycle, the therapist suggested that she and Bernadette spend time working only on the rape to help her come to terms with it. As they talked about the trauma and her reactions to it, it became clear that Bernadette had interpreted the rape in a self-damning way. Unable to face her guilt and vulnerability, she had blocked the rape out. In the same way avoidance forms part of the cycle of hoarding, not thinking about traumatic or emotional events forms part of the cycle of anxiety, depression, and posttraumatic stress.

Bernadette's acquiring, saving, and clutter served a purpose. Buying clothes provided temporary relief from her depression; saving things made her feel safe; and the clutter, especially in the bedroom, shielded her from memories of being raped and feelings of vulnerability. Gaining control over her acquiring, saving, and clutter required that she face those memories and feelings. After spending a few sessions talking about the rape, Bernadette's need to hang on to objects to feel safe began to wane, and she was ready to return to treatment for hoarding.

The main focus of that treatment was the powerful beliefs she had about her possessions and their value. We discussed these beliefs during therapist-assisted sorting sessions. Bernadette sorted possessions into categories — items to save, give away, recycle, or discard. The therapist asked Bernadette to describe her thoughts as she evaluated each item. In one case, she said, "Oh, I should save that sock; we'll probably find the other one. I know it's too small for him now, but maybe someone could use it." In another case, she explained, "I loved those shoes [pink patent leather with black smudges on them]. They don't fit now, but I want to remember [how I felt] when I wore them." After she became good at recognizing the patterns of her thoughts and emotions, she was ready to evaluate and challenge them. One method that worked especially well for her was considering her real need for an item versus her simple desire or want. For example, after considering this question, she concluded that keeping clothes that no longer fit either of her children was a fantasy wish, not a real need. Further consideration of the advantages and disadvantages of keeping things she had no real need for (e.g., the outgrown clothes) led her to conclude that the disadvantages of saving them (taking up a whole dresser that the kids needed for their current clothes) far outweighed the advantages (nice memories, but she had pictures for that). Although these considerations seem rather simple, beliefs such as Bernadette's are usually rigid and strongly held. Our goal was to loosen the grip of these beliefs and get her to start thinking from a different perspective. When she had mastered these strategies (evaluating need versus want and advantages versus disadvantages), her therapist asked her to take the perspective of another person—that of a trusted woman friend from her church community—when trying to make decisions about specific items. When considering each decision in light of what her friend would choose, Bernadette nearly always discarded the item, recognizing her friend's "wisdom" in simplifying her life.

During the early stages of Bernadette's treatment, we didn't emphasize getting rid of things. Instead, we focused on changing the way she thought about her possessions. Once she had some success in challenging or testing her thinking, we put more emphasis on discarding. For most of our clients, this involves a slow and time-consuming process in which they spend many months sorting through the things in their homes. Midway through treatment, if a client has been able to challenge his or her hoarding beliefs and tolerate other people touching his or her things, we recommend a more intense approach.

Bernadette was such a client. She had succeeded in loosening her attachment to the clothes she purchased for her children. Because of the huge volume of clutter in her home and her success in challenging her thinking about the clothing, Bernadette's therapist suggested a "team cleanout." This is a highly structured session in the client's home with a team of therapists and assistants. Gail and five staff members showed up in two shifts at Bernadette's home. Bernadette and her therapist had already decided on and written out the rules for the day. Clothes that were too small for her children could be bagged and taken away for donation without Bernadette's approval. So could duplicate clothing if the team kept the two or three nicest items. Bernadette had already put the children's current shoes in the closet, so all shoes found lying around could be donated. The team agreed to organize papers and other household objects by type and put these in bins for later sorting by Bernadette and her therapist.

Bernadette and her therapist sat in the bedroom on the second floor as team members paraded by with items that fell outside the rules. Bernadette's job was to make decisions on these items. Her therapist's role was to keep up her spirits and ask challenging questions, such as "When will you use it?"; "Where will you put it?"; and "Do you have other things like it?" The process was designed to train hoarders how to make decisions about saving and discarding. Bernadette's typical pattern had been to think only about how great these clothes would look on her or her children. Now she had to consider other issues, such as space and likelihood of use. Her therapist was careful not to put any pressure on her to get rid of things. Bernadette made the decisions. If she decided to keep something after reflecting on the therapist's questions, that was considered a successful decision.

One of the worst experiences for someone with a hoarding problem occurs when another person or crew arrives to clear out the home, usually at the order of the public health department or a frustrated family member. It is easy for an observer to say that the hoarder is overreacting to someone discarding his or her stuff, since the piles seem like worthless trash. But because of the hoarder's difficulties with organization, the piles often contain much more than trash. In many such cases, the crew hired to clean will just scoop up the piles and cart them to the dump. But under the decades-old newspaper may be the title to the person's car or the diamond ring she lost years before. These scenarios almost always leave the hoarder feeling as if his or her most valued possessions have been taken away, which in fact may be the case. Beyond this, most hoarders have a sense of where things are amid the clutter. When someone else moves or discards even a portion of it, this sense of "order" is destroyed. We know of several cases in which hoarders have committed suicide following a forced cleanout.

The time, expense, and trauma of a forced cleanout are not worth the effort if any other alternatives are possible. Although conditions in the home may improve temporarily, the behavior leading to those conditions will not have changed. Moreover, the likelihood of obtaining any future cooperation after such a trauma is slim. One Massachusetts town in our survey of health departments conducted a forced cleanout costing $16,000 (most of the town's health department budget). Just over a year later, the cluttered home was worse than ever.

For Bernadette, who consented to the team cleanout and worked alongside the team to make decisions, the experience, though still very hard, was much more beneficial. She had come to trust her therapist and knew that the team members were operating with her goals and rules in mind. As the day wore on, more and more bags of trash and giveaway items accumulated on the front porch. Bernadette found the process exhausting, but she didn't give up. When her husband and their two children returned from a day-long outing (planned so that Bernadette could concentrate on the cleaning), he was so excited by the mountain of departing stuff on the porch and the now visible hardwood floors in the entryway, living room, and bedroom that he gathered everyone together in a circle in the entryway. Earlier in the day, such a gathering would have meant wading through three feet of clothes, newspapers, and boxes. Then he began to pray, his voice rising high in rhythmic chanting of his praise to God and his blessings for the crew: "Hallelujah! Hallelujah! Hallelujah!" Everyone held hands and swayed to the sound of his voice, basking in the pleasure of the moment.

5

A FRAGMENT OF ME
Identity and Attachment

If I throw too much away, there'll be nothing left of me.

—Irene

Debra began collecting magazines at thirteen. *Seventeen, Young Miss,* and *Life* were her favorites. They gave her a window into the world, and, for a precocious and inquisitive young woman, an entry into all the possibilities it had to offer. She wanted to know the world, "to learn everything," "to experience everything." As she got older, her collecting expanded to include travel, cooking, news, and women's magazines. There were always new magazines with more for her to learn. Before long, she was spending more time collecting than reading. As with many people who hoard, she planned to read them when she found time, but she couldn't afford to miss what was coming her way. The magazines and newspapers began piling up in her room as she found less and less time to read. At least, she reasoned, she had them for when she could find time.

Even when it became apparent to her that she would never have time, her intention to read gave way to a more dangerous motive. She stopped caring about reading the magazines and wanted simply to preserve them. She began to see herself as "the keeper of magazines." Keeping and protecting them would, she told me, "preserve the time in which we live." Soon this idea evolved into an identity. "Having, keeping, and preserving are part of who I am," she declared. Each magazine was its own time capsule, similar to those accumulated by Andy Warhol (see chapter 2). They preserved the time in which Debra lived and provided a physical representation of her existence, or at least what was going on when she was alive. She made a few attempts to fight off this motive. In an effort to convince herself that this sort of preservation was better left to the government, she visited the Library of Congress. She wanted to see if the library had all the magazines she did. "They didn't have half of what I had!" she exclaimed. At that point, she said, she wished she had started her work sooner.

Her preservation expanded from magazines to TV shows. At first she taped only entertainment shows. She didn't watch them: seeing them didn't interest her; preserving them did. She began to spend hours studying *TV Guide,* planning and programming three VCRs to run continuously so that she could tape not only entertainment but news and talk shows as well. Her compulsion to tape these shows was powerful. Shortly before the last time we spoke, Debra had been in a car accident and ended up in the hospital. Her doctors were worried that she might have a serious spinal cord injury, and they put her in a special bed to restrict any movement. Debra could not control her panic at not being able to tape her shows until her husband agreed to go home and program her VCRs.

The *Diagnostic and Statistical Manual of Mental Disorders* published by the American Psychiatric Association is the bible for defining psychiatric disorders. The most recent version lists hoarding as one of eight symptoms of obsessive-compulsive personality disorder (OCPD). There it defines hoarding as "the inability to discard worn-out or worthless objects even when they have no sentimental value."

After speaking with Debra, Irene, and so many others, we found this emphasis on non-sentimental items puzzling. It is a subjective term, after all, and our research indicates that many objects in the homes of hoarders carry intense sentimental value. Sentimentalizing objects—giving them emotional significance because of their association with important people or events—is not unusual. We all do it—ticket stubs from a favorite concert, pieces of a long-ago wedding cake, a scrap of paper with a child's first drawing. In this respect, what happens in hoarding is not out of the ordinary. The difference for Irene and Debra, as for many hoarders, is that intense emotional meaning is attached to so many of their possessions, even otherwise ordinary things, even trash. Their special ability to see uniqueness and value where others don't may stem from inquisitive and creative minds and contribute to this attachment. The desire to "experience everything" may expand the range of attachments hoarders enjoy.

Getting rid of ordinary things upset Irene greatly. As soon as she put her decades-old history book into her sell box, she started to cry. "I just feel like I want to die. This is one of my treasure books. I know I haven't looked at it in thirty years, but it feels like a part of me." Irene's reaction to purging these things was grief, as if she'd lost a loved one. Clearly, strong and wide-ranging sentimental attachments to objects are defining elements of hoarding, contrary to the official description. Hoarded objects become part of the hoarder's identity or personal history. In a sense, they come to define his or her identity.

Most of us keep the things we use regularly and discard the rest. We derive pleasure from using objects and, in this way, determine their value. But Irene kept things she didn't use. It was not their use that she found reinforcing, but the idea of having them. Their *potential* appealed to her. For instance, she had, by her estimation, more than three hundred cookbooks, and she also saved the cooking section of every newspaper and all the recipes she found in magazines. But she almost never used them. In fact, her stove and kitchen counters were inaccessible due to clutter. The mere possession of the cookbooks and recipes allowed her to enjoy thinking about the image of herself cooking and to imagine a potential identity as a cook. Indeed, much of her hoard allowed her to imagine various identities: a great cook, a well-read and informed person, a responsible citizen. Her things represented dreams, not realities. Getting rid of the things meant losing the dreams.

Debra

Debra was in her late thirties when I first met her at an Obsessive Compulsive Foundation meeting several years ago. She attended our workshop and volunteered to take part in a "non-acquiring trip," as described in chapter 3. Her story reveals much about how possessions and identity can be fused.

Debra and her husband lived with her mother and stepfather in a modest home. Although her husband worked and they could have afforded to live on their own, most of their income went to paying rent on three large storage units and purchasing the magazines and other things that Debra collected.

The main living areas of their home were relatively free of clutter when I first met Debra. She confessed at the time that this was because of the efforts of her mother and husband. They maintained control over those spaces and moved anything Debra left there, despite her grumblings and occasional tantrums. In contrast to these areas, wall-to-wall stuff covered the bedroom she shared with her husband. A fortress of papers, books, magazines, videotapes, and more surrounded the bed and reached nearly to the ceiling. She and her husband had to clamber over piles of stuff to get into bed. Amazingly, though we've seen many a person who had to sweep stuff aside to sleep at night, the bed itself remained clear. At the end of the upstairs hallway, Debra's childhood room overflowed with the remnants of her youth. Even if she had allowed it, no one could squeeze into that room. In addition to all this, Debra rented three ten-by-forty-foot storage units, all packed to the ceiling.

In the time I knew Debra, conditions in her home got worse. Her mother and husband got worn down by her never-ending pressure to put her stuff in other parts of the house. When we last spoke, her things had spilled out into the upstairs hallway, and the parts of the house normally cleared by her mother and husband had become cluttered. The corners of her mother's bedroom and the living room now contained growing mounds of videotapes. The dining room had been completely taken over by newly acquired magazines, and the porch now resembled her bedroom.

DEBRA'S PARENTS DIVORCED when she was two, and she lived with her mother and grandmother until she was eight. She had limited contact with her father and knew little about him until after his death three years before we met. It was then that she discovered that he also kept storage units filled with pieces of his life. In sorting through his stuff, all of which he left to her, she found that he had taped and transcribed all of his conversations with her and kept copies of every letter he wrote, just as she did. He had accumulated literally tons of magazines, grocery bags, and papers.

Debra believed that her hoarding began at around age eleven or twelve; at least that was her earliest recollection of significant collecting. Her mother insisted that it began much earlier, closer to age seven or eight, around the time of her grandmother's death. Debra was close to her grandmother and felt safe and comfortable with her. Her grandmother had a calming influence on her, gently encouraging her to keep her room clean. When Debra first learned of her grandmother's death, she locked herself in her room and spent hours in frenzied cleaning, hoping that following her grandmother's advice would somehow bring her back.

The death of her grandmother meant that Debra and her mother had to sell the house and move, although they did keep a small piece of land connected to the property. Debra felt lost and clung to everything that had belonged to her grandmother. These things were now, as she explained, "extensions of me." (Her uncle's plan to sell the remaining property from her grandmother's estate had her crazed with grief. "If it happens, I'll cry forever!" she exclaimed. "I'll never be happy again.")

Just a few years later, Debra's mother remarried and changed her name. Debra felt that she had lost her mother to a man she did not like, and she blamed him for the beginning of her hoarding. He was, by her description, an angry man who disliked children and wanted to send her away to boarding school. She claimed that he stole things from her and tormented her by getting rid of the newspaper before she had a chance to read it. She began trying to rescue the papers from the trash by bringing them back into the house. Her stepfather thwarted her by taking them to work. She resorted to stealing newspapers from the neighbor's trash. (When I met her, she still had many of these stolen newspapers.) Over time, the ongoing battle with her stepfather made her more guarded and secretive about her possessions, and she was careful to keep her room locked.

Just out of school, Debra took a job at a bookstore, which seemed ideal because it allowed her to be around the things she loved. She worked hard as a shipping clerk, staying late every night. Quitting for the day when there were still things to do bothered her. At the end of her shift, she would think, *Let me do this one more thing before I go home.* But one thing led to another. Toward the end of her time at the bookstore, she fell asleep and spent the night at the store on several occasions.

Part of her job involved maintaining lists of all the books in the store and all those on order. Soon these lists became sacred: possessing them gave her a sense of mastery, as though she had read the books themselves. She began duplicating the lists for herself when the thought struck her that she should try to make a list of every book that existed. (When I met her, she still had boxes and boxes of paperwork from this project.) Finally, exhaustion overtook her, and she quit her job.

Debra's own personal history also fell under her preservation net. Ever since she could remember, she had feared change. "I don't like forwards; I like backwards," she complained. The biggest changes in her early life were losses—her father, her grandmother, and, in her mind, her mother. The losses left her uncertain about herself and her identity. It seemed as though she could never quite get a grasp on who she was or where she wanted to go. Instead, she turned to activities that would freeze time. For instance, she photographed nearly everything: "Every second of my life I can document. If I want to remember it, I'll take a picture." She even photographed the trash. In the month before our first talk, she took nearly thirty rolls of film. Her photography began as a coping strategy, a way to get rid of things she couldn't keep—perishable things. By taking a picture, she could keep something of the essence of each item.

Debra's efforts to preserve "the time in which we live" seemed to me to fit the terror management theory (see chapter 2) as some sort of attempt to achieve immortality—to produce something that would outlive her. But when I asked Debra about what she wanted done with her collections when she was gone, she surprised me by saying she didn't really care. In fact, she said, if her husband wanted to throw everything away, that didn't bother her. Her purpose in documenting the time in which she lived was driven by a desire to *experience* everything, not to leave a legacy. Even though she had read few of her magazines and seen few of her taped TV shows, having them gave her the feeling that she had experienced them. As long as she saved them, they were part of her experience. If she got rid of them, she would lose the experiences. For Debra, the driving force for her collecting seemed to be the fear of missing out on life or failing to remember it.

Pristine and Perfect

When Debra started buying magazines, she began to notice details of appearance, minor unintended flaws — a clerk's fingerprint or a wrinkle in a cover. The more she noticed, the more it bothered her. The thought that her magazines were not perfect left her uneasy. She coped by taking her copies from the bottom of the pile, where they were less likely to have been handled and inadvertently altered from their original state. They were as pristine as when they were created. This became increasingly important to her. She explained that when people pick up magazines, "they leave fingerprints and oils from their skin, and they wrinkle the pages."

Soon she searched for magazines without printing flaws as well. Sometimes the "O" on the cover of the *Oprah Magazine* was out of place and touched the fold at the edge. But even when she found a perfect copy, handing it to the clerk to ring up violated its purity. She made friends with the women at Barnes & Noble and convinced them to allow her to ring up her own magazines so that only she touched them. This worked for a while until she began to notice that her own handling of the magazines was violating them. Looking through them changed the creases, the magazines lost their crispness, and she left fingerprints. She started buying two copies, one to read and one to keep pristine. As her things took more of her time, she quit reading the magazines altogether but still continued to buy two copies.

As her quest to obtain perfect specimens continued, Debra began to think that the clerks might be leaving fingerprints when they stocked the bookstore shelves. She convinced her friends at the bookstore to allow her to open the shipping boxes herself. Then no one but her ever touched the magazines; they went straight from the printing press into her possession, untainted.

Before long, she needed a strategy to prevent her own soiling of the magazines when she removed them from the boxes. For this she devised what she called her "theory of threes." She pulled out three copies from the shipping box, being careful to touch only the top and bottom copies. The middle copy remained untouched. She now had one copy to read (though by this time she had given up on reading any of them), one copy to cut up if she wanted special access to an article (although she never did this either), and one copy to save, protect, and preserve.

Her arrangement was not without its drawbacks. One day as she was scanning her own magazines at the checkout counter, a new clerk spotted her and shouted from across the room, "What are you doing?" The whole store stopped to stare at her. It was, she said, like a scene from a movie. Debra tried to explain but was reduced simply to saying, "I'm a hoarder and have OCD."

Finally, her system broke down completely. The cost put a major strain on her family's finances, and the time and effort involved exhausted her. She had to settle for something less perfect, so she ordered magazines by subscription instead, and only one copy of each. She told me that when this started, she was overwhelmed by the sense that these magazines weren't good enough, so much so that she became physically ill when they arrived. For a while, she went to the bookstore to get new magazines as well, until her discomfort gradually lessened. Then her subscriptions, about a hundred each month, went directly into storage. She said that it would have been too much of an ordeal for her to touch them. Although they were not as pristine as those purchased using her "theory of threes," they were still in a state as close as possible to when they were created. She also trained the postman not to make any marks on the magazines and to be as careful as possible with them.

Debra's perfectionism extended well beyond magazines. Although initially her mother and husband kept the clutter out of most of the house, Debra controlled the positioning of the furniture, the alignment of the cans in the kitchen cupboard, and the arrangement of food in the refrigerator. If anyone moved a piece of furniture, she was not comfortable until it was back in its correct place. Cans had to be properly aligned with the labels facing out. Only her husband could move anything in the house without upsetting her.

Her perfectionism presented problems for large purchases as well. When she and her husband bought a computer, it never made it out of the box. After trying for a year, they gave up and bought a floor model so that Debra didn't feel guilty for ruining something that was new. Handling cash was similarly problematic. She had thousands of dollars in cash that she couldn't spend because the bills were too new and too crisp. She couldn't stand the idea of allowing them to get crinkled, so she carefully packed them away in her bedroom. Most of the time, she used credit or debit cards to purchase things, but she needed to use cash occasionally. To allow herself to do so, she insisted on getting old bills when she went to the bank. Similarly, when the *TV Guide* arrived in the mail, her husband "messed it up" so that it was wrinkled and dirty. Without it, her TV recording schedule would have been impossible.

Although conditions in the homes of people who hoard would

hardly lead one to think of them as perfectionists, the intense fear of mistakes is a common characteristic among hoarders. For instance, one of our clients would not recycle her newspapers unless they were perfectly tied up in carefully measured bundles. She did not want the men picking up the recycling to be critical of her. Another was unable to get rid of an old suitcase until she found the key. "It's not all there," she said. "It just isn't right." Like these women, many hoarders interpret minor mistakes as equivalent to failure. Although most of us can accept minor mistakes as part of being human and not cause for self-denigration, many people who hoard can't do that.

Debra's insistence that the furniture be arranged in just the right way and her attempts to keep things in a perfect state are examples of an ordering and arranging compulsion. Such compulsions result from an idea that things need to be arranged in a particular, symmetrical pattern. "Symmetry obsessions," as they are called, are a common but little understood form of OCD. Sometimes the need to arrange things in a particular way is driven by magical thinking that keeping things "just so" will ward off harm. More common, however, is what Debra experienced. When the furniture was moved, she didn't fear a negative event; she just felt uncomfortable, as though things were "not just right." Not-just-right experiences, or NJREs as some OCD researchers and patients call them, are relatively common, and not just among people with OCD. Like an itch, the sensation that one's clothes don't fit right, or the experience of seeing a crooked picture on the wall, NJREs violate our expectations for order.

Most of us learn to tolerate these violations and either don't notice or feel nothing more than simple recognition that something is out of place or off-kilter. But for people with OCD, NJREs can be quite dramatic. I once consulted on a case of a young man who was completely incapacitated by various NJREs and had been hospitalized. For instance, he did not feel right when passing through a doorway unless his shoulders were equidistant from the doorjambs. The discomfort kept him trapped in his room. The only way he could go through a doorway was to leap through so that the experience was as short-lived as possible. Several staff members were needed to clear the hallway whenever he was about to rocket out of his room.

Ordering and arranging compulsions often accompany hoarding. More than three-quarters of children with hoarding problems also have problems with ordering and arranging. Like Debra, a number of our clients have reported to us that as children, they carefully arranged objects in their rooms and felt uncomfortable whenever the items were moved. Some investigators believe that these NJREs originate in the anterior cingulate cortex, the part of the brain thought to be responsible for error detection. They hypothesize that the brain may be sending out messages that things are not as they should be or that a mistake has been made. This results in a sensation like Debra's that the furniture is out of place or a magazine is not the way it should be. In searching for the cause of this error signal, Debra may have concluded that the magazines she purchased were wrinkled or defaced with fingerprints even when they weren't.

Another kind of perfectionism, related to symmetry obsessions, is a deep concern about "completeness." Completeness pervaded many of Debra's saving behaviors. For example, she found it very difficult to separate the content of mail she received from the envelope in which it came. It was hard for her to capture the experience in words. "They belong together," she said, "and if they are separated, it's like they are broken, or like separating a mother and child." She never discarded any mail, even junk mail, without the original envelope. For a while, Debra refused even to open her mail. It seemed to her that mail was meant to be unopened. This stopped abruptly when she lost her driver's license because she failed to respond to a minor traffic ticket that came in the mail.

Violations of this sense of completeness can influence people's sense of themselves. Debra recounted an episode of panic when her recorder failed to work for an Ellen DeGeneres anniversary show. The show was rebroadcast a few days later, but she missed that as well. To get an idea of why this show was so important to her, I asked her a series of questions that form what cognitive behavior therapists call the "downward arrow technique." This technique is designed to uncover important beliefs or reasons for behaviors that the individual has trouble articulating. It also is an attempt to transform these beliefs from statements of fact to hypotheticals. My conversation with Debra went something like this:

ME: Why does missing that show matter to you?

DEBRA: Because it's the only show I don't have. It's like a missing piece of a puzzle.

ME: And if you don't have that one show, why is that important?

DEBRA: That show was special.

ME: How will not having it affect your life?

DEBRA: Because I'll remember forever that I missed it.

ME: Why would that be so bad?

DEBRA: Since I could have taped it but didn't, I blew it. There is something wrong with me that I can't even tape a show correctly.

ME: So if you don't tape the show you want, it means there is something wrong with you, and that will stay with you forever?

The beliefs revealed here had nothing to do with the intrinsic value of the show or its contents; having a copy of the show was all that mattered to her. It mattered for two reasons. First, she worried that her angst at not taping the show would stay with her forever. Second, she thought that failing to tape the show meant that she was inadequate, a failure as a person. Although this is far from the whole story of her hoarding, attempts to avoid that sense of failure may have contributed to the problem.

Debra feared mistakes more than anything. As a young girl, she excelled in school. Even though she was smarter than most of her classmates, any mistake left her feeling worthless and empty. She vividly recalled a weekend at the beach with her mother during the fourth grade. She felt tormented throughout, and when they got home, she told her mother that she had something terrible to confess and hoped her mother wouldn't hate her for it. "I got an eighty-nine on my English paper," she said. Debra had never gotten below a 90 before, and the experience left her feeling "like a loser." By middle school, little had changed. Debra was incensed that although she was getting 100s on her math tests, the teacher's computer grading program could record only two digits, so her test scores were recorded as 99s. Losing a point on every test was intolerable.

Back-to-school shopping trips with her mother were agonizing as well. She recalled her mother looking defeated after she spent hours in the dressing room attempting to find the perfect fit and color. The aftermath tried her mother's patience even more. Debra refused to wear many of her new clothes because doing so would ruin them. She discovered, however, that if she took pictures of the clothes from multiple angles, she could remember what they were like in their pristine state, and then she might be able to wear some of them. Even so, many unworn clothes from her childhood still hung in one of her storage units.

Perfectionism ultimately paralyzed Debra. She realized that there was no way she could come close to making her bedroom conform to her standards, so she gave up trying. It was easier to live with the mess than to experience the frustration of failing to create a perfect room. This is a common obstacle for many of our hoarding clients.

Out of Containment

As a child, Debra closely guarded her stuff. Although she saved a lot when she was young, her room was neat and very carefully organized—so carefully, in fact, that she could instantly tell if anyone had been in the room and moved or touched anything. Everything was at an angle, and she memorized the angles. Anything askew drew her attention as soon as she entered the room. Once when she was twelve, a neighbor girl came over to play. During the course of the afternoon, the girl locked herself in Debra's room. Despite Debra's protests, the girl didn't open the door for thirty minutes. The experience traumatized Debra. As an only child, she wasn't used to sharing and felt violated by this behavior.

Debra described herself as feeling like a mother bear with cubs: "I'll do whatever it takes to protect my things." No one dared to touch her stuff. She allowed her husband to move her things, because she trusted him. Her mother could move them, too, but only a little. She tried to describe this to me one day: "Picture a cartoon with thought bubbles. I have a hundred million bubbles. Junk mail is one of them. If I throw it away, it's out there without me, out of containment. I want a bubble around me and all my stuff to keep it safe. I don't want any of my things out of containment."

When Debra left the house, she took only what was necessary with her. She emptied her purse and her car before going anywhere. Her car looked very different from those of hoarders who can't resist the urge to fill that space. If she went on a trip, she made a list of everything she had with her. This allowed her to keep track of her things and contain them as much as possible.

To get a clearer picture of Debra's experience of not allowing things out of containment, we did an experiment. I sent Debra a postcard with nothing on it but her name and address. Her task was to throw it away and keep track of how she felt. I called a few days after she got the card. She was not happy. She insisted that she had not had enough time with the card. She wanted to get a mental picture of it, to absorb it so that it was easier to remember. She described the stamp it had and the date. Then, as we spoke on the phone, she walked to the kitchen and threw it in the trash. "I hate this feeling," she said. "Why can't I keep it just a bit longer?"

As she sat back down in the living room, she said that she could picture the angle of the postcard sitting in the trash. She thought she would have to write down the details of the postcard, since she hadn't had it long enough to commit it to memory, although she remembered quite a few details: a Martha Graham stamp; a double postmark, including one from Smith College; her name written in blue ink. "I can still pull it back up in my brain, so it's still sort of contained," she said. She rated her distress as 80 on a 100-point scale. She said that the rating would go up as soon as another piece of trash or food from the kitchen was thrown on top of the card, because it would be tarnished—it would no longer be the same as it was when it entered the house. Her rating would go up again, she said, when the trash got removed. Her distress remained high for the rest of our interview. She insisted it would never go down: "I will never forget this card as long as I live. It will never go down to zero. This is a big deal for me. This is the first thing I've thrown away in years, at least the first significant thing, especially because it's personal."

A week later when I called, she told me that other things had occupied her mind and she hadn't thought much about the card since her husband had taken out the trash. At that point, she had still felt anxious, which she rated at about 80, but once it was gone, she was okay. The worst part was actually throwing it away. One week after getting rid of the card, her rating was down to 40. She did not remember saying that the distress would never go down.

But Debra confessed that she had cheated a bit on the experiment. She had written down everything she could remember about the card. She said that she was afraid that she would completely forget about it, and that, to her, would be like an emptiness. "I don't want to lose what was," she said. Cheating on the experiment limited her discomfort, but it may have prevented her from learning that the empty feeling was fleeting and the details of the card meaningless. She was, in effect, keeping the card in symbolic containment. The description went into her storage unit, and although she would probably never look at it again, she was left with the feeling that she had not lost the experience.

About a year later, I spoke with Debra again about the experiment. Despite her previous prediction, she said that "losing" the card had little impact on her now. "It's so minor that it's irrelevant," she said. I wondered whether this fact had caused her to change her beliefs about the necessity of saving such things. She said that there had been some shifts in her thinking about junk mail, but she insisted that the card was different than all her other mail. She had thrown it away only because I had asked her to. She would never have done that on her own. That made the experience different. She admitted, however, that now she knew that if the conditions were right, she could get rid of something important to her without dire consequences. Unfortunately, she had not yet decided to try this herself.

Extensions

In describing her experiences, Debra said that she thought it might feel good if she could just destroy all of her stuff. That way, she said, no one else could touch it. Whenever anyone but her husband touched her things, she felt violated. This held for everything that was associated with her, even junk mail. She explained, "Whatever comes into my life has come for a purpose. I'm supposed to have it. It's a part of me—an extension of me." She described her panic at the thought of discarding these "extensions": "It's like asking me to throw out my children. They'll be dead. I'll kill to prevent that." If her things were thrown out, she said that she would probably kill herself. Suicide would be a better option than facing the grief. Even junk mail that had nothing of interest except her name on the envelope was significant. Her name, written on an envelope by a machine from a computer list, had become a tendril. "It's a fragment of me," she insisted.

Similar reports from many of our hoarding clients link their possessions to their sense of themselves as well as their past. Irene, for instance, had a difficult time discarding anything that represented past events. One day as I was working with her, she was going through the many pieces of paper covering her couch and trying to decide whether to keep or discard them. She picked up an ATM envelope that was five years old, on which she had written the date and how she had spent the cash contained in the envelope. There was nothing unusual about the purchase: drugstore items, groceries, and a few odds and ends. She said that most of the things were long gone, although she thought she might still have one or two of them. When she threw the envelope into the recycling box, she began to weep. She said, "I realize this is crazy. It's just an old envelope, but it feels like I'm losing that day of my life." A bit later, she elaborated: "If I throw too much away, there'll be nothing left of me." Her sense of herself had become so bound up in her possessions that she felt a little piece of her would die with each thing she discarded. We have seen many such cases in which the person likens the experience to the loss of a family member or a part of himself or herself.

Debra's obsessions with preservation and perfection have become her identity. She is "the keeper of magazines." If she were to stop collecting or to get rid of them, her sense of self would be lost. When I asked her about this, she said, "To stop would make all those years a waste of my life. It would make my existence invalid." At the same time, she realized the cost. "This has ruined me," she told me recently. "I'm smart and creative, and I could have been happy. But I'm not anything. I have done nothing. I'm collecting life without living it. My only hope for making some kind of positive contribution is if my story can prevent this from happening to someone else."

6

RESCUE

Saving Animals from a Life on the Streets

All my life, I took care of people. I felt needed but not loved or appreciated. The animals have filled a void inside me. I'm the only one who can love and care for these animals. I am saving them from a life on the streets.

—A woman with sixty-six cats

In her twenties, back in the 1950s, Pamela was a strikingly beautiful woman. Her work as a documentary filmmaker put her in contact with the fashionable elite in New York City. She loved to party, and she loved sex. When she entered the room, she picked out the man she wanted to sleep with and seldom went home alone. She estimated that by the age of forty, she had had more than one hundred lovers who spanned the globe. She lived briefly with a fiancé in Istanbul before their relationship ended. She followed a Peruvian lover to Buenos Aires, only to be abandoned there. She spent much of her twenty-fourth year in Rome studying the Renaissance and having a torrid affair with a plumber/gigolo.

When Pamela was in her thirties, her career took off. She filmed an interview with the Beatles on one of their U.S. tours. She won film contracts around the world and had the kind of adventures she had dreamed of as a child. She was making lots of money and gaining a reputation in the film business. She shot a documentary in Vietnam during the early years of the war. The suffering she witnessed there, especially that of the children, moved her deeply.

A decade later, her career was over and her love life nonexistent. She was struggling to care for the more than two hundred cats she had collected and the more than six hundred cats hoarded by her psychiatrist. At age fifty-two, she found herself running through the streets of Manhattan in the middle of the night, exhausted and skeleton thin, trying to get away from her psychiatrist and the cat hoarding cult that had developed around the doctor.

Pamela was referred to me by a colleague who worked for the American Society for the Prevention of Cruelty to Animals (ASPCA) in New York City and who guessed that I would find this case enlightening. In her seventies when I interviewed her, Pamela provided an in-depth and articulate account of her years as an animal hoarder. Her story is unusual even in the annals of hoarding case studies, with her nearly Dickensian childhood and an adult life fit for the tabloids. Still, it is illustrative of some of the key elements in this particularly damaging form of hoarding.

Whereas the majority of hoarders collect and save inanimate objects, for a small number animals serve as a source of safety, emotional attachment, and identity. Animal hoarding cases are often dramatic and well publicized. The bond between animal hoarders and the animals they collect is a special form of intense emotional attachment. People who collect large numbers of animals, particularly cats and dogs, often see their behavior as part of a mission to rescue animals, and they frequently believe themselves to possess special powers or abilities to do so. But they are usually unaware of the poor health and terrible conditions in which their animals are living. According to the officials we surveyed in our health department study, hoarding cases involving large numbers of animals are the toughest to deal with. Less than 10 percent of animal hoarding cases are resolved cooperatively, and in most both the animals and humans are living in deplorable conditions.

Most neighborhoods have had "cat ladies" in their midst at one time or another, but there is very little understanding of what drives this kind of hoarding. Although there have been dozens of studies of people who hoard possessions, studies of people who hoard animals are almost nonexistent. The few studies that do exist have relied on information from sources such as animal control officers, humane society officials, court records, and even news reports. Rarely has any information come directly from the people doing the hoarding. It is easy to understand why. By the time most animal hoarding cases come to light, the hoarder is in big trouble with the health department, the humane society, the city, and the neighbors. Graphic pictures and personal information have been splashed across the news—hardly an incentive for the hoarder to discuss the case further.

Pamela

Pamela was born into a wealthy family and lived in luxury as a child, but her emotional life was impoverished. Her mother had been forced into marriage by her family following a lesbian affair that threatened the reputation of her status-conscious clan. After Pamela was born, the reluctant bride had little to do with her daughter, leaving her in the care of a series of governesses. Pamela's father, a playboy who had been happy to marry into the mon-eyed family, was seldom around. Her parents weren't malicious, Pamela said, but rather like children themselves: "[My brother and I] were like seeds tossed over the fence" and expected to grow.

Most of Pamela's early years were dominated by a sadistic French governess who terrorized her, unbeknownst to her mother.

"Mademoiselle" repeatedly told the little girl that she needn't bother saying prayers before bed because she was evil and going to hell anyway. Every day she told Pamela, "You're a pig, you're dirty, you're evil." Pamela often hid from the woman, but Mademoiselle always found her; she would chant, "Evil creep, evil creep," as she pulled the frightened girl from under the bed. At times the abuse turned physical. Without anyone to protect her, Pamela withdrew into a fantasy world of Greek mythology, her own brand of Catholicism, and a burning desire to "grow a big body" to escape her tortured life.

When she did "get big," she sought freedom and adventure, but she suffered from the aftereffects of having been physically and emotionally abused. At age twenty, she had a nervous breakdown and sought the help of a highly respected psychiatrist. "The Doctor" practiced an early form of psychoanalysis originated by Dr. Wilhelm Reich, which emphasized the release of pent-up energy by first breaking down "character armor." She introduced Pamela and her other patients to karate, tai chi chuan, and breathing exercises. She encouraged them to scream, cry, and gag as ways of releasing energy and curing everything from emotional distress to allergies and colds.

The Doctor seemed larger than life — highly intelligent, charismatic, strong willed, and emotionally charged. She held rigid views of right and wrong. She demanded absolute honesty and responsibility from her patients, and she was ferocious and punitive when they failed. She believed that she had outgrown her colleagues, most of whom, she concluded, were unable to understand her brilliance. In the beginning, Pamela thought that the Doctor was brilliant. Her insights and teachings transformed Pamela from a frightened young woman into a confident and capable adult. As time passed, however, the Doctor became increasingly isolated from the professional community and moved into uncharted territory with her patients, most of whom had been in treatment with her for decades. Pamela met with her several times each week, sometimes every day, seeing her on and off for thirty-two years. Since the Doctor's patients often attended group therapy together, they came to know one another well, almost like a family.

The Doctor began collecting cats a few years after Pamela started seeing her. At first the cats were an amusement. She found one in her garden, and she thought it was "delightful." She decided another would be "twice as delightful," then she began going to cat shows and brought home more. She was particular about caring for them. She ordered meat from an out-of-state packing company and mixed it by hand with bread. Neutering or spaying was out of the question because that would alter the natural order of things. Animals were meant to experience the totality of life, and according to her Reichian views, that included sex. (Such teachings may have shaped Pamela's sex life as well.) The realities of feline reproduction led the Doctor to keep the male and female cats separated, but somehow nature always won out. The females started to reproduce, and her cat census rose. Still, the Doctor cared for her cats very well, and she kept them out of her clinic offices. She hired people to feed them and clean up after them. Early on, the health department inspected regularly, since the animals were, the Doctor claimed, part of her research, and veterinarians were brought in when needed. But at that time, such oversight was more voluntary than mandatory.

The Doctor soon outgrew her offices and purchased a seven-story building with more than fifteen thousand square feet of space. She intended for it to be a cultural center, but instead she filled it with stuff. (Among the animal hoarders we have interviewed, many of them hoard things as well.) The top two floors held her many collections. Piled to the ceiling were clothes, canned food, carpentry tools, sculptures, and boxes filled with God knows what. Only a small pathway snaked through the middle of the hoard on each floor. The Doctor was ferocious about protecting her things. None of her patients dared to touch any of them. The middle three floors were devoted to cats. The Doctor had arranged for cages along the walls to accommodate her cats, which now numbered near two hundred. She lived on the first floor, amid a growing hoard. (Even the elevator was piled high with newspapers.) The second floor contained her office. Though cluttered, it was at first free of cats. Then the sick ones moved in. Gradually, the whole building became overrun with cats.

The Doctor's interest in cats soon turned to rescuing them from the streets of New York City and protecting them from shelters that euthanized them and from people she deemed unfit to care for them. She spread her mission to her patients, encouraging them to make the "responsible decision" when they saw a cat in need. Images of cats being euthanized, neglected, or abused became searing reminders of their duty. In the Doctor's world, and by extension in the world of her patients, these images required action. Under her tutelage, her patients thought of themselves as the only people who understood the plight of cats and the only ones who could rescue them. These beliefs kept them from seeking help elsewhere when they became overwhelmed with caring for the Doctor's cats. In time, more than a dozen of the Doctor's patients collected cats. They combed the streets looking for strays and other cats in need.

Just as the Doctor's interest turned to cats, Pamela, now in her early thirties, returned from Vietnam transformed by what she had seen there. "The same way I swore when I was eight years old that I would get a big body, I swore that I would help every child and every animal that came my way," she said. Becoming a member of the Doctor's cult was a natural progression. Her collecting began when she learned that her neighbor was going to "castrate" several kittens. "I was against castration, so I took two kittens."

Shortly after that, on her way to group therapy, "this big gray male cat sprang so hard into the tree that his legs were shaking. He was so tough and so cute, I rescued him, and I took him home." Then Pamela made a decision that led her further into animal hoarding. "I thought it would be nice for them to have kittens, because, you know, for nature. So they had many litters of kittens. I tried to find homes for them, but everyone wanted to alter them." Pamela became responsible for a growing herd. When she got to fifteen cats, she had to move from her small apartment in the West Village to a larger one uptown—a fifth-floor walkup with four rooms. For the next five years or so, her life was filled with work, cats, and men. Cats filled an important role in her life. During one of our interviews, she reflected:

> Because I never got any love, any touching, feeling, love that you need to get—somebody once said, "You never bonded with your mother." Well, my mother was not a bad person; she was charming and nice. My friends loved her, but she was in la-la land. So with the animals, you always knew where you were with them, and they were pure love, all of them. And if they didn't like something you did, they told you right away, and they didn't hold any grudge, and they were just love. But I didn't understand that's what it was; I was just drawn to it.

By the time she reached her thirty-sixth birthday, her collection had grown to thirty-five cats, and it had begun taking over her life. Her career was still thriving, but the parties and the men no longer interested her. The Doctor encouraged her to find a larger place to accommodate her cats. She settled on a sixteen-room house in Queens in a block where several of the Doctor's other cat hoarding patients lived. By this time people had learned that Pamela rescued cats and began leaving them on her doorstep, a common occurrence for animal hoarders. She also seemed to attract pregnant cats. Pamela and others in the Doctor's cult shared the belief that they had the ability to understand and communicate with cats in ways that other people could not and that cats understood them and their mission.

Out of Control

At this time, the Doctor began to depend on Pamela and her other patients to care for her own growing herd of cats, which now topped six hundred. At first Pamela worked for her in exchange for the therapy she was receiving. As time went by, her therapy and her own career seemed to give way to caring for the Doctor's cats, and before long she seldom spoke with the Doctor about her own problems. The Doctor's relationship with her patients shifted as the demands of her cats began to overwhelm her. No longer were her patients the center of her attention; all her energy—and that of her patients—centered on caring for and protecting cats. They protested at cat shows and shelters. They spoke out against the neutering of cats and rescued any they found on the streets. Pamela even recounted physically confronting a drunken man over the kitten he was carrying: she pulled it from his arms and leapt into a taxi, which sped away as the man sprawled on the hood of the car to stop them. Patients who did not participate in these kind of activities began drifting away.

None of the patients who stayed would have dared to neuter any of their animals. To do so would have meant certain banishment. Lesser transgressions, such as not working enough with the cats, drew punishment, and the Doctor's punishment could be brutal. For many years, she seemed to single out Pamela for the harshest treatment. Whenever Pamela made a mistake or failed to carry out some chore with the cats, she was forced to slap herself, sometimes for long periods of time, with other patients counting. This was, she admitted, toward the end, when the Doctor was losing it. But Pamela had been with the Doctor for so long that she couldn't see the absurdity of what she was being asked to do. She simply accepted it. In retrospect, she realized how crazy this behavior was, how cultlike the group had become, and how very much the Doctor resembled her long-ago governess.

With so many cats, epidemics were inevitable, and often the Doctor would have twenty or thirty dead cats at once. At first she put the dead cats on the roof, where they mummified, but soon there were too many of them. Pamela and another patient began stuffing them in barrels filled with dirt, which they kept in the Doctor's basement. They would make periodic trips to New England to bury them.

When Pamela moved to Queens, her own cat population quickly got out of hand. Her census shot up to two hundred cats. She received huge shipments of meat and hired people to mix the food. Keeping the place clean became impossible. Feces covered the floors, and the best she could do was pile it against the walls. Neighbors became suspicious because of the smell and the daily meat deliveries. The cost began to overwhelm her as well. She still had a good income, but all of it went to pay people to take care of the cats. After just a few years, she didn't have enough money to pay the mortgage or her taxes. She lost the house to foreclosure and had to move.

She and the cats ended up in a house with another of the Doctor's patients, but the situation did not improve. Pamela, now in her mid-forties, spent most of her time caring for the Doctor's cats and could no longer work. Up at 3:00 A.M., she was at the Doctor's until nightfall, when she went home to care for her own cats.

Looking back on it, Pamela saw that many of her cats were suffering. "I was careless with them. I did the same thing to the animals that my mother did with me," she said. She remembered one cat dying because she was just too tired from working all day at the Doctor's to give him his seizure medication. Finally, the neighbors sued, the health department came, and the ASPCA was called. Pamela panicked. She rented a large truck, loaded up as many of her brood as she could manage, and brought them to a shelter outside of town, hoping to get them all back after the raid. But the ASPCA raided the shelter as well and, according to Pamela, "slaughtered them all." Pamela returned to the shelter with a film crew to try to document what had happened. She found about forty of her cats still alive and "rescued" them once again. Pamela now had no money and no career. She and her cats moved in with yet another patient who had cats of her own. Money trouble plagued them both, and the two women fought. By Pamela's own account, after one fight she nearly killed her roommate, who kicked her out but kept the cats. "I didn't have any cats suddenly," she told me. "I was homeless, and in a way it was the most unbelievable liberation. I had nothing." For a time, she slept on the floor of a factory, let in each night by another friend who worked there.

Despite her "liberation" from her own cats, and despite the upheaval in her life, Pamela's work at the Doctor's continued unabated. She worked from the early hours of the morning until late at night, but still the Doctor wanted more. Pamela slept only three hours each night and lost so much weight that she became little more than a skeleton. The Doctor stuck her with needles when she didn't hold the cats just right for their shots. Pamela toiled in slavelike conditions. Somewhere in the back of her mind, she knew this was wrong, but she felt powerless to end it, as if she were eight years old again and dealing with Mademoiselle. Finally, at the end of a long day, the Doctor sent her out on an errand. At fifty-two years old, dressed like a charwoman and smelling of cat urine, she started to run. She ran block after block through Manhattan until she felt that she was a safe distance away. She never saw the Doctor again.

Rehabilitation

Pamela set about the task of rehabilitating herself. She went on welfare and began collecting food stamps. At a homeless shelter, she learned upholstery, which led to several small jobs. Once she even got a small film contract. She realized that she had to stay away from animals simply to survive. To make sure she did, she issued what she said was a psychic message to all cats in need: "Cats, stay away from me. I can't help you anymore." And they stayed away, except for three cats in her apartment and one in her freezer, which she hadn't yet put to rest. Still, she remained true to her basic mission, "to rescue every cat that came my way," something she had done faithfully for twenty years. Luckily, either cats in need were now staying away or she failed to notice them.

When I asked Pamela if she thought her capacity to care for animals was healthy or enjoyable, she said, "I don't know that it ever was . . . I didn't let myself really enjoy it and feel them ever, until this last period now with these animals, and a little bit as I went along. But I've identified with them so much, and I could see my suffering in them, even though they weren't suffering."

Based on the few studies on this topic and our interviews with several dozen animal hoarders, we surmise that people who hoard animals have several features in common. Most are female, well over forty years old, and single, widowed, or divorced. Cats and dogs are the most frequent animals hoarded, and the numbers vary widely but average around forty, with a few cases of well over one hundred. In about 80 percent of cases, dead, dying, or diseased animals can be found on the premises. Authorities identify between seven hundred and two thousand new cases of animal hoarding nationwide each year. Because only the most severe cases get reported, this is undoubtedly an underestimate.

At the core of most animal hoarding cases is a special feeling for animals, a sense of connection that was hard for the people we interviewed to articulate. Pamela described it as "pure love," while others we interviewed described it as "beyond love" and uncomplicated by less worthy human emotions. Animals were seen as making few demands, while providing unconditional love and devotion. One of our interviewees even sheepishly admitted that she cared more for her dogs than she did for her husband or children. Another odd feature we observed was that the hoarders became more animal-like in their daily habits over time. Their homes were turned over to the animals, which seemed to have greater access and privileges than the people living there. Many said that they wanted their animals to be free and "natural," and so they had no rules for the animals' behavior. They were allowed to eat, sleep, and even relieve themselves wherever they wanted.

Most animal hoarders experienced neglectful, abusive, and/or chaotic childhoods in which rules were absent or hopelessly inconsistent. Pamela grew up without any close connection to her parents and with an abusive caretaker. For her, animals were more reliable and affectionate companions than family members. The frequency with which we have seen this pattern and have heard animal hoarders say that they cared more about animals than about people has led us to think that animal hoarding may be a form of attachment disorder in which already frayed human bonds are easily broken and replaced by bonds with animals, which serve as surrogates for family. One animal hoarder we interviewed insisted that she wanted to find someone to love but hadn't been able to do so. Her cats, she said, "keep my love alive until I can find someone to love." She did not seem to realize that the condition of her home would dampen the enthusiasm of even the most ardent suitor.

Many people we interviewed insisted that they had special abilities that allowed them to communicate with or understand animals more deeply than the rest of us. Several believed that they had psychic abilities that went beyond even their special connections to animals. Such beliefs left them convinced that they knew better than anyone else how animals feel, what they want, and how to care for them. These beliefs actually helped Pamela resolve her cat hoarding by giving her the sense that her "telepathic messages" to needy cats to stay away from her worked.

But not everyone hoards animals for the same reasons, and assessing the motivation behind the behavior is essential to changing it. Based on the limited amount of research that's been done, animal hoarders seem to fall into one of three categories:

- *Overwhelmed caregivers* own multiple pets and care for them well until they experience a significant change in their lives. With the death of a spouse, the loss of income, a sudden illness, or another major event, the demands of caring for a large number of animals become overwhelming. Often withdrawn and isolated by nature, overwhelmed caregivers don't know how to seek help. Once identified, this group often cooperates in resolving the problem more readily than other types of animal hoarders.
- *Mission-driven animal hoarders* represent the bulk of animal hoarding cases. Rescuing animals from death or suffering drives these people to take in and keep too many animals. These rescue hoarders object to the use of euthanasia and often, as in Pamela's case, to neutering animals. Compared to overwhelmed caregivers, who acquire their animals

passively, rescue hoarders actively seek out animals they believe to be at risk. The Doctor and her patients aggressively
targeted any cat they encountered, even some already well
cared for by other people. Like overwhelmed caregivers, rescue hoarders usually begin with adequate resources but are
quickly swamped by caretaking tasks. Unlike overwhelmed
caregivers, they actively avoid and resist intervention by authorities. They consider themselves to be the only ones who
can provide adequate care for their animals, and like the Doctor and her patients, they sometimes have extensive networks
of animal missionaries who enable their collecting. Ironically,
when their animal counts overwhelm them, they end up caus-
ing the very kind of harm they seek to prevent.

• *Exploiters* have little emotional connection to their animals.
For them, animals are simply a means to an end. Sometimes
that end is financial, and animals are used as props for gener-
ating money to run "rescue" operations. Sometimes the driving
force is a more psychologically rooted need to control other
living things, like the Doctor's need to exercise punitive control over her patients as well as her cats. Exploiters are the
most difficult hoarding cases to manage. People in this category possess superficial charm and charisma but lack remorse
or a social conscience. To other people, exploiters seem articulate and appealing, but in fact they are cunning manipulators,
often conning money from others for their "rescue" efforts.
Rejecting any kind of authority, they will go to great lengths to
evade the law, including taking advantage of others if it suits
their purpose. Luckily, these kinds of hoarders are rare.

One of the most puzzling features of animal hoarding is the lack
of recognition of a problem that is way out of control. Many animal hoarders can be standing amid their sick and dying animals,

with feces covering the floors and walls, and still insist that nothing is wrong. This type of assertion, in the midst of clear evidence to the contrary, suggests a distorted belief system—a delusional disorder. Delusional disorders are usually highly specific and do not accompany distorted thinking in other areas of the person's life. Perhaps animal hoarding represents a delusional disorder with a special, almost magical connection with animals as the predominant theme.

Interestingly, all of the former animal hoarders we have interviewed recognized how abnormal their beliefs were, but only well after they stopped hoarding. Circumstances at the time may have contributed to the apparent delusion. Since Pamela believed that she connected with cats as no one else could and that other people would castrate or euthanize them, she had no option but to keep going. Trapped by her own convictions, she may have changed the way she viewed the situation and convinced herself that things were not really as bad as they seemed. The strength of Pamela's belief was evident. Twenty years after she gave up hoarding, Pamela still saw her efforts in a positive light: "For twenty years, I was able to rescue any animal that came my way." To think otherwise would have meant that she had wasted those twenty years, an intolerable idea for most people.

Most animal hoarding cases end up in court. Ironically, the charge is most often animal cruelty, the very thing many animal hoarders are desperate to prevent. Usually charges are dropped or reduced in exchange for their giving up custody of the animals. Often the court orders counseling, but seldom do these orders get followed.

It is evident to us that animal hoarding is a particularly severe version of hoarding, complicated by even less insight and more difficult life circumstances than most object hoarding. We wonder how many animal hoarders also suffer from serious mental health problems, such as psychosis, bipolar disorder, or even PTSD. More research will help us better understand why these individuals allow animals to rule their lives to the obvious detriment of their own health and welfare, as well as that of their animals. The affection of animals can be a therapeutic tool for vulnerable people in the right circumstances. But it also appears to be a dangerous problem for those taken over by missionary zeal.

Like the hoarding of objects, the hoarding of animals may reflect an intellect more expansive or tuned in to the features of the world than most. The people we interviewed displayed an unusual level of compassion and empathy, which would have been commendable if it had not been distorted by compulsion. But the attachment becomes rigid, unaltered by available resources or limitations—an attempt to love that winds up destroying its target. Whatever the causes, animal hoarding remains one of the least understood and most challenging of hoarding problems.

7

A RIVER OF OPPORTUNITIES

Life is a river of opportunities. If I don't grab everything interesting, I'll lose out. Things will pass me by. The stuff I have is like a river. It flows into my house, and I try to keep it from flowing out. I want to stop it long enough to take advantage of it.

— Irene

Betty liked Ralph right away. She met him when he approached the agency where she was a social worker, asking for help with his finances. At seventy-one, he was unable to manage his modest income from a trust set up by his parents. Collection agencies were hounding him, and he didn't know what to do. Along with handling his finances, Betty and other agency officials thought they should help him clear the debris from his yard and do some home repairs. Ralph liked the agency staff and felt important when they paid attention to him. In fact, he liked most people, especially people who took an interest in him. He possessed a boyish charm that affected almost everyone willing to get beyond his speech difficulties. There was something appealing about his enthusiasm for everything and his earnestness. Above all things, he loved trains — toy trains, real trains, pictures of trains, and thinking about trains. He had made elaborate plans for constructing a Jurassic Park model train route in his house, and much of his collecting, especially of cardboard and Styrofoam, was driven by such plans.

On her first visit to help clear his yard, Betty picked up a rusty bucket with a hole in it that she found sitting by the side of his house in a patch of weeds. She asked him about throwing it out. At first he didn't understand her. It seemed as though he couldn't quite comprehend that she would suggest such a thing. When he finally understood that she wanted him to discard it, he explained that the bucket was still quite useful. "But it has a hole in it. It won't hold water," said Betty. "There are other things it can hold," Ralph replied. "But you have other buckets, ones that will hold water and other things. You don't need this one," Betty argued. She continued patiently with the argument for nearly two hours. Finally, Ralph won; he kept the bucket. For her the bucket became a metaphor for Ralph's hoarding. Anything Ralph could imagine a use for had to be saved, no matter how unlikely that use might be.

I found out about Ralph through Betty. He was delighted to learn that someone was interested in his habit of collecting free and inexpensive things, and he agreed to be interviewed. When I first met Ralph, he was standing on his front porch rummaging through a pile of worn and broken shovels, garden carts, and lawn mower parts. His long gray hair stuck out from beneath a hat pulled tightly over his head. His shoulders hunched forward a bit as he stood. Ralph was a well-known fixture in his Boston suburb, frequently spotted pedaling his bicycle, pulling a cart filled with newfound treasures. He grinned broadly when he saw me and eagerly shook my hand. "Doctor, Doctor," he said, "thank you for coming."

Like the homes on the hoarding tour of Berkeley, California (see chapter 4), Ralph's house was nearly hidden by overgrown trees and shrubs, although they were not enough to conceal the cardboard-covered windows, peeling paint, and piles of scrap lumber and metal in the yard. The house stood in stark contrast to the well-kept and expensive homes in the neighborhood. Ralph had lived there for more than fifty years. For the past twenty, since his parents' deaths, the house had received very little attention or repair.

A speech impediment compromised Ralph's ability to communicate. To compensate, he used dramatic facial expressions and gestures to convey meaning. He also augmented his speech by communicating through metaphor, frequently using props such as newspaper articles or pictures from magazines to express his point of view. Sometimes this backfired, such as the time shortly after the September 11 attacks when he cut out a picture of a captured terrorist to use in conversations about terrorism. His intent was to communicate his fear of people like this man, but the effect was to frighten those he wanted to talk to. Even worse was the time he cut out a sexually suggestive picture to communicate that he didn't like such portrayals in the media. The picture, together with his hard-to-understand speech and odd appearance, led to several unpleasant encounters.

Ralph used certain words as metaphors for larger, harder-to-explain concepts. One such word was "privacy." He repeated that he needed privacy whenever he thought someone was trying to force him to do something, especially when it related to his house or possessions.

Ralph's father had been an engineer and a corporal in the army, and the family had moved a lot when Ralph was young. After finishing high school, Ralph lived on his own for a few years, but apart from a long backpacking trip through Europe in his late thirties, he lived at home with his parents for most of his life. He was a devoted son whose life centered on his parents and a very small group of friends. Both of his parents collected things, but neither had a problem with clutter. His father collected cameras, his mother dolls and embroidery. She kept the house well organized and tidy. During my visits to his home, when Ralph found something that had belonged to one of his parents amid his stuff, he made stabbing motions to his chest to demonstrate how brokenhearted he was about their passing. When they died, his life turned solitary, and for many years no one visited his home.

Ralph inherited his father's interest in how things work and how broken things can be fixed. He did not inherit his mother's knack for organizing. She frequently scolded him for not keeping his room neat. Yet as long as she was alive, he had few problems with clutter. Just how long it took Ralph's home to fill up after his parents died wasn't clear, but he first came to the attention of the Council on Aging about fifteen years after his mother's death.

Ralph was devoted to finding an object's usefulness. Once when I visited, he showed me a piece of an old Venetian blind, vintage 1950. The rest of the blind had been discarded, though not by Ralph. "Most people would throw this out," he proudly told me. "Not me." He described how it connected to the rest of the blind and how it could be repaired. He insisted that somewhere there was someone who needed just such a piece. For most of us, this would not be a sufficient reason for keeping it. For Ralph and many other people with hoarding problems, it is more than sufficient. Ralph saw it as a challenge to find a use for such a thing. In deciding to save this piece, however, he, like most people who hoard, failed to consider the cost of keeping it.

Apart from fixing things, Ralph loved newspapers, especially those with articles containing information he found useful. And for Ralph, most newspapers contained something useful. He recalled a newspaper article about a flood that sent six inches of water coursing down a street. The water was powerful enough to wash away a car. "I didn't realize it could be so powerful. I want to be aware of things like that. I want to know everything," he told me. His home contained thousands of newspapers stacked neatly in piles, some as tall as he was and threatening to collapse as he added to them. To clear space, he moved some to his garage, where they grew wet and moldy. Still he couldn't part with them. He told me once that he felt as if he would drown if he didn't get a chance to read these newspapers. This addiction to information was strikingly similar to other cases we had seen. Irene, for example, described herself as an "information junkie," unable to let go of anything containing a useful tidbit. Ralph knew there was a wealth of knowledge contained in those newspapers. Saving them allowed him to believe that he still had access to all that information. Most of us would make the decision to give up such access in order to maintain a comfortable environment, but not Ralph. Old, yellowing newspapers represented opportunities he couldn't bear to pass up.

Despite the arguments about the stuff in his yard, Ralph grew quite attached to Betty and she to him. Even so, she worked with Ralph for four years before he allowed her inside his house. When she finally saw it, she was both appalled and frightened. The house was so full and so dangerous, she feared for his life. "Every room," she told me, "was packed full, nearly to the ceiling." The piles of newspapers could easily tip over and crush him. Most of the doors were packed shut. The front door opened only partway, requiring her to turn sideways to enter. She could barely navigate the narrow pathways. He would never get out alive if his house caught on fire.

Ralph had covered the windows with cardboard to prevent anyone from seeing what was inside, and there were few overhead lights, so even on the sunniest days, the interior felt like a cave. The house was heated with radiators, but there was so much paper, clothing, and other material packed around each one that the house was freezing, not to mention the fire hazard. In the summer, the lack of ventilation made the house unbearable. In the kitchen, the refrigerator door could be opened only partway, and the stove, piled high with papers, had only one working burner. The downstairs toilet did not work. The upstairs one did, but the bathtub and shower were too full of assorted stuff to use, so Ralph showered at the local college pool.

Now Betty faced a dilemma. She knew from working with Ralph on the outside of the house for so long without much success that he would never consent to clear out the inside. If she reported him to the authorities, she could unleash a chain of legal events that might leave Ralph worse off than he was now. But Betty thought that if she did not report him, there was a real possibility that it could cost Ralph his life. She called the city health department. They had seen hoarding cases before, but always in rented apartments, where the housing codes were readily enforceable. The chief of the health department said that there was nothing he could do because this was a private residence.

Betty and her agency did not give up. They enlisted the help of one of the city's health inspectors and kept trying to convince the city to do something. Meanwhile, Betty tried to work with Ralph to clear out the house. After a year of such efforts, with no progress and no action from the city, Betty finally wrote a letter to the city solicitor outlining her observations about the danger Ralph was in. In the letter, she pointed out the city's potential liability. The health department and the city finally swung into action. They pursued an eviction on two charges. The first was that Ralph was running an improperly zoned business. This was stretching it for sure, but the scrap metal he had accumulated in his backyard gave them a basis for the accusation. The second charge was that the house was a fire hazard. This was certainly more justified. The initial order gave Ralph several months to correct the problems. When he failed to do so, the case went to court, and Ralph was evicted. The fire department sealed the house immediately, stipulating that it had to be cleared out, but not by Ralph.

Betty accompanied the sheriff's officers when they served the eviction papers. Ralph didn't seem upset; he enjoyed talking with the officers. The full meaning of their visit seemed to escape him. Betty convinced him to admit himself voluntarily to the local psychiatric ward. He was quite happy in the hospital, enjoying the staff's attention. After some initial confusion about his diagnosis, the doctors concluded that he suffered from OCD and put him on Paxil, an antidepressant. This did little good, and eventually he stopped taking it. Ralph's insurance coverage ended, and he was released. He went to a nursing home to wait for his house to be cleared. He hated the nursing home; it felt like a prison. To make matters worse, he had to share a bathroom with a man who was careless about his hygiene. Ralph's housekeeping not withstanding, he was a fastidious man, and the slovenliness of others upset him.

Meanwhile, Betty and the city were in court seeking a conservatorship for Ralph on the grounds of mental impairment. There was considerable disagreement about who the conservator should be. Betty, who had by then worked closely with Ralph for five years, disliked the idea of appointing a lawyer who did not know Ralph. She was certain that such a person would not gain his trust, and even if he or she did, the lawyer's fees would quickly eat up Ralph's meager trust. The judge and lawyers felt that it was inappropriate to appoint Betty because she was already involved in his life. Despite what had just happened to him, Ralph trusted and liked Betty and felt that he needed her to get through this ordeal. In the end, the judge decided that Betty would be the best choice.

Ralph's "Trauma"

The cleaning, which Ralph was forbidden to attend, took several weeks. Betty did her best to save things of value, though finding them all in the clutter was not easy. The workers removed thirteen dumpsters—the kind used at construction sites, not the smaller variety found behind retail stores—full of stuff. While the cleanout was going on, Betty talked with Ralph about it every day, and it was her impression that he had accepted his fate.

But he was not happy when he returned to his home. Everything, it seemed to him, was gone. Betty's idea of what was valuable apparently did not match Ralph's. The things he wanted to repair, the pictures of his beloved trains, and the parts for his model train setup were all gone. The cleanout, his "trauma" as he described it to me, became a marker in his life, an event against which all others were measured in time or intensity.

When I met Ralph three years after his trauma, he described in great detail how awful it was. As he showed me around his home, every room provoked recollections of things lost—pictures of his trains, the backpack he'd used on his trip to Europe so many years before, and the many things he had planned to use. One especially painful loss was the nameplate for the front door—a brass plate embossed with his father's name that Ralph had taken down to repair. "They dethroned my father's name!" he lamented. As he listed each item, he turned to me and angrily shouted, "Gone!"

To emphasize his point, he showed me a picture he had cut out of a magazine not long after his trauma. It showed an Immigration and Naturalization Service (INS) officer holding a semiautomatic rifle with an angry look on his face. He was pointing the rifle at a terrified Elian Gonzalez, the young Cuban boy at the center of a custody battle several years ago. Ralph had written "the city" in dark ink above the INS agent and "R," for Ralph, above the helpless little boy. In other pictures he had cut out of newspapers and magazines, he wrote short essays stating that the "Confiscators" were evil people who were out to take his house away. The Confiscators were represented as men with guns or menacing cartoon figures. (In a psychiatric interview just after the trauma, Ralph's references to the INS led the psychiatrist to diagnose him as schizophrenic, thinking his metaphors were part of a paranoid delusion. Luckily, the diagnosis changed as the doctors began to understand Ralph's style of communicating by metaphor.) Ralph's fears of being thrown out of his house escalated when seemingly innocuous things happened to him. One day several years after the trauma, a real estate agent approached him outside his home and told him that if he ever wanted to sell it, she would like to list it. The incident left him convinced that someone in town wanted his house and wanted him out. He wrote a lengthy essay, with captioned cartoons, insisting that this agent never come to his house and never mention selling again. He attached her business card to the essay and made numerous copies to show to his friends. The agent was deeply embarrassed and agreed not to bother him again.

After the initial shock of the cleanout, Betty thought that Ralph was adapting well. He began to talk about how nice it was to have a clean house. He invited friends over and even hosted a dinner party for Betty and her husband and some friends. He worried less about people seeing in the windows and generally seemed content.

Even more impressive to Betty, he was more willing to let things go — such as the rusty bucket with the hole in it. She tried to take advantage of the change. For the next few months, she worked with Ralph to clear out his attic. Ralph hated being told what he should throw away. He claimed that when he decided on his own to get rid of something, it felt good. To help him make the decisions himself, they devised a set of simple rules to follow in their work together. Each rule took hours to figure out but in the end saved time.

As they began their work in the attic, where there was no organization and it was impossible to find anything, they established the "trunk rule." Everything in the attic had to be inside one of the many trunks that were there. Other rules evolved over time. The "kitchen rule," which stated that food must be kept only in the kitchen, was developed to deal with mice and insects. (When they had begun, food was all over the house, as were mice.)

Ralph's "utility rule" came from a social worker, Kelly, who had helped him while he was in the nursing home. She was one of the many social workers who had become quite fond of Ralph over the years. Together they devised a scheme whereby Ralph, when faced with a decision about acquiring or keeping something, was to imagine a little Kelly sitting on his shoulder and saying, "If you can't use it right away, don't buy or keep it." This image so tickled Ralph that he planned to take a picture of himself and superimpose a tiny picture of Kelly sitting on his shoulder. When I watched Ralph going through his things with Betty, he frequently patted his shoulder and repeated Kelly's rule.

When making a decision about saving or discarding something, a hoarder often focuses on the usefulness of the item, such as the potential for the rusty bucket, or on the cost of being without the item, such as the information in Ralph's newspapers. Little thought is given to the cost of keeping things or the benefit of getting rid of them. These rules altered Ralph's normal decision-making process. They forced him to consider how objects fit into his life in a more realistic way.

The language Betty and Ralph used to describe their sessions was also tinged with metaphor. Instead of "discarding" or "throwing out" things, they "thinned out" his stuff. This seemed far more palatable to Ralph. He told himself to "prioritize," often with coaching from Betty, to keep his attention focused on deciding about possessions. Like so many others with this problem, Ralph was easily distracted and readily launched into stories about each object. "Be selective" and "Willpower" were other self-instructions he repeated during the sessions I observed.

Ralph said that these sessions were helpful. Before Betty began helping him, he had felt confused when he tried to decide what to do with his things. Now things were clearer to him, and he felt relieved, even happy to work with her. Watching them together, I could tell that Betty kept Ralph focused on "thinning out" when he otherwise would have been distracted by the potential uses of his possessions. Still, the process was difficult for him. An hour into my first session with them, they had worked through a set of videos piled in the middle of the room. He decided to discard some, such as the free videos about buying a condo in Arizona. Betty helped him organize and put away the ones he kept. He was clearly taxed by this activity. He finally said, "I can't think now. It's time for you to go." Betty often gave him homework to complete between their sessions, but he seldom did it. He preferred to work when she was around, and he wanted her to come more often than she did.

Betty helped keep Ralph's home livable. Although it was still cluttered, it posed no health or safety threat. As time went by, however, the thinning-out sessions became more difficult. Ralph grew less willing to comply and began to express more disapproval of Betty. Before one of my visits, Betty had carried off a pile of things they had decided to get rid of, including an envelope with a picture of a train on it. Just how the envelope got into the throwaway pile was not clear, but Ralph was unhappy about it. Maybe he had okayed it originally and was now having second thoughts, or maybe it was a mistake. Whatever the case, he refused to accept Betty's apology or the idea of living without something he wanted. "I don't trust you," he told her. He turned to me and said, "Betty just doesn't understand." For emphasis, he picked up the handle to a garden cart and explained, "I need this for repairs. Betty just doesn't understand. You're a doctor; you understand my psychology."

Ralph's conclusion that Betty didn't understand his attachment to things was unshakable. His refrain continued for the rest of that session and for the next one. Nothing Betty could say or do dissuaded him. When I asked him a question about another part of his house, he did not want to show it to me. He said that Betty would be mad at him: "I need privacy from Betty." Perhaps he had hoped she would come to share his appreciation for things that were used but not used up. When she didn't, he may have given up on her. For her part, Betty accepted the criticism as part of the package, but increasingly it took its toll on her. Especially hurtful were the times he rebuked her in front of other people. Her hope that he would come to share her ability to distinguish useful things from things used up was fading.

But Ralph did show signs of being able to "thin out" on his own. A heavy snowfall over the winter collapsed the roof of his garage, soaking all the papers and other things he'd stored there. The insurance company said that it couldn't authorize payment until the garage was cleaned out and ready to repair. He called me a few weeks later and asked me to stop by and see his progress: he was proud of himself. When he'd first shown me the three-bay garage, it had been packed to the rafters with wood, newspapers, tools, lawn equipment, and junk. He had discarded most of the papers and wood, an enormous amount of stuff in such a short time, even if some of the items had found their way into his house.

Ralph's relationship with Betty continued to worsen until their sessions became battles neither one could tolerate and Betty stopped visiting. No longer employed by the social service agency, Betty was simply helping Ralph as a friend. With her help, Ralph had managed to keep his home livable, if not clutter-free. Without her, his home deteriorated rapidly. When I saw him several years later, Ralph was again in trouble with the authorities. The health inspector had concluded that the pathways were too narrow to allow access by rescue personnel in case of an emergency, and he worried that there might be flammable material near the furnace. No one had been able to inspect the furnace because the basement door was blocked with neatly stacked boxes filled with wood and papers for Ralph's projects.

What's more, Ralph had run out of money. The elder service agency working with him wanted to set up a reverse mortgage on his home that would ensure him a steady income, but the bank required an inspection, impossible to conduct until the house was cleared out. The agency had been to court with Ralph about this problem; the judge had given him a year to clear out his house. At the time of my visit, ten months had gone by with no progress. But Ralph seemed confident that he could make things right: "Come back, Doctor, and see how much progress I can make in a month." I accompanied the caseworker when she visited him a month later. The purpose for the meeting, she told me, was to inform Ralph of the upcoming court date, when the agency would ask the judge for an order of eviction. The agency planned to move him again to a nursing home temporarily so that they could clear out his house.

As usual, Ralph was delighted by our visit and eagerly showed us some of the things he had just collected. He had apparently forgotten his promise to show me what he had cleared out since my last visit. When the caseworker first mentioned the court date and cleanout, Ralph said that he would fight anyone who tried to take over his home. The caseworker tried to convince Ralph that this needed to happen because he couldn't get rid of the things clogging his house by himself. He said he just needed some help and proceeded to look around for things he could get rid of. He handed me a box with a pair of half-worn-out shoes, to which he added a book about needlepoint and a few other odds and ends that he was willing to discard. But he got stumped while looking at a ten-year-old book about computers, unable to convince himself that he could do without it. He sat down and looked pleadingly at the caseworker. "I won't survive," he said. She commiserated and promised to do what she could to save important things, if she could tell what they were. "I won't survive," he repeated, more to himself than to us. And he may have been right. In 2007, the Nantucket, Massachusetts, Health Department abandoned forced cleanouts when three consecutive hoarders died shortly after being returned to their cleaned-out homes. Although it's not clear whether the cleanouts caused these deaths, the trauma of losing a lifetime of possessions may have contributed to them.

Ralph's interest in the utility of objects is common among hoarders. In a way, his devotion to utility was much like Irene's addiction to opportunity. Once Ralph imagined how he could use or fix an object, he felt committed to the plan, though he rarely if ever executed it. During one of my last visits, he eagerly showed me his latest acquisitions, a nearly working band saw and table. A chrome pipe from a bathroom sink sat on the saw. His eyes lit up as he described his plan to drill a hole in the casing of the saw, fit the pipe into the hole, and attach it to a vacuum cleaner. The result would be a sawdust-free band saw that he could operate inside without making a mess. His life was filled with ever-expanding possibilities for construction or repair, but he never got further than collecting the pieces.

Anita and Waste

While some hoarders, such as Ralph, become captivated by the possibilities in things, others are trapped by the fear of wasting them. Both types would save the rusty bucket with the hole in it, but for different reasons. For Ralph, imagining uses for the rusty bucket brought him joy. Anita, a participant in one of our treatment studies, spent little time thinking about possibilities, but a great deal of time worrying and feeling guilty about waste. For her the bucket would bring pain as she thought about what a wasteful person she would be if she discarded it.

Anita was a former schoolteacher and author who impressed me immediately with her insight into her own thought processes. She knew that she had a problem, and she could see it unfolding before her—and articulate it, step by step—but she felt powerless to stop it. Her plight was embodied in the "story of the gloves"—her own painful (and unsuccessful) effort to throw away a single pair of holey gloves.

Anita already had six overstuffed drawers of gloves, but these were her favorite kind—soft wool that fit perfectly and came high up on her wrists. They were striped, which she thought was cute. They didn't show age like white gloves, and they were especially soft. But one of them had a hole in it. She couldn't mend the hole, she knew she'd never wear the gloves, and she knew she should throw them out.

Then she paused and thought that perhaps she should find someone to mend them. But the hole had developed quickly, which meant that the gloves were poorly constructed and probably not worth mending. She thought maybe she could put them in the rag bag, "then I could get rid of them without really getting rid of them." But her rag bag was already overflowing with better rag material. As she pondered this, she finally said, "I hate to put them in the trash. I know it's stupid, but ninety-nine percent of the glove is still usable! They're perfect otherwise, and they're so cute, it seems like such a waste. I've read articles about how wasteful the average American is, and here is this perfectly good fabric that I'm wasting!"

As she continued to talk, she again came to the conclusion that she should throw the gloves out. She also thought that it might help her to write down some of the arguments she'd generated so that she could remember them for the next item she confronted. Her first argument was for things she found cute: "The argument is that there are other cute things, and I don't need this." She went on, "And if I *think* I might use it, in reality I won't."

At this point, she became tearful. "And if I think it's wasteful, the answer is that it's not my fault." She began to cry in earnest. Through her sobs, she continued, "I didn't make the gloves crummy, so I'm not being bad. I'm doing the best I can with a bad situation. If they were well made, and I wore them for two years, and they were worn-out all over, it wouldn't bother me." It took her some time to compose herself after the emotional outburst, and then her distress turned to anger. "It pisses me off at this store. When you shop, you should get things that fit, that are made well, so it's like I got tricked into making this mistake. It's not my fault."

Anita suffered tremendously from a very rigid sense of responsibility and severe perfectionism. She couldn't tolerate mistakes and almost always chose inactivity over the possibility of doing something less than perfectly. Early on in therapy, she had a massive anxiety attack when she thought that she had failed to do the homework properly. She expected me to criticize her and in fact reported that in every social situation she entered, she expected people to be critical of her. To prevent this, she carefully scrutinized her every action to make sure it was correct. Her first sign of progress in therapy came when she threw away a bowlful of pencil stubs. Immediately, she feared that her son would be angry with her, because she had thwarted his attempts to get rid of them in the past.

As might be expected of someone who searched everything she did for mistakes, Anita was influenced in most of her decisions about saving things by the possibility of error. In particular, she worried that throwing things away made her a wasteful person. "It's like I imagine in my head that someone walking down the street may have x-ray vision and can see how wasteful I am," she said. Living in a cluttered home violated her sense of perfection, but at least she was not being wasteful.

The gloves themselves mattered little to her; she just didn't want to give the impression to others—or to herself—that she was wasteful. She could think of other uses for the gloves, such as rags or toys for the cat, but she knew these weren't realistic. Keeping the gloves actually offered her little comfort: "When I see them, I feel guilty and stupid for having bought them. Then I feel guilty for having too many gloves and not being able to keep my drawer organized." Guilt was everywhere.

Anita's concern about wasting things extended to all aspects of life. She recounted feeling guilty for using a Band-Aid on a cut that she wasn't sure really needed it. She described encountering great difficulty one night when she went out to dinner, something she seldom did. She couldn't decide what to order and in the end had to pick something rapidly when the waiter came back for the third time. Before her food arrived, she concluded that she had ordered the wrong thing, and even though she ate the meal, she believed she had wasted it. "It was my responsibility, and I screwed up. I wasted the meal, and I hate that. Even saying the word 'waste' makes me cringe."

Anita, like Ralph, had problems judging how useful her possessions really were. When Ralph looked at his rusty bucket, he saw potential, and that made him feel good. When Anita looked at the holey gloves, she saw waste, and that made her feel bad. Both wanted to save the items—Ralph because of pleasing potential, Anita to avoid feeling wasteful. When Ralph was forced to get rid of his bucket, he got angry at his "privacy" being invaded. Even his attachment to Betty couldn't overcome his frustration. When Anita got rid of the gloves, she felt guilty for wasting them. Beliefs about utility, waste, and responsibility are common among people who hoard. Ownership seems to carry with it the responsibility for making sure things are used to their full potential and not wasted.

Anita saw her clutter as a serious problem and sought help. But her perfectionism and self-criticism got in the way of her treatment. "I have sensitive antennae," she said, referring to her fear of making mistakes and being criticized. Discarding something required perfect certainty that the item was no longer useful and would never be needed in the future. She could get rid of things that met this criterion, but the process was exhausting and didn't match the rate at which things entered her home. Despite my efforts, Anita would not allow herself to experience anything short of perfection. She hated the idea of being in treatment without some guarantee that it would work. She doubted her ability to handle the treatment program, and the prospect of failure frightened her. Her overwhelming priority was to avoid the pain she knew best—the pain of making mistakes—a self-defeating tactic that we'll explore in the next chapter. Anita terminated therapy without much improvement, although she reported some progress in being able to tolerate imperfection.

8

AVOIDING THE AGONY

I just feel like I want to die. If you weren't here, I would avoid doing any of this [sorting and discarding].

—Irene

I first visited Nell's home on a January day when the temperature hovered near zero degrees Fahrenheit. When I knocked, it took some time before a small voice asked through the door, "Who is it?" I called through the door, reminding her of our appointment. "Just a minute," she said. I waited in the freezing cold for nearly ten minutes, listening to shuffling sounds on the other side of the door. Then the door opened just enough for me to squeeze through. Once inside, I was trapped in a space only big enough to stand in, with walls of stuff up to my waist. While I stood there, my hostess, a petite seventy-one-year-old woman with neatly cropped hair and an impish smile, repacked the newspapers and bags against the door, clearing a path into the living room.

I could see why it had taken her so long to open the door. The objects she piled against it were too heavy to allow it to open more than a crack. As the pile grew, I felt uneasy. By this time, I had been in many hoarded homes and gotten used to them, but having the exit barricaded this way was unsettling.

Nell was terribly embarrassed by the condition of her home and fearful of what I would think of her. She normally went to great lengths to prevent anyone from seeing her place. She had become a master at maintaining friendships without allowing visitors into her home. She would offer to buy dinner, suggest going places for coffee, or meet her friends somewhere for a movie. Keeping them from noticing her car posed more of a problem. Her excuses for not being able to give someone a ride usually involved car trouble or temporarily having to store things in her car. For each of her social events, she arrived early and parked at the end of the parking lot, well away from where any of her friends would be likely to park, in order to preempt the inevitable questions about all the stuff in her car. Still, if someone really needed a ride, she would oblige, but only after asking for some time to rearrange things in her car. Her desire to be helpful to others was the only motive that could outweigh her desire to hide her clutter. She knew she had a problem, one she had struggled with for most of her life. Her children knew it, too, and their not-so-subtle pressure on her to clear the clutter had seriously strained her relationships with them. Her son had read about our treatment program and had convinced her to call.

Much of Nell's home resembled her front hallway. In places where furniture should be, boxes teetered on boxes up to the ceiling. She was a Tupperware representative and received weekly shipments, but she rarely sold anything, and the boxes were everywhere. Narrow pathways were littered with cans and bottles, some of which had ruptured, spilling their contents onto the matted carpet. Getting from place to place required skating on top of the debris, and my feet were too big to avoid stepping on soda cans, vitamin bottles, or phone books. I worried about crushing things as I walked down the hallway into her living room. I also worried that she would fall and break a hip.

When we settled into the only seating space available (she on a tiny bare patch of the sofa, me precariously balanced on a stack of cardboard boxes), Nell apologized again for the state of her home and told me how ashamed she felt. Then she said something that astonished me. "When I come home at night," she confided, "I don't even notice the clutter!" In fact, she never noticed the condition of her home when she was there alone.

My visit made her acutely aware of just how bad her living conditions had become. The awareness, she said, depressed her. Noticing the clutter turned her thoughts to what a "worthless" person she was and what a horrible mother she had been. After several visits, she told me that when I was there, she desperately wanted me to leave. And when I did, she became her old self again, unaware of her clutter and back in the world of the worthy. When I showed up, she said, she got depressed, and when I left, she felt better.

There is a flip side to the pleasure hoarders derive from acquiring and owning things, but it is not merely the pain of discarding those possessions. Rather, it is the *avoidance* of that pain, or of any negative emotional experience at all. This is as fundamental to the development and maintenance of hoarding as acquiring things in the first place. The feelings of safety, identity, and opportunity described in earlier chapters also drive the effort to avoid psychic pain. Saving things allows hoarders to avoid the distress of being without their cherished possessions — and all the significant connotations those possessions have. Irene burst into tears one day as she got rid of a treasured art history book. "I just feel like I want to die," she said. She told me that if I hadn't been there, she would have put the book back on her pile and avoided the whole experience. In this and many other instances, saving helped her avoid feeling upset. For Anita, saving things helped her avoid the agony she would feel if she made a mistake about an object's utility. In her therapy sessions, she resisted working on discarding and instead tried to engage me in discussions about her life and struggles. In this arena, she was insightful, articulate, and interesting — but more important, she felt in control and successful. When I convinced her to discard (or even just sort through) possessions, she felt like a failure. Here she had little control and great distress; her perfectionism created consequences that she would do anything to avoid. Indeed, as we saw in chapter 7, it even overpowered her attempts at therapy. She was so afraid of "doing the therapy wrong" that she ultimately avoided the work altogether.

Avoidance behavior and a process called avoidance conditioning are in part responsible for OCD and most anxiety disorders. In the case of OCD, compulsive rituals temporarily alleviate the distress associated with the obsession. For instance, checking to make sure the door is locked provides some people relief from their anxiety over safety. Wiping the back of her dining room chair with a towelette gave Irene some relief from her distress about contamination. These strategies don't address the root problem; they simply allow the person to avoid the difficult work of recovery as well as the anxiety produced by the obsession. Similarly, people with panic disorder avoid using public transportation for fear of experiencing panic attacks; people with social phobia avoid speaking in groups for fear of embarrassment. These sorts of avoidance behaviors are reinforced because they allow the person to escape an unpleasant emotional state, such as fear, sadness, or guilt. Unfortunately, the relief is only temporary, and by avoiding that state, the person never learns to deal with it effectively. Before long, the avoidance behavior becomes second nature, difficult to distinguish from the underlying disorder, even for the afflicted person.

Exactly why this pattern of coping develops is not clear. One theory is that some people are unusually sensitive to anxiety and distress, and this leads them to seek extreme ways to avoid or escape it. In one of our recent studies of people with hoarding problems, we found that this was indeed the case: hoarders were unusually sensitive to even small amounts of anxiety.

For Irene, the sources of distress when discarding her possessions were numerous. Discarding a book or a newspaper might
mean the loss of important information. Simply making a choice
about where to put something was a source of anxiety: what if she
put it in the wrong place and couldn't find it when she needed
it? This possibility terrified her; it seemed it would be too much
to bear, and perhaps it would. Saving things enabled her to avoid
feeling upset, but it also prevented her from learning how to tolerate distress. Each time she avoided a negative feeling, she learned
how to make herself feel better, albeit only temporarily. The more
she did it, the more acute her ability to detect distress became, and
the avoidance behaviors occurred more quickly over time. As she
rarely had to cope with uncomfortable feelings, even mild distress
seemed unmanageable. Over time, Irene learned to avoid even the
simplest decisions and slightest negative emotions. This meant
never dealing with most of her things, since that would involve
difficult decisions and raw emotions. Instead, she just let them
pile up. Most hoarders end up here, avoiding even the stuff they
collect.

Avoiding discarding also prevented Irene from discovering the
true value of her possessions. Less than five minutes after deciding to discard the art history book she had wept over, I asked her
how she felt about it. "It doesn't bother me much at all now. For
thirty years, I've kept that book. Now I realize it didn't matter that
much to me." Had she faced the initial distress over getting rid of
the book years ago, she would have discovered then that it meant
little to her.

Irene's feelings about me, so similar to Nell's, were part of this
process as well. On her first day, as we were making arrangements
to get started, she said, "I want to quit. I just thought I should tell
you this. I realize I have to do this, but I really want to quit, and I
want you to leave." I think the only reason she didn't make us leave

at that moment was that she would have felt guilty about our traveling for more than an hour to get to her home, only to have to turn around and leave. For most sessions, Irene had the same reaction when we showed up at her door: "I sort of wished you had forgotten our appointment." Frequently, she thought about calling to cancel, and sometimes she did. We had come to represent the distress she associated with getting rid of things. We were now conditioned stimuli, automatic cues for Irene's apprehension. People in treatment for hoarding commonly show this pattern, and it translates into missed sessions, attempts to postpone or cancel, not being able to work on clearing or sorting, and sometimes dropping out of treatment. Luckily, Irene understood what was happening, and her general affection for people, including us, overcame her conditioned avoidance.

Anxiety is not the only emotion hoarders seek to avoid. Most people, hoarders and non-hoarders alike, attempt to alleviate or preempt grief and sadness. Anyone who has stayed in a bad relationship or a bad job or has delayed breaking bad news to a friend can understand the urge. The difference with hoarders is a matter of scope: the number of sources for these feelings and the intensity of the feelings themselves, as well as the lengths to which they'll go to protect themselves, are unusually great.

Lydia, a participant in one of our studies, is an example of how broad the range of these three elements (source of feelings, intensity of feelings, and avoidance techniques) can be. Her home was a classic hoarded home, arranged for the containment of things rather than people. She had a particular fondness for vintage clothes, dolls, and anything with a pretty picture, and her home looked a bit like a dark and dingy wardrobe warehouse. The piles of dresses and dolls were actually quite spooky. She had plans to clean and refurbish many of her treasures and donate them to the Salvation Army, but she never seemed to get around to it.

As an experiment, she agreed to let me take something from her home and discard it. She settled on a stuffed toy, a yellow swan, which she'd picked up at a tag sale some years before. It was dirty and ragged but had been around long enough for her to feel connected to it. Although she agreed to let me take it and throw it away, before she let me out the door, she took dozens of photographs: me with the swan, her with the swan, her husband with the swan, my student with the swan. Like Debra (see chapter 5), she was trying to preserve her ownership with pictures. As I reached for the door to leave, she insisted on videotaping my departure and narrating the story of the little yellow swan. I learned that this was standard procedure for her. First she inspected an item to make sure it didn't contain anything important, then she photographed it, and finally she videotaped it while telling its story. She couldn't stand to let anything go without such a laborious procedure, designed to avoid the experience of loss. Had she let herself experience the loss, she may have been surprised at how well she could tolerate it, and subsequent attempts to get rid of unneeded things would undoubtedly have been easier.

A few weeks after my visit, I received a letter from her that contained the following poem:

THE YELLOW SWAN

Oh, yellow swan, you are someplace unknown to me.
It was a struggle to say farewell to you.
I would have been glad to pass you on to a friend.
But I took the suggestion of Randy Frost — like a leap of faith.
He told me that it would help me if I threw you away.
I find it hard to believe, but I did it anyhow.
Because that is what our 12-step program suggests.

Randy asked about my feelings. What are my feelings?
Sadness, a longing for your return, a feeling of missing you.
You were with me for so long,
holding my bangle bracelets so nicely on your stately neck.
I used to think you were beautiful.
I remember how delighted I was when you came to live
    with us.
I guess I am grieving your loss.
I cried at the meeting when I talked about your being
    discarded,
"like an old shoe."
Rhea said she was "proud of me," but I don't understand why.
Rhea always gives things away to people.
I shall have to ask her why she's proud of me.
Throwing away feels like wrongdoing to me.
Little yellow swan, you are the object of my sacrifice.
You are the symbol of new freedom.
Many things will have to follow in your footsteps for my
    husband and me
to gain the space we need to live, to enjoy our home, to have
    our freedom.
In letting go of the old, there will be room for the new.
I enjoyed having you, but perhaps a new family will find you
    and enjoy you.

Accompanying the ode was a note saying that she thought the
experiment had shown her how much energy she invested in the
millions of objects in her home. That led her to think that she could
do more letting go. In the sentences that followed, however, she
described a trip to New York City the previous weekend: "I found
myself hoarding the soaps, shampoos, and conditioners from the
hotel. The more the maid gave me, the happier I felt. I even asked

for the tray they came on as a souvenir." At least she was now more aware of her hoarding behaviors when they occurred, even if more encumbered by her new treasures. I spoke with Lydia a number of times after the yellow swan episode. Six years later, she could laugh about it, but for several years it was a painful memory. Last time I spoke with her, she had made substantial gains in controlling her clutter, clearing out several rooms in her home so that they were livable. It was, however, a constant struggle.

For some hoarders, stopping the avoidance can have a dramatic effect. Recently, we completed a study of the effects of discarding in which we asked people to choose something they had avoided discarding and throw it out. Before, during, and after discarding, they recorded their thoughts and feelings. Most experienced feelings of regret, loss, sadness, or other distress, and most showed a pattern of habituation in which their distress slowly dissipated. One young man was surprised and delighted that his distress went away so quickly. He called three months after the experiment to thank us. He said that the experiment had led him to question how much distress he could tolerate and test himself, and he proudly reported that he had cleared out his entire house.

Avoidance behavior in hoarding is not limited to discarding. It can affect major life decisions and daily routines as well. Remember how Irene coped with her problem with newsstands? She avoided them altogether, crossing to the other side of the street so that she wouldn't have to look at them. She even avoided thinking about newspapers. When I asked what happened when she imagined newspapers she didn't get, she replied, "I could drive myself nuts thinking about all the newspapers in the world, so I don't go there." Janet (see chapter 3) avoided certain stores and even certain aisles in stores because they would trigger her buying.

Buying itself can be an avoidance behavior, because the intense distress and longing for an object that accompanies any attempt not to acquire can be relieved (or avoided) by acquiring it. As discussed earlier, our treatment for acquiring involves teaching hoarders to learn to tolerate the distress they experience at not acquiring something. Several years ago, we organized an experiment after a workshop we gave at the Obsessive Compulsive Foundation's annual conference in Chicago. The conference took place across the boulevard from the second-largest shopping mall in the country. We invited participants in our workshop who had serious buying problems to take a non-shopping trip there and face the discomfort associated with not acquiring something they desired. Each person who volunteered agreed not to purchase anything and to tell us about their thoughts and feelings as they struggled with the urge to buy.

Gail accompanied a woman who was addicted to books—cookbooks, do-it-yourself craft books, mysteries, novels, and, although her own children were grown, children's books. "When they have kids, I'll be able to give these to my grandchildren," she declared. At the bookstore, they found a rack of cookbooks that delighted her. Her eyes lit up as she scanned the titles. At Gail's suggestion, she pulled one out and opened it. It was an Italian cookbook with large color photographs of the food and an appealing, easy-to-read typeface. She found a recipe for a pasta dish and exclaimed over how good it sounded and how easy it would be to make—never mind that she had already reported to the group that her kitchen was so cluttered that she hadn't cooked in more than two years. Her eyes were wide as they bounced over the next few pages, taking in several "wonderful" recipes.

At Gail's request, she closed the book and dutifully put it back, looking disappointed and tearful as she did so. The pull to purchase was written all over her face. She rated her discomfort as 90 on a 100-point scale. She looked miserable but said that she was willing to keep going with the exercise.

The woman and Gail walked toward the entrance to the department store, which took a couple of minutes. At the entrance, Gail paused and asked how she felt. Her discomfort rating was down to 75. They walked to the entrance to the mall. Again she rated her discomfort, and this time, after not more than ten minutes, the rating was less than 20. Gail asked if she remembered the title of the cookbook she had perused in the bookstore. She didn't. Nor could she recall what recipe she'd found so appealing. She couldn't even remember the color of the book jacket. She was shocked. "That's really amazing. I always give in. I would have bought it if you hadn't been here. I can't believe how fast I forgot the book. Wow! I feel fine now. I can't believe it!" Like Irene and her treasured art history book, the woman had avoided the experience of distress for so long that she no longer knew how little value most books really had for her.

This kind of long-term avoidance can have some strange and extreme effects, most notably the "clutter blindness" that Nell experienced. She was a vivacious, lively woman; her days were taken up with work as a private nurse and her nights with church, singing groups, and theater. With all of her activities, she spent relatively little time at home. This is common for people who hoard, most likely another way to avoid thinking about the clutter.

I took pictures of Nell's home on my first visit. It was difficult to do, as is frequently the case in hoarded homes, because the clutter made it impossible to get into position to capture the true magnitude of the problem. Still, the photos were striking: boxes piled nearly to the ceiling, clothes cascading from the piles, and no floor visible. Newspapers and magazines littered most of the home, especially her bedroom. Nell loved to read and reread them, which she usually did in bed. Surrounding her bed and covering part of it were hundreds of magazines and newspapers. Her frequent attempts to organize them were thwarted by her dog and cat, who made a game of sending them cascading across the floor.

Pictures have proved to be a good way to keep track of how clients do in treatment. Photos document progress far better than memory, and reviewing them has been rewarding to our clients later in the therapy as rooms are cleared. For our second session, Nell and I met at the clinic. I showed her the picture of her living room. Her reaction startled me. She didn't recognize her home. It took some time for me to convince her that it was indeed her living room. She was shocked that it looked so incredibly bad. Somehow this two-dimensional image just didn't match the image she had in her mind of her living room as a comfortable and safe place. This picture depicted something abhorrent and bizarre.

We have seen this reaction from a number of clients since then. Seeing pictures of their homes is like seeing through a new lens, the lens most people see through. Although Nell knew she had a problem, when she was at home, everything seemed normal, and she had little motivation to subject herself to the painful process of dealing with her stuff. But when the context changed and she looked through someone else's eyes, a visitor's or a camera's, she saw all too clearly the magnitude of her problem.

In many ways, Nell was lucky. There were some contexts in which she could recognize the problem, and these motivated her to do something about it. For some people who hoard, clutter blindness can be unshakable. This selective blindness allows them to function with less emotional turmoil. Not seeing the clutter allowed Nell to avoid all the unpleasant thoughts and feelings that accompanied it. Of course, it also prevented her from taking any meaningful steps to correct the situation.

Another of our hoarding clients demonstrated her clutter blindness in a slightly different way. At her first therapy session, the therapist asked her to draw an outline of the rooms in her home and to indicate where the clutter had taken over. In her drawing, the living room was a narrow space, more like a hallway. When the therapist visited her home for the first time, he was shocked to find that her living room was nearly three times the size suggested by her drawing. She had drawn a wall where the mountain of clutter began. It was as though the two hundred square feet of clutter packed to the ceiling was no longer a part of her home. Another man simply omitted an entire room from his drawing. The room was completely filled, and he hadn't been in it for years. For him, it no longer existed.

Nell's clutter blindness helped her to avoid distress caused by her hoarding, but she also used hoarding itself to avoid other kinds of distress. One thing she avoided by not cleaning her apartment was a peculiar intrusive thought. Sheepishly, she told me about it one day. "I have a very childlike view of God. I believe he is all-benevolent and would never let me die in this kind of mess." Whenever she began to clean, the thought occurred to her that now God would allow her to die, and the idea terrified her. She had been having the thought, she reported, for more than fifteen years.

As we talked about this thought, she recognized that it was irrational, but still it had a powerful effect on her motivation to clean. Whenever she started to clean, she thought about her own death and the possibility that what she was doing would bring it about. If she stopped cleaning, the distress went away along with the thought. After talking about the fact that *avoiding* cleaning would almost certainly bring about the very thing she feared (she seemed destined to end up like the Collyer brothers, lying dead in the midst of the clutter), Nell was able to start cleaning. The intrusive thought still occurred, but she could dismiss it more easily.

Nell suffered from another common form of avoidance in hoarding. She was a perfectionist, especially when it came to cleanliness and neatness—quite a remarkable irony given the state of her home. Nell had a part-time business cleaning houses (also an irony), and she was very good at it. But when it came to her own home, her perfectionism got the better of her. When she tried to clean something, she did such a thorough job that it took forever to complete. In the end, the time and effort didn't seem commensurate with the result. Doing a half-assed job was equally unsatisfying. Since she couldn't clean the place to her liking, it was less painful to do nothing, and if she was successful in remaining blind to the clutter, the pain was reduced even more.

One feature of hoarding that got in Nell's way was the belief that she could clean and reorganize her home without experiencing distress. From her perspective, this was possible if she simply took the time necessary to go through things carefully. She believed, as do many people with this problem, that the biggest difficulty was not having enough time to go through her newspapers and other items and get what she needed from them. In her view, throwing things away was not a problem once she decided she no longer needed them. All she needed was more time. She could not review one newspaper carefully enough to get rid of it before the next one arrived, however. Papers piled up as she got farther and farther behind. But even if she had taken the time, she may not have resolved her uncertainty over whether she needed to keep the papers. The real problem was not time, but an intolerance of the distress she experienced when she discarded something she was not absolutely certain she would not need.

Even so, she resisted any suggestion that she throw away things such as newspapers without reviewing them for important information. "Don't ask me to do it," she begged. Doing so would make her feel guilty and give her a sense of losing or missing out on something important. She saw no need to experience such distress. In our work together, she wanted me to help her process her possessions in the careful way she had always done it. In a sense, she wanted me to engage in hoarding with her rather than work to change her behavior.

Nell's progress in therapy was slow at first, mostly because her efforts involved spending a lot of time doing the elaborate reviewing and checking that were part of her hoarding. It was not until we did an experiment on experiencing distress that things began to change. Nell had picked up a free newspaper at the supermarket. The newspaper was a community-based publication containing articles and announcements of interest to senior citizens. It had information that might be useful to Nell, but she agreed to discard it and keep track of her distress. The purpose was to see whether her level of distress matched what she expected and whether the distress lasted as long as she thought it would. As we always do in such experiments, I asked Nell to rate her distress on a scale of 0 to 100, where 0 equaled no distress and 100 equaled the most distress she could imagine. Immediately after discarding the paper, she rated her distress at 85. Five minutes after that, it was down to 80. After ten more minutes, it was at 60, and six days later she reported her distress as 15. Although her initial distress was high, in less than a week she had little distress about losing this information. The experiment seemed to rejuvenate Nell. Suddenly, she was able to get rid of more stuff, to discard things without poring over them meticulously. She began to make real progress in therapy.

Another milestone in Nell's treatment occurred when she decided to allow a marathon cleaning session at her home. Her most productive time in working on hoarding occurred when I visited. Most of that time, I simply talked with her and walked her through the steps involved in discarding. Like many hoarding clients, she did not want me touching or deciding about her things. But to make quicker progress, she agreed to experiment with allowing me to make decisions about which things could be thrown away. Normally, we don't make such decisions for clients, but in Nell's case, part of her fear was of other people taking control from her. Facing that fear meant allowing someone else direct control over some of her possessions. After the first such session, I received a frantic phone call from Nell, who was angry with me for putting something in a place where she could not find it. She had found it by the time she placed the call but still wanted to express her displeasure with me. After that, however, she gave up some of her rigid control over her things and allowed me to touch them and even make discarding decisions about them.

A similar thing happened with Irene, who had ended a friendship when someone she'd asked to help her clean had picked up an empty gum wrapper from her floor and discarded it without her permission. By the end of her treatment, when Irene trusted me fully, she allowed me to pick up items and even make decisions about whether to keep some of them.

By the end of our treatment study, Nell had made great progress. Her entry hallway was reasonably clear, her door opened without any problem, and she didn't have to walk on a layer of stuff to get to her living room. The living room itself went from being about chest-high with clutter to having cleared furniture and floor, with only some residual clutter. Open floor space was visible in her bedroom and kitchen as well, and she could once again cook in the kitchen. She had stopped collecting newspapers and magazines. Although Nell had improved, she was still unable to get rid of much of what she had, especially her Tupperware. We moved these items to her basement, out of her main living area, where they formed what she christened "Mount Tupper."

Anxiety, sadness, grief, and guilt are all part of the human experience. When people go to great lengths to avoid them, the results can be devastating. Avoiding distress is a key feature in the development and maintenance of hoarding. It reinforces the belief that the feelings being avoided are intolerably bad, and at the same time it weakens the person's strength to cope with those feelings. Avoidance is a seductive coping strategy that works temporarily but ultimately undermines progress.

9

YOU HAVEN'T GOT A CLUE

When I'm trying to decide what to keep, this outdated coupon seems as important as my grandmother's picture.

—Irene

We could have found the apartment just by following the powerful musty odor that hit us as we stepped out of the elevator. When we got to the door, my guide knocked. No answer. She knocked again, then a third time. I thought of the Collyer brothers, who never answered their door. Finally, a small voice inside said, "Who's there?"

"It's Susan, the social worker. We're here with the cleaning crew. They're here to clean out your apartment."

"Daniel's not here," the voice behind the door told us. "He went to get us breakfast."

"That's okay. We don't need him to be here."

She opened the door just a crack, and the door frame moved, almost imperceptibly. Yet it didn't really move. The world seemed to shift just a bit, and I felt off balance for a moment. The door opened a bit wider, and then I saw them—cockroaches, thousands of them, scurrying along the top of the door to get out of the way.

The door opened the rest of the way. The apartment was dark, and it took a moment to appreciate what was inside. No floor was visible, only a layer of dirty papers, food wrappers, and urine-stained rags. A rottweiler bolted out of the back to see what was going on. He jumped over a pile of dirty clothes—at least they looked like clothes. From the edge of the door, the massive pile of junk rose precipitously to the ceiling, like a giant sea wave. It could have been part of a landfill: papers, boxes, shopping carts, paper bags, dirty clothing, lamps—anything that could be easily collected from the street or fished out of a dumpster. It was one solid wall of trash twenty feet deep, all the way to the back of the apartment. There must have been windows on the far wall, but they were darkened by the broken fans, boxes, and clothing covering them.

Inside the condo the sweet, pungent odor of insects and rotting food enveloped us. Susan had instructed me to wear old clothes that I could throw out afterward. I was grateful for the advice but wished I'd also had a facemask—the heavy-duty kind.

I could feel the cockroaches surrounding me as I stepped in. The walls were coated with their brown dung, and occasionally one dropped from the ceiling onto the piles of debris below. I walked farther in to get a better look at the kitchen, or what I thought was the kitchen. It was impossible to tell, since everything was covered with bags. Food, mostly old and rotting, empty but unwashed tuna cans, and colorful coupons adorned the room. There was a path into the kitchen, though it was atop six inches of trash on the floor. I was afraid to touch anything. I suddenly felt a great deal of sympathy for all the people I'd met with contamination phobias: *This must be what it feels like,* I thought.

Susan, the court-appointed guardian of Edith, who had struggled to open the door for us, had obtained a judge's order for a "heavy-duty cleaning" because she believed that Edith's health and safety were in danger and no more moderate measure had succeeded in improving the horrific living conditions in the condo.

Edith wasn't responsible for these conditions, nor was her sister or her son, Tim, both of whom lived with her. It was all her brother Daniel's doing. And Daniel didn't see anything wrong with the place. "All of this stuff we can use," he insisted. "There is nothing wrong with our home."

Indeed, all four adults living in the five-room condo had become so habituated to the squalor that they barely noticed it anymore. Edith insisted that she was "fine," even when her visiting nurses refused to enter her home to help treat her diabetes. The family was so blind to the severity of the problem that social services took the unusual step of appointing a legal guardian for Edith, a competent adult who lived in her own home.

People who live in squalor and don't appear to notice it exhibit the most dramatic form of clutter blindness. How could Daniel not recognize the bizarre and unhealthy state of his home? How could Edith defend him? Most people who hoard save things that don't decay and aren't particularly dirty, such as newspapers or clothes. In our study of hoarding in the elderly, we found that less than a third of the cases lived in squalid conditions. In younger samples, the proportion is even lower. But some people, like the fifty-year-old Daniel, collect dirty and rotting stuff that invites insects and rodents.

Daniel scavenged his stuff from the streets of Manhattan, mostly from the piles left at the edges of sidewalks for the city trash crews. Anyone walking these streets can see that some of the things piled there have value. Many people avail themselves of these treasures, descending on neighborhoods early in the morning on trash day. But Daniel collected the stuff no one else wanted—broken fans, pieces of lumber, food containers, ripped and dirty clothes. On top of his daily scavenging, Daniel wouldn't allow empty and unwashed food containers to be discarded. Instead, he deposited them on the floor.

Since most of the people we see in our research come to us in search of help for their problems, we seldom encounter people who are completely unaware of their hoarding. But in the social service and public health sector, such cases are the norm. Recently, I attended a local task force meeting about hoarding problems in communities in western Massachusetts. The meeting was attended by representatives from elder and adult protective services, housing and public health departments, and the courts. These officials deal with the toughest hoarding cases, people whose overstuffed homes endanger them and anyone living nearby. The representative from adult protective services, a woman who had handled dozens of hoarding cases in the past few years, remarked that she had never met anyone who actually recognized his or her hoarding problem. Others in the room nodded in agreement.

Clinicians describe individuals such as Daniel as lacking insight, meaning that they don't understand how their behavior harms them or others around them. Most psychiatric conditions that are associated with lack of insight involve deterioration in cognitive functions — people who lack mental capacity, as in schizophrenia or dementia. But there are a few exceptions. For example, people with alcohol or drug problems or those concerned about their appearance (anorexia or body dysmorphic disorder) do not usually lack cognitive abilities. Their reasoning and thinking about most things is just fine; only when it comes to their alcohol or drug use or their body image do they lack insight. Hoarding may be another of these highly specific insight problems. The lack of insight in hoarding appears to be narrow, applying only to the clutter and varying by context. When outside their homes, many people who hoard recognize that they have a problem, but when they are at home and looking at objects they should get rid of, they can't see the problem.

Among social service workers dealing with non-insightful hoarders, attempts to get these clients to recognize the seriousness of

their problems are largely ineffective. No amount of reasoning, ca-
joling, bribing, or arguing has any effect. Week after week, the conditions in these people's homes stay the same or get worse. If the
situation becomes bad enough and there is little hope of improvement, officials are forced to seek a court order to clean out the
home.

Edith and Daniel

In New York City, when a hoarding case has worked its way through
the legal system, the judge can order what is called a "heavy-duty
cleaning," in which a social worker or health department official
arranges for a cleaning crew to come in and clear out what they
deem to be garbage, trash, or other unacceptable items.

The case of Edith and Daniel was a complicated affair involving
medical and psychiatric illnesses, housing and health code violations, and dysfunctional family dynamics. The client that the city's
social services commission was trying to protect was Edith, a fifty-
two-year-old woman who owned and lived in a two-bedroom condo
in a fashionable area of Manhattan with her sister, her son, and her
brother. She had lived there for more than thirty years. Though
plagued with depression for most of her life, she had managed adequately with the help of her husband until his death five years earlier. At that time, her sister had moved in with her and Tim after
becoming too sick with diabetes to live alone. Shortly thereafter,
Daniel had moved in. Edith's meager disability payments barely allowed her to keep up with the condo fees. Although her brother
and sister both received disability payments as well, they did not
contribute to the household. Her son worked part-time, but he
also did not contribute financially. The condo association filed papers to have her evicted for nonpayment of condo fees.

In addition to depression, Edith suffered from diabetes, which left her with limited eyesight and a nearly useless left leg. She relied on a cane to get around the cluttered apartment. Because of her medical problems, she received home health care services to help with basic daily functions, such as getting dressed, washing herself, and preparing food. However, when the conditions inside the condo deteriorated to a certain point, the home health care workers terminated their services. They believed that the condo was unsanitary and unsafe, and things were getting worse.

Their action resulted in a petition by the social services commission to the New York Supreme Court to have Edith declared an incapacitated person, a declaration that would result in the appointment of a guardian. Judges appoint guardians reluctantly, because doing so strips people of their rights to make all decisions about health care, finances, and possessions. Neither depression nor diabetes would normally trigger guardianship, but when the court evaluator visited Edith's condo, he was so shocked by what he saw that he told the court that all of the people living there were in danger. He felt that Edith was being forced to live in these conditions by a manipulative brother and sister and an abusive son. As a result of his report, Edith was declared incapacitated, and a guardian was appointed.

Guardians in New York City walk a thin line, trying to protect people without taking over more of their lives than is absolutely necessary. Hoarding cases make that line even thinner and more precarious. Edith's guardian, Susan, was now responsible for her well-being: if something happened to her because of the clutter, such as a serious fall or a fire, Susan would be legally responsible. But neither Edith nor her family members were willing to acknowledge the danger, and they fought any intrusion tooth and nail. Susan was an experienced social worker, however, and she knew that Edith's life was in danger. She immediately went back to court to get an order to clear out Edith's condo.

Most of the stuff that filled the condo belonged to Daniel. He'd moved in with her two years before because he'd filled his own apartment with things scavenged from the streets, and it was no longer habitable. Although Edith's condo was now full as well, he collected new items daily. Everyone outside the family—nurses, social workers, and lawyers—begged Edith to kick Daniel out, but she refused. She claimed that she depended on him to pay her bills, and furthermore, as she told me, "he's family, and you can't abandon family." Edith's sister felt differently. She hated Daniel but felt powerless to kick him out.

Social workers responsible for cases such as Edith's are usually very reluctant to go into their clients' homes and throw away the things they have collected. A forced cleaning temporarily improves the condition of the home but seldom changes the behavior that created those conditions. In short order, the home fills up again. Furthermore, such cleanings are traumatic events that leave the inhabitants grief stricken, frustrated, and fearful of authority figures. For social workers, who usually choose their profession to ease people's suffering, being responsible for this trauma is painful.

Heavy-duty cleaning is a big business in New York, and private companies offering these services can make a lot of money. Cleaning out a big house can run upwards of $50,000. The crew handling Daniel's case averaged four such cases every day. Even so, their first attempt at a heavy-duty cleaning of the condo failed. Susan sent a less experienced social worker to supervise, and when the cleaning crew arrived, Daniel insisted on taking over. He allowed little to be thrown away, and the crew quit in frustration. The shell-shocked social worker could do little to prevent him from interfering.

A veteran of many such cases, Susan knew that she couldn't leave Edith's case in the hands of a novice again. She combined a tough-minded, no-nonsense approach with an ability to charm her mostly middle-aged and elderly clients. They liked her despite the fact that she took them to court kicking and screaming to arrange heavy-duty cleanings. They stopped by her office frequently to see her, mostly with minor excuses or complaints. She often took them to lunch and listened patiently to their problems.

But Susan was frustrated. She knew that the cleanout of Daniel's trash was not a solution but only a temporary fix. Unless something else happened, the home would fill up again. She desperately wanted a strategy that would work and avoid the trauma these cleanings normally produced. It was for this reason that she asked me along for the second attempt, despite my protest that I had no better solutions for someone who refused help.

Edith's relationship with Daniel was complicated. Daniel's collecting had created problems for the family before. When their father was alive, he protected Edith from Daniel, knowing that Daniel would take advantage of her. Edith's husband also refused to allow Daniel into their home. But now that her husband was gone, Edith passively accepted all of Daniel's eccentricities, never having developed the ability to stand up for herself.

Susan had visited Edith several weeks earlier, before the first attempted cleaning. Just getting into the apartment to see her was an ordeal. When no one answered her knock, she threatened to call the police. Edith's sister told her to come back later when they could contain the dog, a large and aggressive rottweiler owned by Tim. When Susan insisted, Edith's sister locked the dog in the bathroom and opened the door. Susan couldn't see much of the room because of the wall of cardboard, clothes, papers, and junk. Edith was nowhere to be seen. When Susan called out to her, she answered from behind the wall. Susan learned that just before one of Daniel's more successful forays, Edith had lain down on a couch in the living room for a rest. By the time she awoke, the wall had been erected. Edith carried on a conversation with Susan from behind the wall. She insisted that she was okay and would not allow Susan to clear a path through the debris.

The instructions Susan gave to Edith and her family for the cleaning were straightforward. Anything they absolutely wanted to keep should be removed from the apartment before the cleaning. Anything left in the apartment would be kept or thrown away at the discretion of the cleaning crew.

We set out early on a warm summer morning, heading to Edith's midtown Manhattan high-rise. Susan was determined that this cleaning would take place. She worried, and rightly so, that if the conditions inside the condo did not improve immediately, the effect on Edith's already poor health might be devastating. Susan carried with her all of the court orders and paperwork. She knew it was likely the police would be involved, and she wanted everything well documented. If Daniel attempted to interfere, she would have him arrested. Outside the building, we met the four-man cleaning crew and headed up the five flights to Edith's condo.

Syllogomania

Gerontology is the study of aging and its associated problems. In the gerontology research literature, the hoarding of rubbish is referred to as "syllogomania." (*Sylloge* is Greek for "collection.") Syllogomania is widely regarded as one marker of self-neglect among the elderly, along with poor personal hygiene and squalid living conditions. In the early 1960s, two British gerontologists described seventy-two cases of what they called "senile breakdown syndrome." The cardinal features of this syndrome, which they believed to afflict only the elderly, included severe deterioration in both personal hygiene and living conditions, often accompanied by hostility, isolation, and rejection of the outside world. A common feature of these cases was syllogomania.

Somewhat later, another British gerontologist coined the term "Diogenes syndrome," after the ancient Greek philosopher Diogenes of Sinope (fourth century B.C.E.), who was reputed to have traversed Athens looking for "an honest man." Diogenes rejected most social conventions, preferring a hermetic existence and eschewing any form of luxury. For a time, he supposedly lived in an olive oil barrel rather than a house. His indifference to his living conditions probably led to his name becoming synonymous with domestic squalor. However, Diogenes showed no inclination toward syllogomania. In fact, the Cynics, the school of philosophy typified by Diogenes, believed that happiness could best be achieved by living without possessions.

The Diogenes syndrome includes poor personal hygiene, domestic squalor, and syllogomania. (Other names for this syndrome include "senile recluse syndrome," "extreme self-neglect syndrome," and "social breakdown syndrome," although all of these names portray the condition inaccurately, as the syndrome is not restricted to the elderly and involves more than self-neglect or social inadequacies.) More recently, gerontologists have begun to refer to these symptoms separately rather than as a syndrome. The term "severe domestic squalor" has been suggested to distinguish it from neglect of personal hygiene and hoarding, both of which can occur without squalor. In fact, Daniel displayed two of the three Diogenes syndrome features—domestic squalor and syllogomania.

For many years, gerontologists believed that the Diogenes syndrome resulted from other problems, such as schizophrenia, dementia, or frontal lobe damage, and in fact nearly half of the cases do. But more than half occur in the absence of these disorders.

The Diogenes syndrome is not related to income or intelligence. It may be precipitated by life events, such as the death of a caregiver or a serious illness, but these events don't cause it. One theory holds that certain personality characteristics, such as suspiciousness and obstinacy, may be the bedrock of the syndrome. Daniel had both of these characteristics, but most striking was his lack of awareness of any problem associated with his behavior.

The Cleaning

The crew had an efficient system for cleaning such homes. They commandeered one of the building's elevators and lined it with heavy blankets to keep it clean. They brought hundreds of large, sturdy trash bags and set about stuffing everything in sight into them. Once full, the bags were tied off and put in the hallway. When enough bags collected there to fill the elevator, they took them down to the street. There they piled the bags beside a truck. (In the center of the city, trucks are more efficient than dumpsters.) The workers seldom spoke and clearly did not want to be spoken to. Benjamin, their supervisor, showed up midway through the process. He told me that his company had a contract with the city to do cleanings like this, and it kept them very busy. This apartment was worse than some but not as bad as others he had seen. "We did another one in this building just last week," he told me. "It was worse than this."

Daniel arrived about thirty minutes after the cleaning crew started working. He was fifty, with a medium build and lots of energy. He complained about the crew starting without him and insisted that it was his job to direct the cleaning. Susan intervened. She told Daniel that the place was unlivable and asked how it had gotten that way. Daniel appeared offended, but he also seemed to enjoy the prospect of an argument. He objected to her depiction of the apartment as unlivable and suggested that she didn't understand the riches he had acquired. He did concede that the condo had gotten a bit messy, but only because he hadn't had time to straighten it up. He addressed her in a monologue that lasted nearly ten minutes and ended by saying that he appreciated the help she had sent and had enjoyed the conversation with her, but now he needed to get back to supervising the cleaning crew.

Susan asked him another question. He launched into another long answer, telling a story about his life. At the end of the story, he became annoyed and again insisted that he had to supervise the cleaning. Another question by Susan was followed by another story. It seemed that no matter how much he wanted to supervise the crew, he could not stop talking. At the end of one of the stories, he told Susan that he understood that she was trying to distract him from the cleaning, but even then he couldn't keep himself from talking. He seemed to relish the attention. He clearly enjoyed creating intricate stories and making them into formal arguments, as though he were involved in an elaborate debate. He punctuated his arguments with an impish grin, challenging us to find the flaw in his logic.

Finally, he darted into the apartment, jumped onto a cleared coffee table, and started yelling at one of the cleaning crew to put down a broken lamp. The crew member stared at him blankly, leading me to believe that he did not understand English. Later, though, I heard all the cleaners speaking to each other in English and realized that perhaps it was easier to deal with difficult characters such as Daniel by pretending not to understand. Susan asked him to come back out into the hallway and tell her how he thought the cleaning should be done. The question started a spirited description of the ineptitude of social workers and the courts and ended with his interpretation of the judge's ruling. In his view, the judge was giving general guidelines and would never condone what was being done to them.

This pattern repeated itself throughout the day. A simple question produced a long story that sometimes wandered far afield. Daniel's was a world of stories, and during our time there, he communicated almost nothing without one. The question was always answered, after a fashion, but the core of the answer was usually buried in the story. "Novels, no serials" was how his sister described his manner of storytelling. Interrupting the story was nearly impossible. When I tried, he either ignored me or started a new story. On some level, he seemed to understand this problem. When we took him out to lunch, he pleaded, "Please ask me only yes or no questions so I will have time to eat."

Shortly before lunch, we met Tim, Edith's son. Tall and muscular, Tim was in his mid-twenties. He worked at odd jobs but had no steady income. He slept on a single bed on one side of the living room in a niche carved out of the debris. Edith had told Susan that Tim had an anger management problem. One of the social workers had once seen Tim red-faced and angry with his mouth just inches away from his mother's ear, yelling at her for something she had done or failed to do. As he approached us, he looked angry. Susan was afraid of what Tim would do.

"Where are my clothes?" he said, speaking with urgency and anger. "My leather jacket, where is it?"

No one answered. Tim turned to Daniel and asked him to step into the hallway. In the next moment, Tim, who weighed close to two hundred pounds, slammed Daniel in the chest with both hands, sending him flying through the air and into the far wall of the hallway. Daniel slumped to the floor as Tim stood over him shouting, "This is your fault! You were supposed to stop them from taking my stuff!" Daniel tried to placate him, but Tim would have none of it. He continued yelling and threatening: "You haven't got a fucking clue. I should beat the shit out of you."

Susan was already on the phone with the police, and three officers arrived within a few minutes. At Susan's instruction, they pulled Tim aside and began questioning him. They were courteous and respectful to everyone but made it clear they were in control. Once they determined that the papers for the court-ordered cleanout were in order, they focused on Tim. He was still yelling and pacing, threatening Daniel and everyone involved in the operation. The officers surrounded him closely, one of them doing most of the talking. They let him know that he would have to stop pacing and yelling, or they would arrest him. He tried to explain to them what had happened, but they focused not on the cause of his distress, but on controlling his aggressive behavior. I was amazed at how well they gained control of the situation, and through it all, they treated him with respect and courtesy. Tim's anger quickly dissolved into self-pity. He complained to them about his misfortune in having Daniel as an uncle.

By this time, Susan had let her office know of the difficulties we were having. Two more social workers showed up, both of whom had worked with Daniel before. Now standing in the hallway were three social workers, three police officers, myself, and Tim. Inside the apartment were four members of the cleaning crew, Edith, and her sister. Two more police officers arrived. The commotion and the crowd added to Tim's misery. In all the confusion, no one noticed that Daniel had disappeared. One of the social workers set off to look for him. She came back to report that he was out on the sidewalk tearing open the bags the cleaning crew had left by the truck. Now the whole crowd—policemen, social workers, Tim, and I—rushed out to see for ourselves what was happening.

As we got to the street, we could see Daniel tearing madly

through bag after bag. He had a pile of clothing and other things he had rescued sitting beside the bags. The neighborhood was a fashionable one in midtown Manhattan, with lots of well-dressed people walking along the street heading to work. Many stopped to stare.

The policeman in charge asked Daniel to stop and come over to talk with him. Daniel said, "Sure, I just need to find the rest of Tim's clothes," and he continued to open bags. More people stopped to watch.

"No, I mean now. You need to stop that and come over here right now." The policeman was firm.

"Yes, but I have to find these clothes. You can see how upset he is." Daniel didn't even look up as he responded.

The policeman raised his voice above the volume of a simple request. "You need to come over here right now, or we are taking you to Bellevue," he said, referring to the famous psychiatric facility in Manhattan.

At this, Daniel stopped and came right over.

"You know about Bellevue, I guess," the officer said. Daniel didn't respond. Although the threat of Bellevue stopped Daniel's foray, it was a hollow threat. Involuntary commitment to a psychiatric facility requires imminent threat to cause harm to oneself or others. Digging through trash bags would not qualify.

In the meantime, Tim had located the pile of clothes Daniel had rescued. Just as a very nicely dressed woman walked by with her dog, he picked up his leather jacket and shook it. Cockroaches flew in every direction, spraying the woman. She screamed and then froze, looking at once confused and disgusted. The officer who was talking to Daniel saw it happen and turned to Tim just as he shook the jacket again. This time the cockroaches peppered the police officer. He wheeled around with a look of horror in his eyes. "Get them off of me," he shouted at me as he tore at his shirt. I tried to brush them away, but they had gotten inside. He stripped down to his T-shirt, squirming. When he got his shirt back on, he was mad. He rushed at Tim, pulling out his handcuffs. Tim spun around and fell to the sidewalk, breaking down in tears. He pleaded, not with anyone in particular, "Why is this happening to me? What have I done? It's not my fault."

The policeman took pity and put his handcuffs away. "Look," he said, "you're coming with us. We're not going to arrest you. We're just going to escort you away from here. If you don't come back until this cleaning is done, we won't arrest you. If you do come back, the social worker will call us, and we'll take you to jail."

Daniel was again tearing at the bags in the street, and again the officer stopped him. He sent Daniel back upstairs to the apartment, where he set about giving instructions to the cleaning crew, who did their best to ignore him.

At one point, a nicely dressed woman emerged from the condo next door. I wondered what it was like living next door to such a mess. Surely, the cockroaches had migrated into her apartment, and the smell couldn't have escaped her notice.

All morning, the other elevator stopped on the fifth floor, and other residents peeked out until the doors closed. They were curious about the commotion and all the trash bags. Midway through the morning, I went outside for some fresh air. On my way back, I waited by the elevator with several other tenants in the building. They were talking about Daniel.

"They're clearing out Daniel's apartment. He's a collector, you know. He collects junk. You can see him going out and coming back every day with stuff off the streets. He's crazy."

"I knew his father. He had diabetes, like my father, so we had a connection. The collecting, it's an illness, like diabetes."

"That's just like Mrs. Palmer in 63A. Her apartment was packed full. They cleaned her out last week."

In the time we spent with Daniel, he was lucid and could not be considered out of touch with reality. Yet he seemed unable to tell us why he had collected all this stuff. When I asked where it came from, he insisted that his sisters had pressured him into collecting cans and bottles for the refunds and old packs of cigarettes for the coupons they contained. He argued that it was really their problem and not his. But very few bottles, cans, or cigarette packs were visible among the tidal wave of trash in the apartment.

Daniel spent most of the day insisting that there was nothing wrong with him, but for one short period he admitted that his collecting had become a problem. The interval occurred late in the day, after I had listened to a story about his father and asked a question about their relationship. He talked about how he had tried to stop collecting, and how his family had tried to help him stop by telling him what he could bring home and in what quantity. Then, as quickly as his insight came, it was gone, and he was back to arguing with us about the unfairness of it all and about the incompetence of social workers.

We left at the end of the afternoon with the cleaning crew. They had cleaned about two-thirds of the apartment and were scheduled to return the next week. Edith allowed Daniel to stay in the condo, which disappointed Susan.

"He will fill it again," she predicted.

I called Susan a week later to check on how the rest of the cleaning had gone.

"Well, they finished it, but when I went for a visit the next day, the security guard told me he had seen Daniel wheeling in shopping carts full of things all night after the cleanout."

Within a month, the apartment was full again. At that point, Susan, in her role as Edith's guardian, had Daniel evicted and placed a restraining order against him to prevent him from visiting. Then she had the apartment cleaned again, this time without much fanfare. For several months, things went well, and then Daniel sued for visitation rights. Much to Susan's dismay, the judge agreed. The apartment filled up for a third time, forcing yet another heavy-duty cleaning. In the five years after the first cleaning, Susan arranged for a total of eight heavy-duty cleanings, at a total cost of more than $20,000, a high price to pay for one man who could not control his urge to collect junk.

Just how many people have as little insight as Daniel is unclear. In a recent study, we asked family members of people who hoard about this issue. More than half of them described the hoarder as either having poor insight or being delusional with regard to the hoarding. Whether this is accurate and representative of all those who hoard is questionable. Frustration from years of trying to get a loved one to change can make family members believe that the hoarder is delusional. Perhaps people with more severe clutter are especially non-insightful. They have lost the battle of mind over matter, and declaring their innocence may seem easier to them than admitting loss of control over their lives.

In our experience, most hoarders have some degree of awareness of the problem. Even people who insist that they have no problem will go to great lengths to hide the stuff packing their homes. They seem to know, and feel ashamed of, what other people will think of their homes. Some, like Nell (see chapter 8), see their clutter only when others are present. Most people who hoard also experience shame at the prospect of someone discovering their secret. This requires at least the understanding that one's behavior is different. Most of the hoarders we have seen know that they have a problem when they think about it in the abstract. But when a hoarder is holding a ten-year-old magazine and thinking about what valuable information it might contain, that insight evaporates. After all, keeping only one magazine will not matter in the grand scheme of things.

Despite the multiple heavy-duty cleanings and Susan's feedback, Daniel's behavior did not change. He insisted that others misunderstood him and were misguided in their concerns. Daniel was not someone who would volunteer for therapy. Even if he were forced into treatment, it would be unlikely to have much effect. Ultimately, I was unable to provide Susan with the key she'd sought to unlock the problem of obstinate hoarders, for the same reason that no one can help a non-insightful drug addict or anorexic: the patient has to want to change.

For those lacking insight into their hoarding, heavy-duty cleanings are seldom more than a short-term fix. The condition of the home may change temporarily, but the collecting behavior does not. Perhaps it would be impossible to get Daniel to stop collecting, but getting him to organize or store his hoard in a different manner might reduce the risk to Edith and the rest of his family. In such cases, we encourage agencies to take a different approach. Instead of clearing out the home, we recommend working with the hoarder to determine what needs to be done to meet and sustain basic standards of safety. The effort requires the development of a personal and trusting relationship with ongoing contact. Though potentially costly, it may in the long run result in public savings by reducing the number of heavy-duty cleanings. Such an approach requires at least a minimum of cooperation and effort, however, of which Daniel seemed incapable.

10

A TREE WITH TOO MANY BRANCHES
Genetics and the Brain

I see too many options [for things]. I can't control it. My brain needs to be rewired!

—Irene

From observing hoarding in squirrels, some scientists have suggested that the sight of a nut triggers a genetically programmed set of behaviors that is otherwise locked away in the brain. The nut puts the squirrel "in touch with" the feeling of being hungry. Consequently, the squirrel gathers the nut and "squirrels" it away for later. This instinct may have evolved into a similar experience in humans who hoard. The sight of a possession puts the hoarder in touch with the feeling of being without the possession when it is needed. This feeling dominates his or her consideration of whether to save or discard the item.

The possibility that hoarding is genetic has been the subject of considerable speculation. Are these behaviors like the innately driven nest building in birds or nut gathering in squirrels? Ethologists, scientists who study animal behavior, believe that such behaviors are instinctual and not learned. Konrad Lorenz, perhaps the most well-known ethologist, called such instincts "fixed action patterns," or FAPs. He thought that FAPs were inherited programs that, when engaged, follow a distinct and rigid sequence of behavior—like nut gathering in squirrels. They may be passed up the evolutionary chain and stored somewhere in the distant recesses of the human brain. Some ethologists have speculated that brain circuit malfunctions might set off long-dormant FAPs by mistake. The result could be a chain of behaviors that make no sense in one's current environment—such as foraging for and saving useless objects.

Animal models of hoarding have several drawbacks as explanations for human hoarding, however. For most animals that hoard, the behavior is adaptive and part of normal species-specific behavior. This is less clearly the case for humans. Also, most hoarding in animals involves food, while most human hoarding does not. If human hoarding is an evolutionary expression of the hoarding that animals do, we might expect more hoarding of food. It is possible, however, that humans, who are higher on the evolutionary chain, have expanded the category of "needed items" to include nonfood, personal use, or comfort items. This might explain why they hoard clothing, decorative items, and maybe even information. Perhaps human hoarding is closer to nesting behavior in birds and other animals that forage to feather their nests.

The role of the family in hoarding is just now coming into focus, especially the role of family lineage and biology. Since the beginning of our work on hoarding, we've been struck by how often people describe parents or other relatives who hoarded or were "pack rats." In one of our earliest studies, more than 80 percent of our subjects reported a first-degree relative with similar problems. Recent studies have borne out the familial nature of hoarding. The OCD Collaborative Genetics Study (OCGS), a consortium of six sites funded by the National Institute of Mental Health to study genetic linkage in obsessive-compulsive disorder, recently published the results of a study of siblings of people with OCD.

Among the large number of people in the study, those who hoarded were most likely to have siblings who also hoarded.

As a follow-up, the consortium conducted a genome-wide scan for chromosomes and regions on those chromosomes that were linked to hoarding. For families with two or more hoarding members, the scan found patterns of genes in a region on chromosome 14 that were different from those found in families without hoarding members. Why this chromosome would be related to hoarding is unclear. Genes on chromosome 14 are important for establishing immune system responses and have been implicated in the development of early-onset Alzheimer's disease. These problems have no apparent relationship to hoarding, however. A study of Tourette's syndrome found a familial linkage pattern for hoarding on a different set of chromosomes. Perhaps different types of hoarding are associated with different genetic disorders.

The results of the OCGS are still tentative and will need replication with a larger sample of people who hoard and a comparison sample of people who do not have these or other OCD symptoms. Nevertheless, these findings are intriguing and suggest that nature, as much as nurture, may play a role in hoarding. Nowhere is the genetic component of hoarding more noticeable than in identical twins.

The Twins

When I picked up the phone, the caller announced, "Dr. Frost, Brother and I are modern-day Collyer brothers. What can you tell me about hoarding?" Alvin's speech was abrupt, and his words were clipped. I agreed to send him some material on hoarding and described our book project. He hung up without saying goodbye. I didn't expect to hear from him again. A few weeks later, however, he called to say that he could see himself in our writings and was amazed at how close our descriptions were to his world. He wanted to know more. Initially, he expressed an interest in finding treatment, but he was sure "Brother" would not, as "he likes his things too much." Although neither of the brothers pursued treatment in the end, they agreed to be interviewed, and I have since spent many hours with them.

Alvin and his twin brother, Jerry, did resemble the famous Collyers in some ways. Both sets of brothers came from very wealthy families with a father who was a well-known physician. Both were intelligent, highly cultured, and interested in the arts. Beyond that, however, the similarities faded. Alvin and Jerry had a wide circle of friends and acquaintants, nothing like the "hermits of Harlem." And whereas Langley Collyer was the hoarder and Homer simply went along, both Alvin and Jerry hoarded. Bigtime.

Alvin didn't say much about what they hoarded as we chatted in the sitting room of the hotel where he lived. Tall and slender, around fifty years old, dressed in a slightly rumpled suit and bow tie, Alvin quickly took control of the conversation. He spoke at the same rapid pace as in his phone call. He asked a number of questions about our research and about hoarding in general, but he avoided the topic of his own hoarding. He was not yet certain he wanted to speak to me about such a personal subject. After thirty minutes, Jerry—dressed identically in a rumpled suit and bow tie—arrived and reminded Alvin that he had an appointment. He spoke in the same rapid pace and tone, but with a hint of hostility and without the apparent curiosity of his brother. I got the impression that the interruption was staged to give Alvin a way out if he wanted to take it. Luckily for me, he didn't. From my initial encounter over the phone, I expected an angry and unpleasant man. Nothing could have been further from the truth. Alvin was engaging and inquisitive and cared deeply about the people in his life.

His descriptions of his and "Brother's" lives were vivid, literary, and nuanced.

Their family wealth left them without the need for an income. However, Alvin worked as an event organizer and was very good at his job. Most of his events were dinners and fundraisers celebrating the accomplishments of others, including authors, artists, musicians, politicians, and athletes. I attended several and watched as he worked the room. He knew everyone there—not just their names and what they did, but the details of their personal histories. It was clear that he liked all kinds of people and used his charm and grace to "collect" them. His collections of people formed his community, and I had become a part of it. Both brothers were always eager to meet with me and talk about their attachments to possessions, as well as other aspects of their lives. Although I suggested that they call me by my first name, they always addressed me as "Dr. Frost," a designation Alvin said was more comfortable and consistent with the way they were raised. He spoke excitedly about his work and his friends and disparagingly about his hoarding.

Although Jerry's rapid speech and intonation matched that of his brother, his affect was different. Whereas Alvin was exuberant and outgoing, Jerry was apprehensive and reserved. He, too, cared deeply about those around him, but his caring came out as worry. He worried about anything that could go wrong. He worried that he might run out of gas when he drove his car, so he was forever stopping to fill his tank. On his most recent trip to their boyhood home, a nineteen-room mansion several hours away, he kept a close eye on his gas gauge. When it moved off the full mark, he felt compelled to stop for gas, even if he could only add a few gallons to the tank. The trip took an extra hour.

Mostly, Jerry worried about Alvin. He worried that Alvin did not know how to take care of himself and that he was too trusting of other people. Jerry took care of many of Alvin's day-to-day responsibilities: paying his bills, sorting his mail, arranging his doctor's appointments, and doing his taxes. The details of life never troubled Alvin, perhaps because Jerry took care of those things for him. Alvin was absent-minded about money, seldom keeping track of or even carrying cash. On several occasions while complaining to me that Alvin was naive about others and easily taken advantage of, Jerry mentioned the sad case of Jonathan Levin, the son of former Time Warner CEO Gerald Levin. Jonathan eschewed the life of luxury and instead became an English teacher at a Bronx high school. One of his former students learned of his identity and, convinced that he was hiding great wealth in his apartment, attempted to rob him. When he found little money, he tortured Levin for his ATM pin number and then killed him. The story captured Jerry's imagination in a profound and ugly way. He repeated it to me more than a dozen times, always in the context of worries about Alvin: "Dr. Frost, I think about this every day. Alvin doesn't have the common sense to stay away from these people." Jerry worried that Alvin would likewise be murdered by one of the many people he befriended.

Jerry's worries about Alvin consumed him. Whenever Alvin was within earshot, Jerry complained to him about his carelessness, the people he associated with, and the activities he pursued. At times the relationship between the brothers was so tense they could not be in the same room. Even in the presence of friends and business associates, they bickered. The topic was always the same—Alvin's risk-taking behavior. In private, Jerry insisted to me that Alvin could never survive without him and that it was his job to protect his twin. He seemed to have no clue that his worry was over-the-top. "He treats me like I'm ten years old," Alvin complained. "Jerry is just like my mother. He will invade my life in every way, and he can be nasty." When Jerry felt Alvin wasn't paying attention to his concerns, he became increasingly angry and upset. Although Jerry felt that Alvin discounted him, it was clear that Jerry's distress registered with Alvin. After one of their episodes, Alvin said to me, "When he gets upset, it's like wind chimes inside me." Alvin had access to a number of other rooms in the hotel, and he admitted using them sometimes to hide from Jerry.

Jerry took me on a tour of his and Alvin's separate apartments. Each had an identical penthouse apartment in the hotel with a huge "great room" of approximately eight hundred square feet and a two-story-high ceiling. Adjoining the great room in each apartment were a dining room, bedroom, bathroom, and galley kitchen; there were two upstairs bedrooms and an upstairs bathroom. We went into Alvin's apartment first. Every square foot of the great room and dining room was packed with works of art and period furniture: eighteenth- and nineteenth-century paintings, sculptures, busts, antiques, lamps, jewelry, and more. Most of the works were extremely valuable. He pointed out several large seventeenth-century vases that he estimated would each sell for more than $10,000. It is hard to imagine how much the art in this room was worth, but it had to be at least hundreds of thousands of dollars.

In contrast to many homes of hoarders, the great room had no pathways. Crossing the room meant stepping over or on things. In some places, the objects were piled up to six feet high. No floor was visible. Although Jerry's apartment was in just as much disarray, he was more concerned about the safety of the things in Alvin's apartment. He complained that Alvin was not careful about keeping the great room locked, so he took it upon himself to put some of the heavier urns (ones no one could easily walk away with) in the hallway blocking the door. The room reminded me of the Ming Tombs in China, where the emperors had stuffed their burial chambers with all the treasures of their reigns. The layers of dust indicated how long these objects had lain dormant. Jerry found this comforting since it meant no one had touched any of these things.

Both twins had a form of photographic memory. For each of his rooms, Jerry carried a mental image of exactly how it looked. When he entered the room, he knew immediately if anything had been touched or moved. Given the chaotic appearance of the rooms, this was a remarkable achievement. If something had been moved, Jerry's image of it was no long "placid." This was more a sensation of disruption than anything else, a not-just-right experience, or NJRE (see chapter 5). He had to study the room to decide what had been moved and then "recalibrate" his image. It usually took him about thirty minutes to do so.

In addition to the works of art, there were clothes strewn about and hanging from every conceivable hook. They covered most of the kitchen, making it unusable. There were few papers but thousands of business cards, each with notes written on the back. Jerry complained bitterly about Alvin's penchant for collecting cards and never looking at them or being able to find them when needed. Jerry confessed that he had taken to throwing away some of them for his brother. The stairway was covered with things as well, and although he never showed me the upstairs rooms, he assured me that they were at least as cluttered as the downstairs.

After seeing Alvin's apartment, we visited Jerry's. We had to move a large and very heavy pot away from the door to get inside. The apartment was nearly identical to Alvin's place, except for the absence of business cards. It contained large eighteenth- and nineteenth-century paintings, Italian busts, tapestries, furniture, and jewelry—at least as many objects as in Alvin's apartment. As in Alvin's space, there were few unobstructed paths. Most of the great room was inaccessible, blocked by vases, antique lamps, and grandfather clocks. Clothes lay everywhere. Unlike Alvin, Jerry apparently never hung his clothes up. All these things, Jerry explained, came from their parents' home or from buying sprees. Jerry knew a lot about each piece in the room. "Everything here has a story, and I remember them all. If I get rid of any of it, the story would be lost."

Jerry spoke with dismay about the state of the apartment. He recognized that the works of art were in danger of being damaged by the clutter, but he was at a loss about what to do. "Our parents would be horrified if they saw our apartments," he said. We spoke briefly about strategies for organizing Jerry's great room. He said that at one time, early in their stay here, the room was beautiful, and they had used it to entertain dignitaries, politicians, and royalty.

The next day when I returned to meet Alvin, I waited in the lobby of the hotel. Jerry came in, obviously upset with Alvin. He said that Alvin had blown off the appointment. I asked Jerry if he would like to talk without his brother. He thought for a moment and with a wave of his hand and a pained expression said, "No, it's just hopeless." At that he walked off, and I wondered whether either of the twins wanted anything more to do with me. Jerry explained later that shortly after I had left the day before, he had returned to his apartment and tried to do some of the sorting we had talked about. He got confused and frustrated trying to make decisions about what to move and ended up breaking a wooden sculpture. At that moment, he gave up all hope of changing. Apparently, Alvin felt similarly. He called me a few days later to apologize. He said, "This is like a stool sample, and Doctor, there's blood in this stool. I don't like to think about it." The odd analogy was apt.

The Parents

Over the next several years, I learned a great deal about the twins and their history. Their father had been distant and strict, clearly not one to communicate warmth. Alvin described him as "verbally rough." Jerry recalled that his maternal grandmother intervened on several occasions when she felt her son-in-law's strictness had crossed the line with the boys and his wife. Both of the twins were afraid of him and his temper, and their relationship with him grew worse as they got older. Our recent research indicates that an absence of warmth, acceptance, and support characterizes the early family life of many hoarders, perhaps leading them to form strong emotional attachments to possessions.

Their father collected books, magazines, and travel information, but he always kept his things well organized. "Everything in its place" was his motto. His mother, the twins' grandmother, also collected. She was a schoolteacher who had acquired and inherited a great deal of things and had kept all of them. When she died, the moving company that cleaned out her house wrote to the twins' parents to say that they had never seen a Victorian house so full.

The twins' mother saved things as well—vases, china dolls, and teddy bears—and she was a world-class shopper. Both brothers reported never having seen her throw anything away. Only the intervention of the twins' maternal grandmother kept the house uncluttered. By the time their parents reached their sixties, however, the home had begun to fill up. When their mother became ill near the end of her life, Jerry estimated that there were five thousand paper bags scattered about the house. Although the twins kept their parents' house, they spent little time there. The basement was still filled with Kleenex boxes, paper towels, and more than one hundred dried-out deodorant tubes from the 1960s. Most of the other rooms were too crowded to use. Jerry said that when he visited the house, he slept on the floor in the living room because none of the beds were accessible.

Jerry had a special relationship with his mother. He spent hours with her watching soap operas and shopping. During the twins' early twenties, their relationship with their father soured. According to Alvin, "Father used to say we had minds like snapping turtles. We just bit the wrong things." He became more and more critical of them. Their mother tried to make up for it by taking them shopping. They shopped for everything from bric-a-brac to fine art. When Jerry spoke of his mother and her death, his eyes filled with tears. "I think about her every day, Dr. Frost. Do you think I'll ever see her again? I keep the house just the way it is thinking she might return. If I get rid of anything, it's like giving up on her." He admitted that this was an irrational thought, but not one he could easily ignore. Before she died, she asked him to do two things for her: not to let any of her things be sold to relatives and to look after Alvin. Jerry had fulfilled both of these promises, but at quite a price.

The twins' mother was overprotective and did not allow them to have much contact with other kids in the neighborhood. She preferred to keep them at home, studying. She never permitted other kids to come over and play, fearing they would mess up the house. According to Alvin, "Too much change upset Mother." He remarked that most of the time his mother stayed home, where she felt safe and protected. "She treated our home like a cocoon," he said. Few of the mansion's nineteen rooms were accessible to the twins. Once their mother arranged the rooms the way she wanted them, she allowed no one to use them.

She even refused to let the twins organize their shared room or their dressers. She insisted on doing it for them. She laid out their clothes each day, choosing what they would wear without consulting them. They could keep only a very few clothes in their room. Their closets full of newly purchased clothes were off-limits. Many of these clothes were never worn and still hung in the mansion with the sales tags attached. The house remained much the way it was when their parents died nearly a decade earlier. Jerry visited sometimes, but Alvin did not.

Although the twins occasionally played at other kids' homes and they had friends at school, both felt that many of their peers resented their wealth and their intelligence. Both boys qualified as geniuses and found it difficult to relate to their classmates. Alvin said that the first time their parents noticed their penchant for collecting was when they were three years old. On a walk with their nurse, they filled their "perambulator" with a collection of sticks and leaves. They wouldn't allow the nurse to get rid of any of them. When the boys discovered a particular branch missing on reaching home, they put up such a fuss that the nurse had to retrieve it. The boys also collected other things, such as shells, pinecones, and, later, porcelain figurines. Jerry recalled having great difficulty getting rid of school papers. He still had his first- and second-grade papers stashed away somewhere in his parents' house.

Living in Clutter

Neither Alvin nor Jerry actually lived in the apartments Jerry showed me. They had moved out because living there had become impossible. Instead of clearing some space to live, they simply left everything as it was and moved into other apartments in the hotel. Jerry lived in a small suite that was also filled to the point of being nearly uninhabitable. Mostly, the suite contained a random scattering of papers, clothes, and books, as well as a few pieces of art. As in their penthouse apartments, there were no pathways, and when we entered, we had to wade through a foot of stuff littering the floor. In the kitchen, the piles were not as high, but little of the floor showed. The kitchen sink was full of an assortment of junk and jewelry, with no place to make a meal.

Beyond the kitchen was the bathroom, the floor of which was covered with vitamin bottles. To use the sink, Jerry had to straddle the pile of pill bottles. The bathroom light fixture was broken, but Jerry would not allow anyone in to fix it because he was embarrassed by how the place looked and worried that someone might steal something. He relied on the light from the kitchen to see in the bathroom. He said, "I don't know what I'll do if the kitchen light breaks. I guess I'll have to move to yet another apartment." In fact, he confessed that he was considering doing just that because it had become difficult for him to live in this one. Occasionally, he slept in one of the other rooms in the hotel to which he had a key when he was too tired to navigate this apartment.

The bed was covered as well, and Jerry admitted that he often just slept on the floor, or on the papers and clothes piled on the floor. Sometimes he swept things off his bed onto the floor so that he could sleep in the bed. This left him feeling uncomfortable, though, because he lost the sense of where things were in the room.

Jerry had brought some of his artwork from his penthouse apartment to this one, mostly smaller pieces. One kitchen cupboard was filled with jewelry and a second with crystal vases and decorative glass. Jerry said that there were several larger paintings under the clothes on one side of the room. He explained that he liked to have these works nearby. "These things make me feel safe. This is like my cocoon." It was a refrain we had heard before. He said that when he had gone out of town recently, he had been afraid that someone might come into the apartment and steal his things, so he had piled clothes on top of them, and he just hadn't gotten around to removing them.

Unwittingly, both Jerry and Alvin had repeated their childhood experience of owning a large number of clothes but wearing very few of them. But instead of keeping them neatly packed away in their original wrappings, the twins strewed their clothes helter-skelter about their suites. The piles of clothes on the floor had been there for months and in some cases years. Jerry wore none of the clothes from the floor. The few clothes he did wear hung from the upper cabinet knobs in the kitchen. A small armoire built into the wall contained more unworn clothing.

Two years earlier, a heating pipe had burst, and water had leaked throughout the apartment, soaking all of Jerry's things. The paint had peeled and blistered from the water damage. He had let workmen in to remove the soaked papers, but he wouldn't allow anyone else in to fix the pipe or the walls. The apartment had been without heat since then. During the previous two winters, he had slept with a stocking cap and heavy blankets to ward off the cold. Jerry hated being in the apartment and seldom spent time there. He took all his meals at the restaurant downstairs and spent most of his days at his brother's workplace.

Complex Thinking

Though identified as geniuses early in life, neither of the brothers was able to finish college. Alvin complained that his mind was "too difficult to navigate." He went on, "It's like a tree with too many branches. Everything is connected. Every branch leads somewhere, and there are so many branches that I get lost. They are too thick to see through." He said his thoughts came so rapidly and spun from topic to topic so fast that he couldn't keep things straight. He likened it to an old episode of the TV comedy show *I Love Lucy* in which Lucy and her friend Ethel work in a chocolate factory picking chocolates from a conveyor belt and putting them into boxes. As the conveyor belt speeds up, Lucy and Ethel fall behind. As it continues to accelerate, chocolates collect everywhere, resulting in chaos. The mess resembled not only the twins' minds but each of their rooms as well.

Jerry echoed Alvin's description in a note he sent me.

> I think somehow this "paper" situation is like an embarrassing secret—normal people cannot fathom or understand this predicament or overwhelming situation. Also, keeping my important stuff (driver's license, credit card, garage key card etc.) together is a real daily feat! My head has so many spinning plots and my dreams at night are turbulent and unsettling—Every day I wonder if I will ever have freedom from chaos.

Alvin's experience of getting lost in the complexity of his thoughts is common among hoarders. At first we thought that people who hoard might be more intelligent than those who don't. Although that is probably not true, hoarders do appear to think in more complex ways. In particular, their minds seem flooded with details about possessions that the rest of us overlook. Irene frequently commented, "I'm a detail person, not a big-picture person, but I've been saving the details for so long, I need to put them together."

The complexity of thought extends beyond possessions. A curious commonality among people who hoard is how they talk on the telephone: they leave long, rambling, almost incoherent messages filled with irrelevant details. My voice mail records up to six two-minute messages. Often it is filled with messages from a single caller, such as one woman who contacted me recently. At the end of two minutes, when the machine cut her off the first time, the woman still had not gotten to the point of her call. She called back and repeated half of what was in the first message. She described her background and how she thought she might need help, then told a story about a comment her brother had made regarding her collecting. She argued with herself briefly about exactly when he had made the remark, concluding that it had been about Christmastime. That was the year her mother burned the turkey and it snowed on Christmas Day. The machine cut her off again. In her third message, she apologized for the first two and launched into yet more details about her life. She left her phone number just as her time ran out. She never asked a question or asked me to call her.

Dr. Sanjaya Saxena, a University of California, San Diego, psychiatrist who studies the neuroscience of hoarding, described this tendency as giving "a twenty-minute answer to a twenty-second question." People who hoard often speak in overly elaborate ways, including far too many details and losing the main themes, as with Daniel's tangential stories in chapter 9. It seems as though they are unable to filter out irrelevant details. Each detail seems as important as the next. People with hoarding problems can't sort them out or draw conclusions from them. Alvin tried to explain his predicament this way: "Everything is compelling, like it's attached to something else. I can't interrupt the stream of things without ruining it."

This might explain the problems with decision making that accompany hoarding. Even making simple decisions such as ordering from a menu can be excruciating. Alvin showed me a wad of twenty ties in his room. He said, "I have trouble deciding which of these ties to put on in the morning. I could spend all day just deciding that." Jerry reported similar problems: "If I'm going away for the day, I have to pack six or seven sets of clothes. I can't decide what is too much." Alvin recalled his mother having similar problems. When the boys were young, their parents booked a cruise but nearly missed it when their mother couldn't finish packing. Their grandmother came to the rescue once again and did the packing.

Even filling out questionnaires poses a problem for hoarders. More than once, we have waited for more than an hour for a research participant to complete a ten-minute questionnaire, only to throw out the data because the person wrote a paragraph about each question rather than circling one of the answers provided.

Our diagnostic interviews can take six to eight hours instead of the usual two or three, as hoarders provide endless details or sit silently, unable to make up their minds about how much a symptom bothers them. The process of sorting out important from unimportant details is clearly impaired in hoarders, who can't see the forest for the trees. Jerry described it as "like a kaleidoscope—broken pieces that don't fall just right."

Alvin first noticed his difficulty with organizing things when he was nine years old and away at camp. As the other children packed to go home, Alvin remembered sitting alone among his things, trying to figure out how to arrange them in his case and watching the other children leave one by one. Their efficiency startled him, and his own comparative inefficiency distressed him. Alvin's father prided himself on his ability to organize his collections of books, pictures, and magazines. His motto, "Everything in its place," rang in Alvin's head on the trip home from camp. Alvin resolved to do something about his organizing problem and asked his father if he could watch him sort and organize the mail. Perhaps not quite understanding his precocious son's odd request, he refused. The incident stands out in Alvin's mind as a lost opportunity.

Jerry thought little about organizing problems until taking a ten-day trip to visit friends in Vancouver. A week into his stay, his friends hosted a dinner party. Jerry remembered sitting in the kitchen as his friends gave the guests a tour of their home. When they got to Jerry's room, there were gales of laughter. When Jerry asked about the laughter, they told him that they were debating whether he would ever be able to organize the chaos and get all his stuff home. Their reactions to the mess in his room embarrassed and confused him. Alvin had a similar experience when he visited a friend in Chicago. After just four days, his host tried to get Alvin to allow him to hire someone to organize Alvin's room for him.

Other experiences of our clients have led us to suspect that deficits in attention and the ability to stay focused constitute a large part of hoarding. While Jerry and I were in his room once, he said he wanted to show me an article he had clipped out of the newspaper. He knew vaguely where to find it. Before he could find the article, though, he got distracted by a story about a picture of him and Alvin with a member of the British royal family. Next was a story about the jewelry in the sink, another about the inscription on a jewelry box, and another and another. Everything he spotted in his search had a tale he had to tell. In the end, he never found, or even remembered that he was looking for, the original article.

In one of our research projects, we compared people with hoarding problems to people with other mood or anxiety disorders and to people without any kind of emotional problem. We found that most of the hoarders reported frequent childhood experiences of distractibility, attention deficits, difficulty organizing tasks, failing to finish projects, losing things, being forgetful, and talking excessively. All of these are symptoms of attention deficit hyperactivity disorder (ADHD). As adults, the hoarders displayed even more pronounced symptoms. Also as adults, they described a tendency to avoid any work that required sustained mental effort. Jerry is a good example of someone with this problem. He spent almost no time trying to organize his things because the intense effort required and frustration from getting confused caused him to give up. "Everything I do is so hard. I have to think about it so much," he complained.

My Life in Shards

The brothers coped with their inability to keep things organized by turning their living space into storage and simply moving into new living areas. Luckily, they had the financial means to do so. Even so, their new homes filled up so quickly that they lived in perpetually dysfunctional spaces. A week before one of my visits, Jerry got up in the middle of the night to use the bathroom. He tripped over one of the many piles by his bed and knocked over an exquisite Venetian vase. It shattered when it hit a metal case sitting on a pile of clothes. As he tried to step over the pile, he stepped on a piece of glass that lodged in his foot. He could barely walk after digging it out. He admitted that it was buried so deep, he should have gone to the emergency room. Despite the pain and trouble caused by his accident, he had not yet cleaned up the glass. I asked him why.

"I don't know, it just feels so stupid," he replied.

"Have you tried to clean it?"

"Well, I went up there yesterday and looked at it. But I got depressed."

"Can you tell me exactly what you were thinking when you went up there?"

"I thought, *How terrible is this? What would my grandparents think? What's wrong with me? How stupid was this? I must be stupid to allow this.*"

Then Jerry told me about many of the other things that had been broken over the years, including an antique lamp of his mother's, an expensive chandelier, and the wooden sculpture that he broke after my first visit.

"Lots of things have been broken in the past and will get broken in the future," he said. "Then I also think of other things, equally precarious, in my rooms that I should clean up. At that point, I pretty much give up trying."

He concluded, "I have come to this. It's like my life—in shards!"

Cleaning up the glass would have taken less than an hour, but during that time he would have had to endure those depressing thoughts. By not cleaning it up, he could avoid the thoughts, at least as long as he wasn't in the room. Unfortunately, he had to endure them every night when he returned to the room and every morning when he awoke. With some effort, however, he could distract himself with other thoughts during these times.

I convinced Jerry to let me go with him while he tried to clean up the glass. He was reluctant to face such an unpleasant task but agreed for my sake. He spent about forty minutes on his hands and knees picking up glass shards and sweeping up the dust and other trash with his hands. "My father would pass out at my technique. He was big on systems. Maybe I should get a vacuum sweeper to do this." Yet he continued with his hands. Jerry seemed to experience very little distress during the cleaning, although he did say that if I wasn't there, he wouldn't be doing it. When we are doing therapy with people in these kinds of situations, we seldom do more than talk them through the task of cleaning and sorting. Much of what they need is someone simply to keep them focused. My presence seemed to distract Jerry a bit from the discomfort and kept him working.

Although Jerry threw away most of the broken glass, he set aside two large pieces. He said, "I just want to save these." When I asked why, he responded, "I'm remembering how it looked before it fell. If I throw them away, it's like I'm giving up on it, and I hate to do that. It's like I think maybe somehow it will get back together. I know that's crazy, 'cause it can't, but that's what it feels like. I don't want to give up on it. I guess I just like to know it is there." This sentiment reminded me of how he felt about maintaining his boyhood home: selling it would feel like giving up on his mother.

When I asked how he would feel if he were to throw away those two pieces, he said, "It would be just as bad as when it broke, and it would feel that way for a long time." This was another refrain we'd heard before. When I pressed him some more, he said, "Maybe a glass blower can use them for another piece." Finally, he said that he would get rid of them in a month or so, when he got over the loss of the vase. When I visited four years later, the pieces were still there.

Memory: Things Speak Out

Although many hoarders avoid spending time in their homes and feel depressed when they notice the clutter, paradoxically they retain an intense attraction to individual items in the hoard. Alvin told me that he visited his penthouse apartment for a short time nearly every day to get away from his business and to enjoy his things. He didn't organize or try to cull when he was there; he just enjoyed being amid his treasures. I accompanied him on one of his walks through the apartment. He scanned the room with his eyes and said, "Most people would look at this and see a mess. Really, it's layered and complex." When his gaze fixed on something, he inspected it, and the effect was intoxicating. He spotted an Orrefors crystal goblet and launched into a description of the Ariel versus the Grail technique used by the designers, but it was really the shape and contour of each piece that excited him. His eyes found another treasure. "Here, let me show you this, Dr. Frost." He picked up a bronze elephant with a man sitting inside a basket atop it. He recounted how he had found this piece in an antique store more than a decade before, but the detail with which he described the store and the purchase made it sound like yesterday.

"But wait, Doctor, look at this." He pointed to a stained-glass panel with a wall lamp in it. "This came from my parents' house. There are still eight of them there on the wall and working. I saw one like this go at Sotheby's for over four thousand dollars."

"Wait, here, look at this, Doctor!" His voice rose with excitement as he found a ring. The ring, he thought, was from western India. It was huge, almost the size of a walnut, with a large sapphire in the center, a Buddha on each side of the stone, and elephants around the edges — silver with gold inlay.

One of the many clothes racks in the apartment had fallen over and caused a shift in the landscape, burying his box of prized rings. Alvin's ring collection numbered more than five hundred. Each had a story, and each was personal, from his father's moonstone ring to the signature ring he had bought one night at an upscale restaurant. He'd seen it on the finger of the man standing at the urinal next to his in the restroom and offered him three times what it was worth. Alvin appreciated the artistry of each of his rings, but more than that, his rings recorded his life. They were his way of organizing and remembering events. They provided a vividness not available from simple recall. I asked why he had a Hula-Hoop in his room. He'd bought it on a recent trip. "In my mind, it's like a reel that can put that movie back on."

But it wasn't as simple as needing things to aid his memory. It was more like the things allowed him to reexperience a past event. He described a recent experience of losing a folder containing his notes from an event he'd organized. For the life of him, he couldn't remember anything about the event — who had been there or what had happened. When he found the folder, his memory returned. He said, "I didn't even have to look through the folder. I remembered it all. Memories associated with things are vivid. The things are like holograms."

"But wait, Doctor, look at this!" Again his voice rose as he spotted a nineteenth-century Russian icon hanging haphazardly on a nail next to the doorjamb. It was a masterful piece, and I could see his appreciation as he carefully caressed the wooden backing and the inlay. "There must be a dozen more of these around here some-where," he said.

"But wait, Doctor." Now he rushed from thing to thing. I ex-pected another valuable artifact as he reached across the cluttered top of a nineteenth-century French dresser. Instead, he picked up a pair of green plastic dime-store glasses. He handled and admired them with the same reverence as he had the icon. They were, he recounted, from an "Emerald City" party he had once organized.

"When I walk in here," he said, "it's like walking into the past. Here, let me show you." He opened a drawer and pulled out a stack of business cards. "I collect these. I must have over twenty-five thousand of them. I can tell you something about each of these people—mostly where I met them and what we were doing. Be-ing handed a card forms a physical connection to them and to that past. There is a physicality to my memory. I have to have the physi-cal connection."

The way Alvin's memories were tied to objects is reminiscent of sympathetic magic, in which someone sees a physical object as forming a connection with the original owner or event, much like Jerry Seinfeld's shirt did for my student (see chapter 2). Once Alvin was at a dinner with the former governor of Puerto Rico. The governor gave a speech that Alvin admired, and Alvin asked if he could have the governor's notes for the speech. At some point during the meal, the waiter picked up the notes and threw them away. The governor promised to e-mail a copy to Alvin, but Alvin insisted on the original. He spent more than an hour going through the kitchen garbage looking for the notes. He said that the original notes carried the "physical memory" of the dinner, and he had to have them.

Many of the things Alvin collected connected him to people he did not even know. He showed me a ring he had bought years before at a flea market. It was engraved with the words "To my daughter." The affection from parent to daughter struck Alvin as beautiful, and he had to have the ring. He described such things as "footprints to the soul of the former owner."

We spent nearly an hour looking through Alvin's stuff. By the time we left, his hands were blackened with dust from the treasures he'd caressed. Possessions connected him to his past and the pasts of others. They had a meaning far beyond their physical existence. "It's like a language," Alvin said. "The things speak out."

Alvin's experiences with his possessions were far richer in detail and complexity than they are for most people. Each of his treasures contained a vast amount of information, and seeing an item conjured up all of it. It was easy for him to get lost in the memories stored in each thing or in the stories they contained about others. But these objects also had a physical presence — they had shape, color, and contour — and these characteristics were as captivating to Alvin as the memories. Alvin's excitement at showing me his treasures reminded me of Irene's bag of bottle caps. His appreciation of the physical attributes of each thing was remarkable. His attention to every physical feature of an object expanded its value and meaning. As Alvin once said to me, "Visual art bounces my electrons." We have noticed an inordinate number of hoarders who describe themselves as artists. This might be because hoarders are more intelligent or creative than the rest of us, their worlds filled with an appreciation of the physical world that most of us lack. This part of hoarding is a kind of giftedness, a special talent for seeing beauty, utility, and meaning in things.

But along with this gift comes a curse. Alvin's complaint that his mind was "a tree with too many branches" may prove to be the most accurate description of the worst part of hoarding — an overabundance of information paired with an inability to organize it.

Disorganization makes what would otherwise be a gift into a seriously problematic, dangerous, and sometimes deadly affliction. Maybe hoarding is creativity run amok.

Brain Circuits

Irene had struggled with hoarding for more than thirty years by the time I met her. She complained about her seeming inability to control it: "I was born this way, and I'll probably die this way. I see too many options [for things]. I can't control it. My brain needs to be rewired!" Brain circuitry may indeed be involved in the development of hoarding.

In the fall of 1848, Phineas Gage, the foreman of a Vermont railroad construction crew, set gunpowder in a hole in a rock he wanted to clear. He packed sand on top of the powder with a tamping rod, a three-foot-long iron bar that tapered from one and a quarter inches in diameter down to one-quarter inch at the tip. As he tamped, the powder accidentally exploded, launching the tamping rod through Gage's skull. It entered just under his left eye, exited through the top of his head, and landed twenty-five yards away. Miraculously, he survived and lived nearly a dozen more years. Changes in his behavior after the accident made Phineas Gage the first and most celebrated neuroscience case study.

Among many changes in his behavior, Gage developed a "great fondness" for souvenirs. Although little has been recorded about Gage's apparent hoarding, other cases of hoarding following damage to the frontal lobes of the brain have been reported since then. Researchers at the University of Iowa have taken the next step in localizing this effect. They compared brain-damaged patients who began abnormally collecting things following their injuries to brain-damaged patients who did not collect. All of the abnormal collectors had damage in the middle of the front portion of the frontal lobes, while the non-collecting patients' damage was scattered throughout the brain. The prefrontal region of the brain is responsible for goal-directed behavior, planning, organization, and decision making—all activities that represent challenges for people who hoard.

Brain scan studies have added additional information about what is happening in the brains of people who hoard. Sanjaya Saxena found lower metabolism (an indication of the level of activity in that portion of the brain) among hoarders in regions of the brain roughly corresponding to those identified in the University of Iowa study. In particular, hoarders had lower metabolic rates in the anterior cingulate cortex, one region responsible for motivation, focused attention, error detection, and decision making.

Saxena's study examined people's brains while they were at rest, or at least not engaged in a task. Subsequent studies have examined what is happening in the brain when hoarders try to make decisions about discarding possessions. Our colleague Dave Tolin at Hartford Hospital in Hartford, Connecticut, devised one such ingenious experiment. Hoarding patients and a control group who didn't hoard brought their junk mail to the lab. Their brains were scanned while they watched a monitor showing the experimenter picking up their mail and holding it over a shredder. The subjects were then asked to decide whether the experimenter should shred or save the item. In contrast to what happened when their brains were at rest, hoarders had significantly more activity in areas such as the anterior cingulate cortex than control subjects did when trying to make the decision.

Because these areas of the brain are responsible for many of the functions with which hoarders have difficulty, these studies support the idea that something may have gone wrong there. Perhaps Alvin's tree did have too many branches. Although it may seem easy to conclude that hoarding occurs because of dysfunction in these areas of the brain, the science doesn't yet allow us to do so. What happens in the brain *seems* to match what hoarders experience, but that doesn't mean brain dysfunction caused it. The function and even the structure of the brain can change as a result of experience.

Even if hoarding is inherited or driven by problems in the wiring of the brain, people with hoarding problems do seem to be able to learn to control them. I spent several hours working with each of the twins sorting and discarding. Progress was slow, but both were able to sort and discard, and it appeared to me that with effort, they could both learn to control their hoarding. It seemed that these men needed someone they trusted to sit with them while they went through their possessions. Perhaps having someone else there kept their attention focused on the task at hand. My attempts to get them to do this work on their own failed, as had Betty's efforts with Ralph (see chapter 7).

Jerry tried hiring a professional organizer, but he got frustrated by someone else making decisions about his stuff. I tried on several occasions to find a therapist for Alvin and Jerry, but no one seemed good enough for them. They continued as best they could. It was easier for Alvin, who had his business and spent much of his time away from his apartment. For Jerry the situation was more troubling. His stuff had become his life, and although it gave him some degree of pleasure, worrying about it took a huge toll.

Alvin and Jerry's story is a remarkable one. The similarity in their hoarding behaviors, the early onset, and the fact that their mother also hoarded suggests that their hoarding was heavily influenced by genetics. But nurture may also have been at work, as they grew up in a cluttered home with a mother who taught them her ways. At this point, geneticists are betting that hoarding has at least some significant genetic cause, but exactly what is inherited is not clear. One possibility is that hoarders inherit deficits or different ways of processing information. Perhaps they inherit an intense perceptual sensitivity to visual details, such as the shapes and colors of Irene's bottle caps. These visual details (overlooked by the rest of us) give objects special meaning and value to them. Or perhaps they inherit a tendency for the brain to store and retrieve memories differently. If visual cues (i.e., objects) are necessary for hoarders' retrieval of memories, then getting rid of those cues is the same as losing their memories. Whatever is inherited, it is likely that some kind of emotional vulnerability must accompany this tendency in order for full-blown hoarding to develop.

11

A PACK RAT IN THE FAMILY

It was my BIG SECRET. I always had to make up something to keep my friends from coming over.

—Ashley

Growing Up in a Mess

Ashley panicked as soon as she walked into the apartment. It was worse than ever. The pathways through the mountains of stuff were narrower than she remembered. The piles were higher, and the closed-off feeling struck her sooner than ever before. "It felt horrible—unnatural," she told me later. *I can't do this anymore,* she thought. She had just gotten away a few weeks earlier—to college and a room that was hers to control. No more walking on eggshells. No more worrying that she might touch or move the wrong thing. She could relax and look after only herself. As she looked around her mother's apartment, she realized that she no longer considered this home.

Children who grow up in a hoarded home are dramatically affected. Their childhoods are markedly different from those of their peers, and their adult lives can be shaped by the experience. Ashley was one such case. She started her sophomore year at Smith College troubled by a variety of things, not least of all worry about her mother. She made an appointment with the college's counseling service and began to talk about her mother's eccentricities for the first time. She was shocked when her therapist recognized her mother's behavior and surprised to find that it had a name: hoarding. Her therapist told her about the work we were doing in studying hoarding. She called me immediately after the session.

Ashley was the kind of student professors love: bright, thoughtful, responsible, and curious. She was quite open with me about her mother's difficulties and about what it was like growing up with them. Eager to learn more about hoarding, she worked in my research lab during her senior year. Not surprisingly, her research project was on the effects of growing up in a hoarded home. Ashley reviewed interviews with more than forty children of hoarders who described their experiences growing up. The information she gathered formed the backdrop for our subsequent studies on the topic.

When I first met her, Ashley was at once relieved and saddened that her mother's condition was a subject of study. Knowing that it was identifiable meant that there was hope that something could be done, but her mother had needed that hope years before. When Ashley's father left, partly because of her mother's hoarding, her mother became extremely depressed. "Just knowing it had a name," Ashley said, "would have protected her and given her some self-respect—knowing that she wasn't a freak of nature." Ashley also thought that if they could have named her mother's condition, she might have been able to discuss it with her mother. As it was, Ashley's attempts to do so always ended in frustration and anger.

She first noticed that there was something "wrong" with her home when she was very young and needed a babysitter when her parents were going out. The entire weekend before the event, Ashley and her parents cleaned like demons. Since her mother would not allow anything to be discarded, most of the stuff was relocated to a studio apartment they kept primarily for storage. Ashley remembered trip after trip to the apartment and a mad rush to the finish. Afterward, the stuff came back.

Major chaos accompanied any planned visitor, so very few visitors ever crossed their threshold. Ashley took these episodes in stride, but her father was frustrated and resentful. He took her aside after one such event and said, "You don't have to live this way when you get older." Ashley wasn't sure whether he feared that she would inherit this behavior and was warning her, or he was apologizing for what she had to endure.

With her house too messy for play dates, Ashley went to her friends' homes. "I liked that," she said. "Their houses were clean." But she always held back a little even around close friends. There was a part of her life that she couldn't share. She felt funny when her friends asked, "Why can't we play at your house?" She made up clever excuses to hide the truth. She didn't think of it as lying exactly—more like protecting. Her parents needed a shield—from what, she wasn't sure, but she knew from the way they behaved when visitors were expected that their home was something to hide. This was, she told me, the worst part of it. She called it her BIG SECRET, and she felt obliged to keep it. What's more, she had no words to describe the situation at home. "It's hard to talk about something when you don't know what it is," she said. "I knew things weren't normal, but I acted as though they were." While at camp one summer, she confided her secret to a new friend. She wanted some sympathy and understanding, but instead got what she characterized as "morbid interest—like I had just described a cool bird I'd seen at the zoo." She shut herself off and didn't try again for some time.

When Ashley was young, the house was full of newspapers, books, boxes, and memorabilia scattered everywhere. Her mother liked projects, especially those involving the creative use of things—old squeeze bottles, plastic containers, cardboard, whatever was at hand. She could imagine hundreds of projects for these objects. Her things occupied most of the floor and all of the horizontal surfaces. Still, the family could, with Herculean effort, move enough to make the apartment presentable, at least temporarily. That changed when Ashley was eleven and her father moved out. While the hoarding was not the only problem between her parents, it was a significant one. His departure sent Ashley's mother, Madeline, into a tailspin. The apartment grew even more cluttered, with piles of things beginning to overwhelm the furniture. Making matters worse, the acrimonious divorce resulted in the loss of their studio apartment, so most of the stuff stored there suddenly appeared in their home. Every room but Ashley's was quickly being overtaken by stuff. At times her mother made some headway against the clutter, but the newly cleared space always filled up within a week or two.

Madeline grew increasingly concerned about other people touching or moving her things. Ashley obliged by not touching anything outside her room. She accommodated her mom on nearly everything. If she didn't, the cost was high. Her mother's temper was volatile, and Ashley learned to walk on eggshells to prevent a tantrum. At least her room was her own. She kept it neat and protected her things from getting lost in the sea of her mother's stuff. It was an oasis for Ashley, a place to hide from the chaos.

Ashley's first experience away from her mother came at age thirteen when she went to sleep-away camp for a month. It was freeing for Ashley to be away from home, independent and responsible only for herself. But while she was gone, her mother's stuff invaded her room. Madeline thought that she could use the time to clear out the apartment, and she used Ashley's room as a staging area. She piled things from the rest of the apartment on Ashley's bed. By the end of the month, Ashley's room was full of stuff, and the rest of the apartment looked no better. "I felt bad about that,"

Madeline admitted later, "and I kept telling myself I'd fix it up, but it never happened."

By the time Ashley returned from camp, all of her things were buried under a thick layer of her mother's possessions. She could barely even walk into the room and had no hope of sleeping there. Since her mother would not allow her to move anything, Ashley effectively lost her room. From that time until her departure for college, Ashley slept with her mother in her mother's bed — an island in a sea of stuff.

Ashley suffered through adolescence. "I couldn't create enough space for myself," she reflected. "With all the hormones and my development, my body was changing, but I couldn't change because I was sleeping with my mother!" Even under these conditions, Ashley didn't rebel. "This was my life. I had to learn to live with it," she said. "I wasn't just her daughter; I was her partner. I had to be the one to fix things. I had to be the responsible one. I couldn't think about myself or the things I wanted." She had grown used to protecting her mother and keeping the BIG SECRET, first from the babysitter, then from her friends, and now from her father. When he asked how things were going at the apartment, Ashley led him to believe that they were no different from when he'd left. "Nothing good would have come out of being truthful," she said, but she wasn't sure he believed her. All of this tied Ashley to her mother and left a lasting mark. "I couldn't separate from her," she said, nor did she learn to pursue her own interests. "I still have trouble with that," she said. When she left for college, she worried about how her mother would get along without her. She had gotten used to cushioning her mother from life's blows and being her mother's constant companion. After she left, her side of Madeline's bed was taken over by stuff.

Ashley could not understand her mother's need to acquire, although she marveled at Madeline's astute (albeit unusual) way of observing the world. "The pieces of the physical world she picks out to focus on are incredible, things I would never notice," Ashley explained, like the colors on a milk carton or the shape of a vitamin bottle. Madeline spent an hour trying to describe to Ashley why the contrast between the blue sky and an old building was so compelling in a photo she'd taken. "She's like a savant," Ashley said. "Her brain can see things mine can't. I can see the beauty in objects, but it's like she sees the atoms of objects. She sees more than anyone I know and attaches more meaning to each piece of it."

Madeline could not understand Ashley's point of view about possessions and sometimes got angry at being "betrayed." Once, after Madeline was able to clean a small corner of the bathroom—a major accomplishment for her—Ashley failed to compliment her or act excited about it. "To me it was unexciting, 'cause I knew it wouldn't stay," Ashley said. "She got mad, then I got mad. Most of our arguments were like this." When Ashley eventually found a therapist for her mother, Madeline again felt betrayed. "She felt I was handing her over to someone else and washing my hands of her. She didn't say, 'Ashley cares so much she's gone out and found a therapist for me,' but rather that I'm making her pay someone to work on this."

Ashley thought that perhaps at some level Madeline might have had an inkling of what her problem meant for her daughter, but "she's never been able to say that to me." In Ashley's view, her mother understood little if anything about the effects of growing up in such a home.

On the weekend of her college graduation, Ashley brought her mother to my office to meet me. As we chatted, the topic turned to hoarding. Madeline was open about her problem, but it was clear that she had little hope of overcoming it. I was surprised by the exchange between mother and daughter. In all of my discussions with Ashley, I had gotten the impression that even though she didn't like her mother's hoarding, she had resigned herself to not being able to do anything about it. "I had to live with it and not fight back," she had once told me. But in my office, she challenged her mother aggressively about her hoarding. Madeline tried to explain why she had five storage units, but Ashley interrupted, insisting that the stuff in them wasn't worth the money she was paying for them. "Why don't you just get rid of it?" Ashley asked. Madeline reacted stiffly, and I could see the pattern that had developed between them. Despite knowing from her study of hoarding that such a direct challenge was unlikely to help and might even hurt, Ashley couldn't seem to get past the years of frustration and worry.

Madeline, for her part, was as baffled by her hoarding as her daughter was. She didn't know she had a problem until late in life. She spoke bitterly about the failure of numerous mental health professionals she had seen to diagnose her problem and treat it effectively. Her recent therapy had left her with the realization that she'd been living with this problem since she was nine years old. Madeline thought that her own mother had a lot to do with it.

When Madeline was nine, her mother wanted her to clean the stuff off her desk. To Madeline, the small pile of odds and ends — school papers and Brownie clothes — hardly amounted to a problem. But a few days later, she came home from school to find all of the stuff from her desk in the trash can. She felt violated and reacted angrily, but the "invasions," as she called them, continued. Every day she dug through the trash to retrieve her stuff, and the yelling and screaming began. "I felt like I had no control," Madeline told me.

It was at about this time that her rituals started as well. She began with prayers. At bedtime, her fears were at their worst — spiders, fire, darkness, the possibility of not waking up. So Madeline prayed. When she finished one prayer, she prayed once more, and once more after that. "Soon I was doing the entire evening service," she said. When she became a teenager, it wasn't prayer that occupied her, but tapping and touching. She felt compelled to touch the marble-topped table beneath the mirror in the hallway. The number of taps was based on the date. She couldn't say exactly why she felt compelled, just that she had to do it to make sure she would be alive the next day. Her rituals helped her feel calmer, in control. Although her rituals were not as bad when I met her, she still had to touch certain things a prescribed number of times based on the date.

For a long time, she kept her rituals secret, not realizing that other people also suffered from such compulsions. After her husband left her, her therapist suggested that she read a book about Prozac, which made reference to touching and counting rituals. *Are you kidding me?* she thought. *You mean other people do that?* When she saw Jack Nicholson compulsively tapping his foot on the floor in the movie *As Good as It Gets,* she reddened with embarrassment in the theater. Then she got annoyed: *He stole my thing!*

Madeline got her first period at age twelve, but her easily embarrassed mother said nothing to her about how to manage it. Madeline hid her used sanitary pads in a clothespin bag. She didn't know what else to do with them and feared that her brothers would see them if she put them in the garbage. More than that, however, her menstrual flow felt like a part of her, and getting rid of it made her uncomfortable. When her mother discovered the bag, she was horrified and forced Madeline to throw it away. Despite the drama, Madeline continued to save used pads secretly until the grossness outweighed the discomfort of losing these parts of herself. We have observed a number of instances in which people hoard used tampons, nail clippings, even urine and feces — critical parts of themselves, from their point of view.

During her junior year in college, Madeline started piling clothes, papers, books, and memorabilia such as playbills in a pile in the middle of her dorm room. She always meant to organize the stuff and put it away, but she didn't. Finally, the dome-shaped pile began to remind Madeline of an ancient burial mound, with an aesthetic mixture of textures and colors. Both Madeline and her roommate came to see it as an odd piece of art—a "stuff structure." The shape and colors pleased her, and the things sticking out seemed to contain the memories of the events they represented. Taking the pile apart was unthinkable. Even changing it was too hard to contemplate.

After college, when Madeline got her own apartment, she created another "stuff structure" from the dirty dishes in her sink. The mound occupied her kitchen for two years, and Madeline had to get by with only a single spoon, fork, knife, bowl, and cup. Stuff structures seemed to appear naturally in whatever space Madeline occupied. No planning went into them. They grew on their own until she noticed their aesthetic quality. Then they could not be broken.

Initially, her stuff structures posed few difficulties. Her first real problem began when she moved into a small studio apartment in New York City. Unread newspapers piled up, overtaking her small space. Depressed over the suicide of a close friend, Madeline just couldn't seem to dig out. She knew that those papers contained important information that could help her acting career, but she had neither the time nor the energy to tackle the piles. When she finally moved to a bigger apartment, her parents solved the problem by throwing the papers out despite Madeline's pleas. Once again she felt victimized by her mother and angered by her loss of control over things she valued.

At her new apartment, Madeline left everything packed in boxes, living as she had before, using only a few of her possessions. Soon pathways appeared, and, as with her stuff sculptures, once she created a pathway, it seemed impossible to change it. When she tried to unpack, she couldn't decide what to do first.

She would start on a box, become distracted by a different box, and end up moving from box to box without accomplishing anything.

When she got married, she had more incentive to control her hoarding. "I can keep things clear for other people," she told me, "just not for myself." She and her husband had minor arguments over her newspapers, but she insisted that their apartment was clean enough for comfortable living and even having parties. This changed in the years that followed as life began to overwhelm her.

According to Madeline, she and her husband had few problems with clutter during the first four years of Ashley's life. Madeline had a career as an actress, and although she suffered from various physical ailments, she was happy. As Ashley got older and Madeline's acting career ended, she felt isolated and depressed. "She's not a networker," Ashley told me of her mother. The small piles of unread newspapers began to grow and, according to Madeline, merge with Ashley's toys, artwork, and clothes. Piles of unopened mail got stuffed into plastic bags and thrown in the back of the closet. When Ashley was five, the family moved to a new apartment, where most of their things remained in boxes so that Madeline could paint the walls. Her unreasonably high standards delayed the process, and they lived amid the boxes for years. She described the one wall she finished painting with some pride: "This was my perfect wall!" Caught by the perfectionism afflicting so many hoarders, she never painted the rest of the apartment.

At the time, Madeline didn't worry much about how her behavior might affect Ashley. She said that until Ashley was four or five years old, she had friends over to play at the apartment. One of them, Madeline claimed, lived in the same kind of cluttered apartment. The rest, she rationalized, had much more space in their apartments, so naturally they lived in less clutter. But by age six, Ashley no longer wanted to have friends over. Madeline felt relieved.

Madeline knew that the apartment was in bad shape while Ashley was in high school, but she couldn't control it. Her perfectionism meant that any project she began had to be flawlessly done. She couldn't just throw away the old newspapers; she had to examine them for important information. It would take years to go through all of them, so she avoided the task and went through none of them. When she got up the motivation to clean, she couldn't stay focused long enough to make any headway. Life events and illness always seemed to intervene. Whenever she was able to clear an area, the open space made her feel empty inside, and she refilled it quickly.

Only in the past few years had Madeline recognized what Ashley endured growing up, "but by that time," she said, "Ashley was in college, a little late for me to change the past." Recently, Madeline's own mother developed Alzheimer's. Madeline moved in with her mother to care for her. Ashley told me that her grandmother had thrown out Madeline's driver's license. Ashley thought it ironic that Madeline was once again going through the trash, making sure her mother wasn't discarding anything of value. She wondered whether, in addition to her license, Madeline was still retrieving plastic trays and old newspapers.

Ashley's independence didn't come until she left for college. Only then was she able to separate her interests from her mother's and let her mother struggle with hoarding (and life) on her own. Still, a legacy remained. Years of learning how to avoid her mother's tantrums had left her with an aversion to conflict. She would gladly suffer almost any consequences in order to avoid conflict. Ashley recently found herself in a park admiring a tree. She noticed the contrasting hues and textures of the trunk and leaves, and she thought, *I am like my mother. She's given me an appreciation of the physical world that I would not have had without her, but without the bad parts.*

The impact of growing up in a hoarded home can be substantial, so not surprisingly, Internet groups have been formed to provide information, comfort, and support. Overcoming Hoarding Together (O-H-T) was created by the leaders of a hoarding self-help group to provide a place for hoarders and family members to interact with one another in a supportive and cooperative way. Children of Hoarders (COH) was started by adult children of hoarders who recognized a need to share their experiences of growing up in a hoarded home. The COH Web site has expanded to provide a comprehensive overview of hoarding, including synopses of current research and information about hoarding. In a COH survey, more than 80 percent of the group's approximately fourteen hundred members reported that when they were growing up, they thought their family was the only one that lived amid extreme clutter. The founders of COH hope to ease members' isolation by providing a forum for people to share their stories and hardships.

As with any endeavor in which people expose the secrets of their youth, emotions are sometimes raw and unfiltered. This has explosive potential, especially since some children of hoarders struggle with the same problem themselves. On one online discussion board, a member vented her anger about how her mother, and by extension all hoarders, put her own interests ahead of those of her children. Another member, a mother with a hoarding problem, took offense. The conflict erupted into a nasty dispute. Such conflict notwithstanding, it seems that the majority of posts on such sites are expressions of gratitude and relief at finding others who not only understand their experiences but also share them.

We recently conducted a study of relatives of hoarders that revealed the harmful consequences of growing up in a hoarded home. We found that the effects varied depending on the age of the child when the hoarding began. Children who lived in a hoarded home before the age of ten were more embarrassed and less happy, had fewer friends over, and had more strained relations with their parents growing up than did those whose parents' hoarding began later. As adults, they were more likely to experience social anxiety and stress and continued to have more strained relationships with their parents. Children who spent their early years in a cluttered home held more hostile and rejecting views of their parents than did children whose parents' hoarding was not apparent at that time—but even the latter group expressed a very high level of hostility toward their parents, higher even than that expressed by the relatives of people with other forms of serious mental illness. It is clear that the negative effects of hoarding stay with many of these children for a lifetime.

Children with hoarding parents find ways of coping with the problem. Ashley became the protector, ignoring her own needs. A woman from one of our studies, the middle daughter in a family of six children, described elaborate rituals the family adopted to deal with her father's rage at losing things. When her father couldn't find a newspaper article he wanted from the thousands of copies of the *New York Times* cluttering the house, he became belligerent and insisted that the family search for it. As his distress grew, her mother concocted a plan to calm him down. She organized the children to chant to Saint Anthony, the patron saint of lost items, while they searched:

Saint Anthony, Saint Anthony please come around
Something's lost that can't be found.

They chanted in unison faster and faster as they searched. Although they never found the article, the chanting seemed to ease her father's distress.

Besides the emotional costs of growing up in a hoarded home, children of hoarders bear the responsibility of figuring out what to do with an aging parent who is living in such unsafe and unhealthy conditions. Most children are frustrated and angry after years of unsuccessful attempts to get their parents to do something about the problem. At the same time, they love their parents and are worried about them. Conflicting feelings of love and resentment put the children in an impossible position, and understanding a parent's problem does not change the condition of the home. One woman on the COH Web site wrote about how her mother died in squalor, leaving her scarred by shame, guilt, embarrassment, and anger. She advised, "I don't care what the cost for the rest of you whose parent is still alive and living this way, WHATEVER IT TAKES, have an intervention."

Some interventions involve clandestinely removing things from the parent's home. But forced cleanouts can be long, acrimonious, and, in the end, ineffective. Wholesale cleanouts may temporarily resolve the health or safety crisis, but they do little to change the problem behavior or the causes of hoarding, and the problem often resurfaces (see Ralph in chapter 7 and Daniel in chapter 9). From a mental health perspective, we strongly recommend that the hoarder be included in the de-cluttering process when the cleanout is legally mandated. Even when the person is mentally incapacitated by conditions such as dementia or psychosis, some involvement in the intervention is likely to reduce the trauma. A hoarder's attachment to his or her things and decisions about acquiring and saving will not change if he or she does not participate in the disposition of the stuff. Of course, when the situation is at a crisis level or the person's life is in danger, immediate action to ensure the person's safety is essential. But whenever the process can include the hoarder, even if this slows things down considerably, the quality of the family relationships (and the relationships with legal authorities) will be improved.

When children, siblings, and parents intervene by discarding items against the wishes of the hoarder, things generally turn out badly. Usually the family fractures, with the hoarder feeling angry, resentful, abused, and sometimes suicidal, and the family members feeling frustrated and angry. At this point, the family members often abandon the hoarder, concluding that there is nothing they can do. The hoarder becomes more isolated and suspicious of others.

The key is for families to evaluate the pros and cons of different courses of action and to figure out where the leverage lies. Dr. C. Alec Pollard and his colleagues in St. Louis have developed a telephone consultation program to help family members decide how to engage a loved one with a hoarding or other OCD problem in seeking help. The starting point for any family member is to understand what his or her loved one experiences when dealing with possessions.

Therapists face an additional burden when severe hoarding cases appear for treatment. Every state in the United States now mandates that mental health clinicians report suspected cases of child or elder abuse and neglect. Severe hoarding qualifies as neglect, and as a result, someone with a serious hoarding problem who comes in for treatment may find himself or herself dealing with child or adult protective services. Once a therapist, by legal and ethical obligation, reports a suspected case of abuse or neglect, the chances that the client will return for treatment are almost nil. Protective agencies typically—and sometimes unfairly—have a bad reputation. Although agency employees who are familiar with hoarding as a disorder and educated about dealing with it may be useful resources, when workers aren't familiar with hoarding, the outcomes can be traumatic for everyone involved. The unfortunate consequence of the mandated reporting law is that it reduces the likelihood of the hoarder voluntarily engaging in treatment. As the case unfolds, treatment may be mandated by the court, but the therapist will have to overcome a mountain of resentment before therapy can begin.

With Ashley's help, Madeline found a therapist familiar with hoarding and began treatment. When I last spoke with her, she happily told me that she had made progress in clearing out her apartment. She had removed more than ninety boxes of stuff, although most had gone into storage. Although the apartment was getting better, Madeline's room at her mother's house was getting worse. There were narrow pathways in the room, and getting to the window required climbing over the bed. Despite this setback, Madeline was hopeful. Ashley, after years of watching her mother's previous attempts, was understandably pessimistic.

Marrying into a Mess

Research on hoarding clearly shows that people with this problem are less likely to marry, and when they do, they are more likely to get divorced. Among the participants in our first study in 1993, only 42 percent of the hoarding group was married, compared to 80 percent of the non-hoarding group. In our 2001 study of elderly hoarders in Boston, 55 percent had never been married, compared to only 5 percent of the general population over age sixty-five. So the marriage rate alone makes hoarders a very atypical group, even compared to people with conditions such as anxiety disorders or depression, whose marriage rates are much higher. Something about this syndrome keeps people isolated. As long ago as 1947, Erich Fromm suggested that people with a "hoarding orientation" tended to be isolated figures who distanced themselves from others.

Clinical lore has followed this trend. The stereotype of a hoarder among clinicians is of someone who is withdrawn and difficult to get along with. But our experience indicates that people who hoard vary widely in their interpersonal skills, just like the rest of the

population.* At one end is Irene (see chapter 1), a delightful conversationalist, and at the other end is Daniel (see chapter 9), extremely isolated and detached.

There's a prosaic explanation for why so many hoarders live
without spouses: no one wants to live with all that stuff. The chaos
created by hoarding reduces the chances that the hoarder can find
and sustain intimate relationships. Most people who hoard are intensely ashamed of their failure to control the clutter and try to
hide the conditions of their homes from others. Since the problem
has usually escalated enough to create significant clutter by the
time they reach their mid-twenties, hoarders enter adulthood with
a reluctance to let anyone into their homes—which makes dating
(or even friendships) next to impossible.

The shame surrounding hoarding may also contribute to the development of social anxiety. Nearly a quarter of people with hoarding problems have social anxiety severe enough to warrant a mental health diagnosis of social phobia. This kind of anxiety—which
can come across as shyness or even rudeness—can cripple the development of intimate relationships, as it leads sufferers to avoid
parties, dining out, and dating.

For some, the intimacy struggle is more complex. One woman
who hoarded animals told me that she was desperate to find someone to love. Nearly fifty, she had never had a serious relationship.
She attended social events and even took evening classes at a local university in order to meet men. But getting serious with a
man would be difficult if he visited her home. Although she did
not have piles of clutter, she did have dozens of cats—so many
that the humane society had taken some away and put her on no-

---

*We recently published a paper on the interpersonal difficulties of people with hoarding
problems. Although hoarders had more interpersonal difficulties than people who had no
psychological problems, they were no different from people who suffered from depression
or other forms of anxiety (Grisham, Steketee, & Frost, 2008).

tice. Unless she kept her cat collection to a minimum and sub-mitted to periodic inspections, they would remove all her animals. Her home smelled so strongly of cat urine that my two-hour inter-view with her left me with a splitting headache. She insisted that her cats were "keeping my love alive" until she found a boyfriend. Once she found someone, she believed, she would be able to get rid of most of her animals.

More tragic for this woman was the fact that after the animal control officers raided her home and removed most of her cats, her New Hampshire town held a town meeting (a tradition in New England) to discuss the threat she posed to public health. This so-cially anxious woman sat in the front row while her fellow citizens admonished her for her behavior. This public humiliation drove her deeper into isolation.

Sharing space with another person proves difficult for many hoarders, except perhaps when both partners have hoarding ten-dencies. These folie à deux couples may live together contentedly until lack of space provokes conflict or the authorities invade their territory and insist on a change. In our experience, a different prob-lem arises when one partner recognizes the hoarding problem and wants to change but the other does not. It's hardly surprising that we've had limited success in breaking the hoarding cycle in such families.

Not surprisingly, most hoarders' marriages follow a rocky course. Frustrated spouses criticize their hoarding partners until the mar-riage breaks up or an icy standoff occurs. Irene's marriage was typi-cal. Her hoarding got progressively worse as her efforts to control the clutter failed. Her husband responded by criticizing her for these and other shortcomings. As his criticism escalated, so did her depression, which further reduced her ability to control the problem. Finally, he left. By the time she regained control of the clutter, it was too late to save her marriage. In other cases we've known, non-hoarding partners disengage from the marriage, relieving their frustration by avoiding the partner and the home and arranging their social lives with others on the outside.

In a different and probably less common scenario, one spouse acquiesces to the other's hoarding behavior and simply learns to live with it. Bella and her husband, Ray, had been married for several years when her hoarding began. Twenty years later, much of their house was unlivable. Through it all, Ray never complained or pressured Bella to change. Over the next ten years, Bella, with the help of a therapist, learned to control her hoarding, and the couple regained much of their living space. Although Ray didn't hoard, he wasn't bothered by the clutter and was happy to follow Bella's lead, both in collecting and in cleaning up.

At War over Hoarding

Some couples make an uneasy truce in which the non-hoarding spouse controls the living areas of the home, restricting the clutter to the basement, attic, garage, or storage units. The success of this arrangement depends on how well the afflicted partner can resist cluttering the living areas. If the urge to clutter is controlled and the collecting behavior doesn't cause financial or other problems, the marriage often survives and may be quite happy. But when keeping clutter out of the living space is an ongoing battle, the truce is fragile.

Such was the case for Helen and Paul. Half a generation apart in age, Helen was in her mid-fifties and Paul nearing seventy when I met them. According to Helen, Paul's hoarding started some ten years after they were married. Before the hoarding began, they lived in a small and very neat apartment without any clutter. But according to Paul, he had been collecting seriously since his mid-twenties. He had concealed it from Helen by keeping his stuff in storage sheds, at work, and spread among his friends. Paul collected objects from behind department stores and machine shops—junk by most people's standards.

He told me that he felt bad when he went out and didn't return with something. Before long, his collecting expanded to buying, mostly surplus items from shops and stores. When Paul and Helen married, years before Helen knew the extent of his problem, Paul said that he was "buying like a drunken person." Helen knew he liked to pick things up and save them, but to her it seemed a harmless eccentricity. It wasn't until they moved to France and bought a house that the extent of the hoarding became apparent. Paul's stuff quickly filled the yard and both porches of their new home, and soon it began to creep into the house. From that moment on, battles over clutter defined their marriage.

When I first spoke with Helen, their home and marriage sounded like a war zone. She controlled the kitchen, dining room, and parlor. He controlled the bedroom, living room, and laundry room. The porches and yard were disputed territory—the frontlines. Rules of engagement evolved. If any of his hoard found its way into her territory, she could move it and scold him, but she dared not throw anything away. If she got rid of something, he became unreasonable, sometimes even violent.

Paul gained some territory when he retired and had more time to scavenge. She reconquered it when she got the health department to take him to court over the condition of the property. His charm and vigor swayed the judge, however, who gave him an overly generous amount of time to clean it up, at least in Helen's view. Paul convinced the judge that he needed the extra time to sort, clean, and store his possessions. He cleaned, or attempted to clean, everything that came into the house. He then tied things into neat bundles and stored them, usually never to look at them again. His interpretation of the problem was that he simply didn't have enough time to clean and put away what he had collected, and with new things coming in daily, he had little time for anything but sorting, cleaning, and storing his things.

Paul was dedicated to the proposition that if a thing exists and is free or cheap, it must be had. He foraged throughout the neighborhood behind paint stores, grocery stores, and Laundromats. Anything with a "castoff" appearance, obviously not of use to the proprietors, was his treasure. Before long, he won the battle for the yard and porches.

The kitchen formed part of Helen's territory, but in Paul's forages, he frequently acquired discarded vegetables and produce from grocery stores. Some of the produce rotted in the yard and prompted a lawsuit from their neighbors. Some of it he brought into the kitchen. Retrieved at the point of spoilage, the rotting food sickened Helen but didn't seem to bother Paul. For some reason, Helen didn't feel that she could throw it out. Somehow it transcended their rules of engagement.

Another battle was waged over sex. The bedroom was his domain. To sleep there, she had to move part of the hoard off the bed. She took the offensive and refused to have sex with him until he cleared the hoard from the bedroom. He refused. They had reached a stalemate. Her use of sex as a weapon in the war had failed. He argued that she was ruining the family and forcing him to seek the comfort of prostitutes.

Helen stayed in the battle, refusing to surrender or to quit the marriage. Finally, after many years, something changed. Paul declared that he was through collecting and that he was going to get rid of much of what he had accumulated. Helen described the turnaround as nothing short of amazing. In the months preceding this change, Helen had taken to reading articles about hoarding to Paul. He enjoyed being read to and was attentive, providing critiques of the research. After she read portions of a draft of our treatment manual to him, he stopped collecting. When I met him a few years later, he told me why. His rationale had always been that someday he would need and use the things he collected. But it finally dawned on him that at his age, this was terribly unlikely. As another of our clients on her way to overcoming hoarding once remarked, "You can't hook up a U-Haul to a hearse." Helen attributed Paul's sudden change to pressure from the city and his friends, as well as her threat to leave him at the end of the year if nothing changed.

When I last spoke with them, the situation was much improved, but their perceptions of the extent of the remaining problem differed substantially. Helen's account of the condition of their home indicated that using the refrigerator, eating at the table, finding important papers, and sleeping in their bed were still difficult because of the hoarding. Paul thought that none of these things was a problem. Helen also described parts of their home as extreme fire hazards and very unsanitary. Paul considered their home safe and clean. His perceptions of the value of objects also differed substantially from Helen's and from most people's. One day a visitor asked him why he washed and hung out to dry so many rags and why he never used them. The questions enraged him. He couldn't understand how someone could describe his used clothes and bits of cloth as "rags." In his mind, he would never have picked up or kept something that was just a rag.

Helen and Paul came to a fragile truce in their marital war. Skirmishes still occurred on a regular basis, and whether they would be able to keep the peace remained to be seen.

12

BUT IT'S MINE!
Hoarding in Children

> If she ever owned it, it's hers; if she wished she owned it,
> it's hers; if in the future she might own it, it's hers; if it be-
> longs to anyone she loves and who loves her, it's hers.
>
> —Amy's mother

Many people who see hoarding cases—psychologists, psychiatrists, social workers, housing and health department officials—insist that it is a disorder of older people. Most people who get in
trouble with the health or fire departments because of their hoarding are middle-aged or older. A survey of the existing research
might lead to the same conclusion. The participants in our studies, for example, have ranged from ages eighteen to ninety, with an
average age of just over fifty. But our studies of people who suffer
from hoarding problems indicate that hoarding begins early in life.
Although few published case studies of hoarding in children exist,
some of our colleagues have described the symptoms in their child
clients. Aureen Wagner, a clinical child psychologist at the University of Rochester and author of *Up and Down the Worry Hill: A
Children's Book about Obsessive-Compulsive Disorder and Its Treatment,* told me about an unusual case: a six-year-old girl who col-

lected nearly everything she found—crumbs from a restaurant, pencil shavings at school, empty juice cartons, whatever came her way. When her parents were remodeling their home and workers removed the drywall from her room, she threw a fit. On another occasion, she was with her parents at Wal-Mart when some mud dropped off her shoe. An alert store clerk happened by and scooped it up. The little girl fell apart in the store, demanding to get her mud back. "But it's mine!" was the only explanation she could give.

By some estimates, more than 90 percent of children have a collection of something: rocks, dolls, bottle caps, action figures. But the story of Alvin and Jerry in chapter 10, who recalled an unbreakable attachment to sticks they found on walks, and stories like this six-year-old's seem extreme. When does normal collecting behavior in childhood turn into hoarding? Perhaps the best way to make the distinction between hoarding and normal collecting is to determine whether the behavior creates a problem for the family. Ted Plimpton, a colleague of ours and a child psychologist specializing in OCD, became interested in the topic of hoarding in children late in his career. He had seen very few such cases but admitted that he had never asked his OCD kids or their parents about it. When he did, he found he had several hoarding cases in his practice. Apparently, hoarding was not the most troublesome problem for these kids, so it hadn't come up in therapy. Still, it was serious enough for the parents to take steps to deal with it. Several of these parents agreed to tell us about their children who hoarded. We describe four of these cases here based on descriptions by one or both parents. Work such as this may lead to more and earlier diagnoses of hoarding problems in children, for whom treatment may be more effective than it is for adults, whose habits have had years to solidify.

Amy

For the first five years of her life, Amy lived with an abusive and neglectful mother who suffered from a host of problems, including alcohol and drug addiction, OCD, and AIDS. Both Amy and her younger sister were in and out of foster placements until they landed at the home of Krystal and her husband. Krystal's household contained a mixture of foster, adopted, and biological children, many suffering from various disorders, including Asperger's syndrome, attention deficit hyperactivity disorder (ADHD), Tourette's syndrome, and OCD. Amy and her younger sister arrived as foster children and were adopted by Krystal and her husband within two years. Krystal was a very bright and capable woman who seemed undaunted by the problems in her brood. She spoke of them all lovingly, without minimizing the significance of the problems they faced. At the time I interviewed Krystal, Amy was twenty-two, had just finished college, and was living with several roommates and working in New York City.

Krystal and her husband noticed Amy's hoarding immediately. Even at age five, she saved every paper from school regardless of its importance. Both Amy and her sister hoarded food, hiding it under their beds. At first Krystal attributed this to the girls having been neglected and suspected that in the past they had needed to hoard food to keep from starving. She kept telling herself, "If I can just feed them enough, they will realize there will always be food there." Amy's sister's hoarding gradually stopped, but Amy's grew worse. Krystal worried that the food would attract mice and insects and that if Amy ate the rotten food, she would get sick. She finally decided to make Amy keep the food in a box so that it would be sanitary. Her approach paid off, and food hoarding became less of a problem, but Amy's other hoarding behaviors escalated.

Like many moms, Krystal hung school papers on the refrigerator. In a houseful of children, these papers needed to come down regularly to accommodate the newest ones. It didn't take long before Krystal realized that Amy's refrigerator displays, as well as all her other papers, never left the house. Amy collected homework, notes passed in class, handouts, and magazines under her bed and in her closet—stacks and stacks of them—until by the fifth grade, they had become unmanageable. Krystal made Amy get rid of them, prompting an angry outburst.

Despite the struggles, Amy settled into her new family and community. She was a remarkable child: beautiful, dramatic, engaging, and extraordinarily bright. After three weeks of kindergarten, the teachers suggested that she move on to the first grade. She could already read fluently, and her math skills were at the second-grade level. But she was a challenge for the teachers, too. Easily bored, she was also loud, abrasive, messy, and disruptive. Krystal suspected that this was another reason the kindergarten teachers wanted to bump her up to first grade.

Amy developed a wide circle of friends, and when she went to friends' houses, they and their parents would give her things, especially if she hinted or asked. "She was such a sweet, charming, and beautiful child, how could you not?" Krystal observed. There seemed to be little logic to what she brought home. It might be a movie they already owned or clothes she didn't need. At first her friends and their parents were generous toward this interesting little girl. After a while, however, her behavior became more annoying than interesting. Krystal began receiving embarrassing phone calls: "Amy appears to have gone home with our daughter's shirt, her sneakers, and her doll." She didn't steal; she borrowed or begged these items. She couldn't seem to leave anyone's home without something. Often the item was on loan, but Amy seldom returned these things to their rightful owners.

Amy's childhood was otherwise remarkably normal and active, with tennis, soccer, prom, and boyfriends. The charming and attractive child grew into a strikingly beautiful young woman. "She could be Miss America," said Krystal. "Her features are perfect. Her teeth are perfect. Her dimples are perfect. Her hair is perfect." No matter how she dressed, she caught the eye of every person in the room.

But her "collecting" habits belied her personal charm. When something left the public domain and entered Amy's bedroom, it became hers. A family DVD in the den was hers as soon as it crossed her threshold. When a friend asked her to return a sweater, Amy felt insulted. "How dare they? They're accusing me of stealing!"

"But, hon, you've had it for seven months. It looks like stealing," Krystal would reason.

"I'm a nice person. I don't steal things!"

When she was in her sophomore year, a friend's mother called Krystal and demanded that Amy return an expensive camera she had borrowed. Amy was livid. She couldn't understand how the woman would have the nerve to call Krystal. In fact, Krystal found four digital cameras in her room, only one of which belonged to Amy. She knew to expect more angry phone calls.

Family members' personal stuff migrated to Amy's room as well: clothes, jewelry, hair clips, and more. Sometimes she talked family members out of them, and sometimes she just took them. Mostly they were small items, but sometimes she took expensive things, such as her father's binoculars. Krystal recalled a time when they had just taken in a new foster child, a young girl who had been neglected and came with only the clothes she was wearing. Within a few hours, Amy was wearing the child's sweatshirt. "But it's a cool shirt, and she didn't mind," Amy explained. Never had Krystal been so angry with her. "How could she take the only shirt off this child's back?"

Retrieving things from Amy's room required a confrontation. Typically, Amy ended up angry and hurt, and the fight became about the insult to her rather than the missing item. When Krystal suspected that Amy had added her tape recorder to the treasure trove in Amy's room, she avoided trying to get it back because she didn't want to spark an argument.

Discussions with Amy about taking things frustrated Krystal. "Amy, if it doesn't belong to you, and you don't have permission, it's stealing. That's the long and short of it."

"But it's not stealing if it's your family," Amy would insist.

Confrontations about the number of things she acquired were equally frustrating. "Just how many pairs of nail clippers do you need?"

"Well, I don't know, but I can never find them."

Amy just didn't have the same understanding of ownership that most people did. Krystal described Amy's philosophy to me this way: "If she ever owned it, it's hers; if she wished she owned it, it's hers; if in the future she might own it, it's hers; if it belongs to anyone she loves and who loves her, it's hers."

Amy's recognition of her hoarding fluctuated. If she was in a good place, she could acknowledge that her life was more difficult because of the hoarding. But if she was in a bad place, she would say, "It's nobody's business but my own." At those times, even the criticism of friends and the anger of family members didn't have an impact.

Amy shared a room with her biological sister. Both girls suffered from OCD but couldn't have been more different in their symptoms: her sister had symmetry obsessions and ordering compulsions, while Amy feared contamination and germs. Krystal knew that Amy didn't like to be dirty, but she didn't realize it was a problem until Amy was about fourteen. On a trip to the mall, Amy stopped at the door. With a baby in her arms, Krystal couldn't open it and motioned for Amy to do so. Amy said, "I gotta wait until someone else goes in."

"Why?" Krystal asked.

"I'm wearing short sleeves!"

"And?"

"I can't touch the doorknob!"

Krystal realized then that she had never seen Amy touch a door-knob in the nine years she'd known her. Although Amy managed this problem better as she got older, she still wore long sleeves to the mall so that she could pull them down and not have to touch the door.

Amy's side of her bedroom was a sea of stuff, chaotic and dis-organized. In contrast, her sister's side was picture perfect and clutter-free. She spent a great deal of time lining things up just so. Like Debra (see chapter 5) and Alvin and Jerry, she knew the instant she entered the room whether any of her things had been touched or moved. If she found that a hairbrush on her dresser had been moved even a little, she exploded. Amy didn't want anyone to touch her things either, but she left her stuff in such disarray that she wouldn't have noticed. The line down the middle of their room made the space look like a before-and-after shot. The sisters strug-gled constantly with these conflicting demons.

Although every possession seemed important to Amy, she drew some distinctions between her things. Krystal thought there were some things that mattered to her more than others, and although she couldn't part with any of them, she took better care of the ones that mattered. For instance, cluttering Krystal's house were boxes of notes from Amy's friends — "every note every friend ever wrote her in the history of the world" — each folded carefully into a tiny triangle. Amy's clothes, however, didn't matter to her. She couldn't get rid of them or give them away, but she usually ignored them, leaving them scattered about the room. Krystal doubted whether she would notice if any of them went missing.

Amy also saved mementos from every place she'd ever been. Krystal pointed out that she saved pictures that were out of focus or showed the back of some unknown person's head. When Krystal suggested that Amy try to get rid of them, Amy reacted strongly. "You know I loved that concert. How can you suggest getting rid of these pictures?" Just as we've seen in many adult hoarders, Amy's things seemed to be parts of her personal history and identity that she had to keep close. Krystal found it ironic that Amy fiercely guarded her third-grade spelling tests and blurry photos but had lost the "Life Book" Krystal had made for her. The "Life Book" contained all the information Krystal could find about Amy's biological family and her early history. It even contained her adoption decree. Krystal lamented, "She keeps stuff that isn't important, but the stuff that genuinely matters, she doesn't have."

These behaviors plagued the family even after Amy moved out. A few days before our interview, another of Krystal's foster daughters asked when Amy was coming for a visit. When Krystal said "tonight," the young woman spent the next few hours working in her room and came back to report. "I think everything is okay. I packed the things I really care about away in the back of the closet, and I put them behind all those boxes of books. And I hid all my hair stuff and jewelry."

Amy had another characteristic we often see in adult hoarders: the "just in case" syndrome. Wherever she went, she carried an enormous amount of stuff with her. Krystal noticed that compared to her classmates, Amy always had a bigger, fuller backpack or duffel bag. Our studies have indicated that people with hoarding problems believe that they need all the stuff they carry in order to be prepared for any sort of emergency. One of our clients always carried two shopping bags full of things other people might need—a comb, Band-Aids, a sweater, even extra shoes. She felt obliged to have these things on her person, or she would feel guilty and inadequate.

Chaos and disorganization typify hoarders. Many could probably function quite well if they could simply keep their stuff organized. As mentioned in chapter 10, our research has shown high levels of attention deficit problems characteristic of ADHD among adult hoarders. Although Amy was never diagnosed with ADHD, Krystal wondered in retrospect whether her behavior fit the syndrome. She was always losing things, and her room was pure chaos. Her difficulty focusing at school also seemed to fit. At twenty-two, she remained as disorganized as ever. Krystal recalled the last time Amy had come home for a visit. No one had been able to reach her for three weeks. Amy said she had lost her phone charger for a few days, and before that she couldn't find her cell phone, so she had missed all her calls. When Amy finished her explanation, Krystal handed Amy her driver's license.

"Where'd you get that?" Amy asked.

"Somebody mailed it to us. Why did they find it at Fenway Park? Give me a reason that your driver's license was at Fenway Park!" Krystal insisted.

"Oh, man, I took it out. Now I remember. I took it out, and I guess I didn't put it back."

It was her fifth driver's license. "ATM cards we can't even count," Krystal said. As Amy was leaving, Krystal asked her, "Amy, you forget something?"

"Oh, yeah, yeah, yeah, the other backpack."

"Anything else?"

"No, I don't think so."

"Your cell phone?"

"Oh, where is it?"

"You're charging it. It's over there."

When Krystal finished telling me the story, she let out an exasperated sigh. "If it wasn't so tragic, it would be funny."

Out of college and working, Amy now shared an apartment with several friends. It was not exactly neat and tidy, but it wasn't as bad as her room at home. Amy believed that smoking marijuana helped both her OCD and her hoarding. Krystal didn't like to hear about Amy's drug use, and she thought it was particularly ironic since Amy refused to try any psychiatric drugs to treat her symptoms. But Krystal had noticed a difference in Amy's hoarding and the chaos surrounding her since she'd started smoking pot. (Although there is no evidence suggesting that marijuana helps hoarders, several testimonials to this effect can be found on the Internet.)

I was in awe of Krystal's insight into Amy's problems and of the fact that she did not display any disappointment or regret about them. In our study of family members of hoarders, most expressed a striking level of frustration, disappointment, and hostility. Not so with Krystal. She described Amy as "my charming, beautiful, and sweet daughter." Amy's ability to learn how to live successfully despite her hoarding was undoubtedly due in large part to her remarkable adoptive mother.

Eric

Eric, a smallish twelve-year-old with thick glasses and an anxious smile, began having trouble with objects just before the third grade, when he was eight. At that time, he started to save the boxes things came in. Since then, it had been a constant struggle. He came from a family with a history of hoarding on both sides. His paternal grandmother filled her home and her car, making it impossible for anyone to ride with her. His maternal grandmother saved virtually everything and even hid money and savings bonds in the pages of old magazines stacked in her home. Eric's mother described her as "a world-class hoarder."

Eric hoarded three types of things, each for different reasons: Lego-related products, school papers, and mementos of special events. Playing with Legos was Eric's favorite activity. He spent hours by himself building or planning construction. He kept not only his creations but also the boxes, instructions, and packing material the Legos came in. Eric was proud of his elaborate structures, and his parents believed that creating them gave him a sense of competence in a world in which everything else was a struggle. For this reason, they were reluctant to push him to dismantle or get rid of his creations. Eric was intelligent, but he had to work extremely hard to compensate for a learning disability and a lazy eye that made reading difficult. His intense perfectionism and desire not to be seen as different made school tough for him.

Eric's Legos lined the perimeter of the family room. No one was allowed to touch or move them. Whenever they impinged on the center of the room, however, Eric's parents insisted on a cleanup. These were major events for Eric, who needed weeks to prepare for them. He insisted on doing all the moving and cleaning himself because he couldn't tolerate anyone else touching his things. Still, the cleanings were accompanied by major meltdowns. These were not temporary emotional outbursts that subsided quickly. Rather, they began with crying and screaming and then escalated, sometimes lasting for hours. "He will really let everyone know he's having a rough time," said his father. The episodes exhausted Eric, as well as the rest of the family.

Once, when Eric was younger, a few neighborhood girls came over to play, and one of Eric's Lego constructions got knocked over, perhaps by the girls or perhaps by Eric's cat. Eric erupted and physically attacked one of the girls; his father had to restrain him. After that, no children came to the house to play with Eric. When his brother's friends visited, his parents sent Eric to his grandmother's house, where he would fret about the safety of his things.

In the summer before the fourth grade, Eric developed some odd rituals. He began touching things in a peculiar way. If he thought he hadn't done it correctly, he would do it again, until it felt right. He gave no reason — just that it felt like the right thing to do. A short time later, at the fourth-grade Halloween party, one of his classmates got sick and vomited in the classroom. Eric became convinced that germs from the vomit had contaminated the school and anything associated with that day. He no longer enjoyed Halloween, and for a long time he refused to wear anything blue, the color of the shirt the boy who vomited was wearing.

Most problematic for Eric was that anything he brought home from school was contaminated with "school germs" and had to be kept separate from his treasured Legos. The Legos were kept in the family room because Eric's room, and much of the rest of the house, was contaminated with "school germs." School papers piled up in the kitchen and his bedroom. He couldn't throw them out because handling school germs at home was too upsetting. This saving behavior was less about hoarding than about a fear of contamination, an OCD symptom. As soon as Eric got home from school, he went to his room to take off his contaminated school clothes. When something got contaminated by accident, he washed it thoroughly. His father remembered an episode in which he washed a letter in the sink until it disintegrated. His germ fears and washing rituals were more serious problems than his hoarding and had a much worse effect on his life and that of his family.

Eric hoarded an odd assortment of things other than Legos. In the corner of the room in which his parents and I talked was a collection of things from his birthday party a month earlier — several balloons, a bathrobe, and a few other items. They had stayed there, untouched, since the party. The night before the party was tough for Eric. He worried that the people coming—only family members since he had few friends—would touch or move his Legos. But the day was a good one, and his party was a lot of fun. He got many presents, including the bathrobe, a book about rocks and minerals, a pair of jeans, and a shirt. Eric loved the presents but had no intention of ever using them. These things were now associated with his special day. It was as though they contained all the memories and feelings of that day. He was afraid that if he wore the bathrobe on an ordinary day, it would become ordinary, and its connection to the special day would be lost.

Eric's "special event hoarding," as his mother called it, reflected almost the same reasoning process as his contamination fears and exemplified the contagion effect we described in chapter 2. Just as any object associated, even remotely or symbolically, with the vomiting episode had "school germs," the bathrobe and clothes he received for his birthday were infused with good feelings and memories. Interestingly, though, these things could not spread the good memories. Instead, if these items were used on an ordinary day, they would lose their specialness and become ordinary. Eric's father convinced him to wear the jeans and shirt on Easter, but only because it, too, was a special day. His dad could not convince him to wear them to school, nor could he convince Eric to wear his bathrobe at all. Similarly, Eric became distraught when the dishwasher had to be replaced. The dishwasher, he said, reminded him of that special feeling he had on summer mornings in the kitchen with his mother. He begged his parents to let him keep some metal pieces from the dishwasher. They agreed, not knowing that he had secretly hidden several other pieces of the dishwasher in the yard. When his father discovered and discarded them, Eric had a meltdown.

Like many hoarders, Eric was easily distracted and had difficulty keeping his attention on anything but his Legos. Most likely he would have qualified for a diagnosis of ADHD. His mother described him this way: "He gets very distracted from one thing to the next. I'll ask him to brush his teeth, and he'll go from here, maybe five feet, pet the cat, another five feet, turn around, come back in, straighten out his Legos—you get the picture. Even if we're on our way to Toys "R" Us to buy a new Lego set, it's the same thing. My mother was like that." It seemed that Eric's foibles had been handed down from family members, although they may have skipped a generation. Last we heard, Eric's contamination OCD had improved with medication, and his hoarding was under control due to firm limit setting by his parents.

James

A friend of mine who tutors autistic children called me one day about a sibling of one of her clients. James was a beautiful child— bright, fun, inquisitive, and a wonderful conversationalist. But beginning at age two, he craved clutter. According to his mother, he only seemed happy when surrounded by things, *his* things. James was six when I interviewed his mother, and the family, especially his mother, had struggled with his addiction to things. He wouldn't allow his parents to throw out so much as a candy wrapper. Like many young hoarders, James had a host of other problems. He had worn thick glasses since he was just sixteen months old. He also had ADHD and what his evaluation team called "sensory issues" (perhaps a mild form of autism), which made school and getting along with other kids difficult.

James's room was cluttered but didn't look all that different from the room of a normal, if somewhat messy, child. Toys and stuffed animals were scattered about. James's hoarding problem, like Eric's, was not about how much he accumulated, but about his relationship with the things he owned. Chief among his troubles was his need to completely control his things. James's mother said that if anything was moved or touched, James would know and be upset. "Upset" was putting it mildly. His mother used the words "mournful" and "grief-like" to describe his reactions; it seemed to her that he felt physical pain. He complained to her once about it, saying, "Mom, my whole body hurts." What seemed to worry him most was that he wouldn't know where his toys were if other people had touched them. Not knowing was intolerable.

On a broader level, this discomfort applied to any kind of change in his environment or routine. James followed a set routine every day and got upset whenever it changed. Transitions between activities had always been a problem. Perhaps his things were comforting because they didn't change.

James had always been perfectionistic. He couldn't stand not doing things right the first time. His mother tried to get him involved in team sports, but his first episode on the basketball court was a disaster. When he missed a shot, he collapsed onto the court in tears at his failure. His mother had to carry him off. He also tried karate, but when he couldn't master one move on the first try, he quit in frustration. Even small failures were more than he could handle.

James's mother thought that some of his problems were associated with his failure to comprehend time. When he wanted something, he couldn't tolerate waiting. He couldn't even bear to wait the ten seconds it took the computer to boot up. His mother had to give him a toy to distract him until the computer was ready. "He's the most 'I can't wait' person in the world," his mother said. He also had a hard time with the idea of forever. Things seemed to fall into two categories for James: things that would be gone shortly and things that would last forever. Things that would be gone shortly included mostly trash and routine garbage. Things that would stick around longer he incorporated into his own sense of permanence.

When someone moved his things, his mother couldn't console him, nor could he console himself. Although she reported that he was a little better now than he had been a year earlier, a minor infringement on the sanctity of his things could still cost James a whole day. His mother kept bags full of broken toys, fearful of his reaction to her discarding them. He seemed somewhat comforted by his stuffed animals, so she often sent two or three of them with him to school in case he had an episode. This caused some trouble at school, however. The teachers complained that he was distracted by the things he brought, so they eventually limited what he could bring to school. Otherwise, James would cram his backpack with toys he couldn't bear to be away from—more of the "just in case" phenomena we've seen in adults.

According to his mother, James bonded with things, especially things in his collections. His favorite collections were his stuffed animals and his Star Wars objects. But he also bonded with anything he could incorporate into his imaginary play. Once a thing was included in his fantasy world, it was hard for him to let it go. From his mother's perspective, these things seemed as important to him as human beings. He talked to them as if they were alive and often assigned them human qualities. Once he picked up one of his Star Wars soldiers and told his mother, "He has a sense of humor." On another occasion, he said of a stuffed animal, "He feels sad." Although this degree of personification is not all that unusual in children, James extended it to a surprising range of objects. One day he started to cry when he spilled his fruit drink on the driveway because he thought it was getting burned on the hot pavement. At one point, he stopped eating for a time because he thought eating would hurt the food's feelings. He couldn't articulate much more than the distress he felt, but his mother observed that these things seemed to have become like parts of his body: they felt pain, and he empathized. We've seen this in other child hoarding cases and also in adults. For example, one young girl believed that her toys would die or feel betrayed if given away or discarded. Another child described his toys as having personalities and opinions. One middle-aged woman feared that the dishes on the lower level of the dishwasher would feel upset because they weren't on top.

James bonded not only with things he owned but also with things he touched. Once when a friend lent him a toy light saber, his mother had to buy the friend a new one because James wouldn't part with the one he'd been loaned.

Even taking James to the grocery store was an ordeal. One day he touched a robot he wanted for his collection and became inconsolable for the rest of the day when his mother refused to buy it. He went through a grieving process even though he had never owned the item.

As in other cases we've seen, there was a history of hoarding in James's family. His paternal grandmother hoarded things for most of her life. Now, at age eighty, she was unabashed about it. James's mother said, "She's the curmudgeonliest person I've ever met." She had strong opinions about everything and wasn't shy about expressing them. Brought up in the Depression, she attributed her saving to frugality and considered it a virtue. She had canned foods from the 1940s and multiple freezers full of food in her basement. Her house was cluttered with newspapers, magazines, and whatever else she could collect. Small pathways cut through the clutter. Several years ago, she added on a room to accommodate all her stuff, but it quickly filled up, and her house was worse than ever. The family had recognized her eccentricity for years and often joked about it, but now they were worried. Even though the conditions in her home bordered on dangerous, no one dared bring up the topic with her.

James's extreme attachment to his things, his family history of hoarding, and his perfectionism fit a pattern repeated again and again among children who hoard. Like Eric and Amy, he felt intensely emotional about objects and sought to control his environment with an unusual ferocity. More recently, his mother began to notice a shift in James. He had an easier time managing his emotions and tolerating other people having control over his things.

Julian

At the age of seven, Julian broke his arm while on a hike with some friends. His ordeal involved trips to several emergency rooms over a thirty-six-hour period, and the bones had to be reset multiple times. Through it all, Julian never cried. His father marveled at that. But shortly thereafter, the hoarding started.

His parents first noticed an odd reaction from Julian about some of his Valentine's Day candy. He refused to eat or even unwrap the special red Hershey's Kisses. He asked, "What if they don't come out with [them] again?" Before long, his concerns spread to virtually everything he touched: papers from school, empty milk cartons, napkins, paper plates, paper towels from the bathroom at school, and even empty potato chip bags. When his parents insisted that he throw some of these things away, he began to hide them under his dresser or in his pockets. His teacher noticed this problem as well. After completing a project that produced scraps of paper to be discarded, he would walk up to the trash can and have a hard time throwing his scraps away. On a bad day, Julian could not even part with lint he found on his clothes.

When his parents tried to talk to him about it, he came unglued. The stoic young man who did not cry when his arm was shattered dissolved into a flood of tears when faced with the prospect of parting with the paper towels stuffed in his pants pockets. Before the accident, his mother had noticed some reluctance to get rid of things. It wasn't so much that stuff collected in his room, she said, but that he hesitated before throwing things away. "Broken toys were always an issue," she said. Still, it was no cause for alarm. This new reaction, however, caused them enough concern that they contacted a psychologist for help.

The psychologist asked Julian to draw a picture on a piece of paper. When he finished, the therapist asked him how hard it would be to throw it away. Julian's eyes filled with tears before he answered. He rated the difficulty as 7 on a scale of 1 to 10. The doctor asked him how hard it would be to throw away a blank piece of paper. Julian rated that as 4. Most things the therapist could think of gave him some trouble, the lone exception being used toilet paper.

Julian could offer little in the way of an explanation for his behavior. Initially, he told the psychologist, "I don't know why I have to save things. I just can't throw them away." To his parents, who were good at getting him to talk, he described "that sadness feeling" when he had to throw something out or when he recalled something he had thrown out. At night the feeling kept him awake. "I worry about stuff I might have forgotten about, stuff I didn't save and I think I might need to use. I try to close my eyes and not think about it. I try to think about country music."

Julian's father thought that his son's major worry was waste. Julian seemed obsessed with making sure nothing he handled got wasted, even things such as used napkins. He took personal responsibility for all the materials he used, as well as those his family used. Julian often asked about saving napkins and paper plates after meals. His concern also extended to food. He insisted on finishing the food on his plate, and if other family members didn't finish theirs, he had to eat it, too. In contrast to the other child hoarders we have seen, he had no trouble sharing his toys with others or even giving away or selling old ones. In his mind, they were not being wasted but going to someone who would use them.

Talking with the psychologist seemed to help Julian. His father observed that it didn't make the problem go away, but Julian did accept getting rid of things more easily. After the first session, he asked his parents to throw things away for him when it was just too hard for him to do so.

By the second session with the psychologist, Julian was able to throw some things away himself. But at the end of the session, he told the psychologist he was sad about the things he had discarded. After a few more sessions, things quieted down for Julian, and it looked like the problem was abating. The cast came off his arm, and Julian resumed the more active life he was accustomed to. The hoarding faded into the background, and he was able to throw things away in a normal fashion. His father noticed, however, that he sometimes put things that he knew needed to be discarded, such as empty potato chip bags, on the edge of the trash can rather than inside it. When asked about this, Julian admitted that he didn't want to get rid of them completely.

About six months later, Julian's parents called the psychologist again. Julian had told them that he was having "that sadness feeling" again when throwing things away. His biggest worry was that he would start to cry in math class about the things he had to throw away. Julian had just been moved up to an advanced math class where speedy problem solving, something that had always caused him trouble, was emphasized. Fear that he might fail at this new challenge seemed to have triggered the latest episode of hoarding. After a few weeks in the class, when it was clear to him that he could handle the work, his worries disappeared, and so did "that sadness feeling." The hoarding faded again, though he occasionally asked his parents if they could wash and save their used paper plates and napkins. In contrast to his earlier state, however, he accepted their insistence that the items be thrown away. His father thought it ironic that the day before our interview, Julian was given the class citizenship award for insisting that everyone in the class, including his teacher, recycle water bottles instead of discarding them.

Julian had always been an anxious child with a "nervous stomach," afraid to take risks. His parents had also seen signs of indecisiveness, particularly when it came to spending money. He struggled with what to order at a restaurant or what to buy if he had some money. He showed some attention problems in the first grade and sometimes had to stay in at recess to finish the work he couldn't complete during class. His father described his style as deliberate, like his grandfather's. He wanted things done just right and was careful and meticulous in his work. Despite this tendency, Julian didn't seem perfectionistic in other ways. The only OCD-like rituals Julian displayed were his rigid rules for saying goodbye to his parents. He showered them with multiple hugs and kisses before he felt comfortable parting. If his father did not wave to him at the window, Julian would complain to him later in the day.

In contrast to the other child hoarding cases we've seen, Julian had no family history of OCD or hoarding. His problems with saving seemed closely tied to his general fearfulness and to traumatic events. Small, irrational concerns or habits can spin out of control when people are very fearful. Although Julian's hoarding had ceased to be a problem, his father was cautious: "My intuition . . . is that we're not done with this."

From Childhood Collections
to Compulsive Hoarding

The diversity of hoarding behaviors in these children mirrors what we see in adult hoarders. Worries about waste drive some child hoarders. For others, their identities fuse with possessions so that getting rid of something feels like losing a piece of themselves. Most experience an intense need to maintain control over their possessions, and they become extraordinarily upset, even aggressive, when their control is challenged. Most of the parents we interviewed found that getting their children to understand the difficulties their behavior created was a real challenge as well.

Hoarding in children may be more closely related to OCD obsessions and rituals than it is in adults. Two of the cases discussed in this chapter had significant OCD symptoms in addition to hoarding. What little research exists on this topic suggests that up to half of children with OCD hoard. Among adults, somewhere between 25 and 33 percent of OCD patients have hoarding problems. Dr. Eric Storch and his colleagues at the University of Florida found that certain kinds of OCD symptoms, including magical thinking and ordering and arranging compulsions, occur in hoarding children, though not in any of the children described here. This reflects some research on adult hoarders showing an association with symmetry obsessions and ordering and arranging compulsions, like those of Debra in chapter 5.

Outside the OCD sphere, some genetic disorders are associated with hoarding. Hoarding occurs in more than 50 percent of children with Prader-Willi syndrome, a genetic condition associated with the absence of paternal contribution to chromosome 15. Prader-Willi patients typically suffer from mild mental retardation and problems with satiety, resulting in obesity. A high frequency of hoarding in children with autism spectrum disorders has also been reported. Among the cases we reviewed here, only James may have had a mild form of autism. Whether the causes of hoarding are the same for children with developmental disabilities as for those without such problems remains to be seen. Foster care workers have long been aware of hoarding in the children they serve, but no studies have been done to document hoarding among foster children.

The University of Florida study found that hoarding kids also experienced more anxiety and somatic problems and displayed more aggressive behavior than non-hoarders. All of these themes were present to some degree in the four children described here. Whenever anyone touched or moved their possessions, or even threatened to do so, they responded with intense emotion that included fear, anger, sadness, frustration, and guilt. Interestingly, these are the same emotions we see in adults with hoarding problems. James, Eric, and Julian were all anxious, easily frustrated boys who had great difficulty recovering from emotional upset. Eric also displayed aggressive behavior. Storch and his colleagues think that children's lack of insight into their problems might explain their aggressive behavior. The hoarding kids in the Storch study had a harder time seeing their symptoms as problems than did the kids with other OCD symptoms. If they didn't believe their hoarding was a problem, their parents' attempts to prevent their acquiring and to make them throw things away were more likely to be met with anger, resentment, and aggression.

For all four children profiled here, hoarding was one problem among many, and usually not the most serious one. But it was one the parents could control with some clear rules and careful planning. Perhaps parents' ability to control this problem explains why so few clinicians have seen hoarding in children. When kids are brought to therapists for help, it is usually for other problems, such as OCD, ADHD, or Asperger's syndrome. Hoarding is often not mentioned at all. In addition, mental health clinics do not ask questions about clutter and saving possessions as part of their routine diagnostic interviews.

Julian's hoarding was episodic and seemed to occur mostly when he was upset about something—such as his broken arm or his new math class. For most adults, however, hoarding is chronic and unremitting. In our study of the course of hoarding, for instance, less than 1 percent of the cases reported that the hoarding became less severe over time. Other OCD symptoms, such as compulsive cleaning or checking, fluctuate over time, but hoarding remains stable. Among children, the situation may be different. Some parents, especially those whose children had other OCD symptoms, have reported to us that their children had clear starting and stopping points for their hoarding. Perhaps by adulthood, hoarding that began as a reaction to stressors solidifies into a chronic habitual response.

The strong emotional reactions by child hoarders to any interference with their possessions can wreak havoc at home. To preserve the emotional climate, parents often accommodate hoarding by allowing unusual collecting and saving. Similar family problems arise when parents hoard and the rest of the family must accommodate them, as we saw in chapter 11.

It seems that a number of children develop fears and rituals when they are young, only to outgrow them during their adolescence or early adulthood. Whether this is also true for hoarding, we simply don't know. We do suspect that when behavioral patterns are rigid, to the point of perfectionism and extreme avoidance of distress, a knowledgeable mental health professional can help parents mitigate the strong reactions.

13

HAVING, BEING, AND HOARDING

> Without these things, I am nothing.
>
> —A hoarding client

Although there are a few societies in which notions of owner-ship are absent or downplayed, in most cultures the interaction be-tween people and their things is a central aspect of life. As noted in chapter 2, we see cases of hoarding throughout the world, and references to it can be found as far back as the fourteenth century. But never has hoarding been so visible as it is today in westernized societies. Perhaps the abundance of inexpensive and easily acces-sible objects makes it the disorder of the decade. At the end of the 1990s, PBS aired a one-hour program called *Affluenza*. The pro-gram documented an American culture of materialism and over-consumption and defined "affluenza" as a contagious social afflic-tion in which possessions take over our lives and drain us of the very things we seek by acquiring them.

As has been apparent to us from studying hoarding, we may own the things in our homes, but they own us as well. Objects carry the burden of responsibilities that include acquisition, use, care, storage, and disposal. The magnitude of these responsibili-ties for each of us has exploded with the expanding number of items in our homes during the past fifty years. Having all these possessions has caused a shift in our behavior away from human interaction to interaction with inanimate objects. Kids now spend more time online, playing video games, or watching TV alone in their rooms than interacting with family or friends. Possessions originally sold on the promise that they would make life easier and increase leisure time have done just the opposite. Often both parents work longer hours to support an ever-increasing array of new conveniences that lead them to spend less and less time together.

This is partly a function of the commercialization of our culture. Never has there been so much stuff for people to own and so many ways of peddling it to consumers. As pointed out by John De Graaf, David Wann, and Thomas H. Naylor in their book *Affluenza: The All-Consuming Epidemic,* which followed the PBS show, there are twice as many shopping centers in the United States as there are high schools. A great deal of effort and money is invested in finding out just how to present objects to create a desire for them. More than a hundred professional journals are devoted to the science of marketing and selling consumer goods.

The success of this marketing has been remarkable. Increasing numbers of rental self-storage units cater to an apparently insatiable appetite for stuff. Forty years ago, facilities for storing unused personal possessions were virtually nonexistent. Now nearly two billion square feet of space can be rented for storage in more than forty-five thousand facilities, and most of that space is already full! In March 2007, the *New York Times* reported that self-storage unit rentals had increased by 90 percent since 1995 and more than eleven million American households rented outside storage space. According to the *Times,* the number of multiunit and long-term storage renters was increasing steadily. These were not people who had just moved and needed temporary storage. They were people who were simply unwilling to part with the beloved treasures that they "might use one day" and that their own homes could no longer accommodate. Alongside this growing appetite for rented storage space, the average house size had increased by 60 percent since 1970—although this trend may be changing since the real estate crash of 2008. Many of these oversize homes, often referred to as "McMansions," also come with their own storage sheds. Perhaps we are becoming a nation of hoarders.

A generation earlier, in 1947, the psychoanalyst and humanistic philosopher Erich Fromm forecast a society obsessed with possessions. He argued that humans can be characterized by one of two basic orientations toward the world, "having" or "being." These orientations determine in large part how people think, feel, and act. A person with a "having" orientation seeks to acquire and possess property and even people. Ownership is key to the person's sense of self and meaning in the world. According to Fromm, a culture driven by commercialism is doomed to foster the "having" orientation and result in hollowness and dissatisfaction. In contrast, a person with a "being" orientation is focused on experience rather than possession, and he or she derives meaning from sharing and engaging with other people.

Modern-day social scientists describe the "having" orientation as "materialism" and have made it the subject of considerable research. Much of what Fromm predicted has been borne out by this research. Possessions play a central role in the lives of materialists. They are a means to self-enhancement, identity, and social standing, and the driving force in daily activities. Materialists expect possessions not only to enhance their sense of self but also to make them happy. Ironically, possessions seem to do the opposite. Many studies have documented the fact that highly materialistic people are less satisfied with their lives and less happy than people without such an orientation toward "having." It's not clear from this research, however, whether materialism leads to reduced satisfaction and happiness or whether people who are unhappy pursue materialistic goals.

The recently developed field of positive psychology, which is devoted to the study of personal virtues, is concerned with questions such as "What makes people happy?" Not surprisingly, positive psychology has turned its attention to the role and meaning of possessions. Surveys asking what types of purchases make people happier than others have found that purchases associated with an event or experience, such as going out to dinner or taking a trip, create more happiness than those associated with acquiring an object. Other studies asking people to describe their reactions to their most recent purchases have shown the same thing. Also, when asked to think about recent purchases, people usually report that they are happier when thinking about experiences than about objects.

Leaf Van Boven, a positive psychologist from the University of Colorado, says that there are three reasons why experiential purchases create more happiness than material ones. First, material purchases are not subject to recall and reliving in the same way as experiential ones, except perhaps among the avid collectors described in chapter 2. Recalling a vacation with the family creates a better feeling than recalling the purchase of dining room furniture. And with each retelling of vacation stories, the feeling gets better. Second, the appeal of material purchases fades as comparisons are made with similar purchases by neighbors and friends, but the effect of experiential purchases is not dimmed by social comparison. Finally, material purchases are often solitary actions, whereas experiential purchases tend to be inherently social events that more often engender lasting positive moods. Van Boven and a colleague took this idea a step further by asking people who didn't know each other to discuss a recent material or experiential purchase that made them happy. Following these conversations, participants rated people who discussed experiential purchases more favorably and as more likely to be someone with whom they would like to pursue a friendship. It seems that experiences carry more social potential than things, and "being" versus "having" brings people closer to happiness.

These findings suggest that our expectations for the happiness potential of owning objects has come not from our own experience but from clever marketing strategies emphasizing the "having" orientation. Scientifically developed ways of selling stuff largely emphasize utility, security, and identity motives. Interestingly, these are also among the most frequent rationalizations for excessive acquiring among people with hoarding problems: "I can use it," "It will give me comfort," and "It's part of me." Perhaps hoarders are the casualties of marketing—acquisition addicts who can't resist a sales pitch, like the compulsive gambler who can't pass up a lottery ticket or the alcoholic who is drawn irresistibly to the neon sign of a tavern.

But our research with hoarders indicates that although materialism is a part of the hoarding syndrome, there is a fundamental difference between people who are simply materialistic and those who suffer from hoarding. For materialistic people, possessions are outward signs of success and affluence. They are part of a persona designed for public display. Showing off one's material wealth communicates success and status to one's neighbors and is a major feature of materialism. In contrast, the typical hoarder will go to great lengths to hide his or her possessions from view. The hoarder's motivation for saving things is to create not a public identity but a private one. Objects become part of who the hoarder is, not the façade he or she displays to the world. As one of our clients put it, "Without these things, I am nothing." This quote is similar to Fromm's comment on "having": "If I am what I have and if what I have is lost, who then am I?"

Affluenza—both the PBS show and the book—hit a nerve in American culture and prompted efforts to counteract this trend.

The voluntary simplicity movement was born out of the concern that lives full of consumption were losing their meaning. The movement promotes a lifestyle minimizing consumption and emphasizing the enjoyment of life without a large number of possessions. It is consistent with the growing environmental movement to reduce each person's carbon footprint, or impact on the planet. Materialism produces a large footprint and fosters the tendency to replace perfectly good items with brand-new ones. Much of the stuff we collect is readily thrown away and replaced when a new model comes out or styles change. Many barely used items end up in landfills across the country. Based on the rate at which we are acquiring and disposing of possessions, the earth's natural resources will be exhausted within a few generations. Voluntary simplicity and green living are natural outgrowths of such dire predictions.

Ironically, many people who hoard do so partly in response to these concerns. Recall Langley Collyer telling his lawyer that he and his brother were simplifying their lives by living the way they did (see the prologue). Consider Ralph, who saw utility in worn-out things, and Anita, who was racked by guilt over the slightest waste (see chapter 7). Many hoarders see special value in society's unwanted trash and consider themselves custodians — even protectors — of things no one else wants. They are de facto archivists of objects others have left behind, inverted versions of materialists who crave the new. In our culture of collecting, hoarders hold a unique if unenviable place, wherein impairments of the mind and heart meet the foibles of the wider culture. As one non-hoarder once joked, "Every community needs a hoarder. Without them, trash would be everywhere. At least they gather it up in one place." Embedded in this comment is an irony that highlights the plight of both hoarders and our society.

Hoarding might be a behavior with a social benefit if the collected objects were used and didn't foul living spaces. Unfortunately, simply collecting things others throw out does not save material possessions from the landfill. Because few of these items are ever used, hoarders simply provide temporary way stations until they die and their stuff is hauled off to the dump. But some developments in the reuse/recycling world have improved the lives of people who hoard, at least among those plagued by guilt over wasting things. Many of the hoarding participants in our early studies told us that the advent of recycling in the 1970s allowed them to get rid of substantial volumes of stuff, especially newspapers. Both traditional organizations such as the Salvation Army and newer ones such as the Freecycle Network are great resources for hoarders looking to get their treasures back into circulation. Unfortunately, they are sources of new free stuff as well.

In our attempts to help people who hoard information, we frequently emphasize the fact that most information in print is easily accessible over the Internet. We haven't found this fact to be very helpful in convincing hoarders to change their information-saving habits, however. There is something compelling about having a physical representation of the information that makes it seem more accessible. Many hoarders have also complained to us that their computer hard drives and e-mail accounts are stuffed with files and messages too numerous to sort but too valuable to discard. We suspect that this may be a function of the same information-processing problems that contributed to their hoarding.

We live in a materialistic culture rich with stuff, so why should a passion for collecting be considered pathological? People often come to our talks uncertain whether their collecting habits and the piles in their homes and offices are problems or simply eccentricities. The acquisition and saving of possessions is not inherently problematic. In fact, within our culture, it is normative. However, for the people described in this book, who represent up to 5 percent of the population, these behaviors are out of control and result in serious impairment and distress. This group is the subject of the mental health and neuroscience research on compulsive hoarding that we have described here.

Interest in and attention to hoarding has been heightened in recent years by reality TV shows featuring messy homes. The heroes of these shows are professional organizers who save the day by turning cluttered homes into showplaces worthy of *House & Garden*. Professional organizers market their services to people who can't seem to get organized on their own. The National Association of Professional Organizers (NAPO), which represents this profession, has grown rapidly, from sixteen members when it was founded in 1985 to more than four thousand today. A subgroup of professional organizers, the National Study Group on Chronic Disorganization (NSGCD), specializes in dealing with what it calls the "chronically disorganized," a euphemism for hoarders. Their services are often helpful to people who hoard but insufficient for those with serious problems.

The rapid growth and high profile of professional organizers have led some to question the necessity or wisdom of eliminating disorder in our lives. Eric Abrahamson, a professor of management at Columbia University, and David H. Freedman, a writer and editor, wrote a book called *A Perfect Mess: The Hidden Benefits of Disorder*. In it they argue that messiness and clutter are markers of efficiency and creativity and that spending too much time and effort organizing may not be wise. They describe examples of highly successful people who lack basic organization and planning skills and conclude that messiness should be celebrated rather than treated as a disorder. Our observations lead us to agree with them to a point. For most of us, a certain degree of disorganization is not harmful and can help us be creative and productive. But at the point where severe disorganization begins to impinge on quality of life, the detriments outweigh the benefits and may qualify as a disorder.

Pinpointing the moment that quality of life is impaired enough to consider the behavior a disorder is not always easy to do. To some, an active response to hoarding may seem like a civil liberties violation, in which people's homes are invaded by the "clutter police." But after standing in the living rooms of the people described in this book, we find it hard to agree with that point of view. To illustrate this dilemma, each year the students in my seminar watch segments from the BBC documentary series *A Life of Grime*. The segments feature Edmund Trebus, who emigrated from Poland to England shortly after World War II. Mr. Trebus settled into life in London, where he married, had five children, and began his life as a collector. He started by filling the upper floors of his four-story Victorian home by theme: vacuum cleaners in one room, cameras in another. By the time his children had grown up and moved out, much of the house was full, and he was spending his days collecting whatever could be had for free. His wife held out as long as there was space for her, but eventually she left, and he filled up her space. He never saw his wife or children again. The documentary follows Mr. Trebus's subsequent battles with the local Haringey Council over the rat-infested hoard in his garden. His defiance of the council led to his arrest on several occasions, and the debris in his garden was forcibly removed three separate times. Each time, the crew was met by a defiant Mr. Trebus telling them to "stick it up your chuffer."

The image of the frail, elderly Trebus confronting the burly cleanup crew over his prized but unused and dilapidated possessions highlights the ethical dilemma faced by anyone responsible for the public's health. He comes across as an unlikely, but likable, hero, one oddball against the implacable force of the government. Mr. Trebus has become something of a cult figure in Britain. Since his death in 2002, Web sites have celebrated his life and battles with the Haringey Council. After showing the segments, I divide the class into "pro" and "con" groups to debate the ethics of forcibly cleaning out the property of someone like Mr. Trebus. The debate ranges widely from property rights to civil liberties to community responsibility and liability, and in the end students often end up agreeing with both sides.

Therapy Outcomes

For Irene (see chapter 1) and many others like her, possessions provide pleasure, opportunity, comfort, safety, and a sense of self and personal history that make up an identity. Detaching from her possessions led her to feel wasteful, guilty, and distressed. Possessions provide similar feelings for all of us, but for Irene and other hoarders, the drive to acquire and possess things is stuck in high gear, and changing it is difficult. At a recent research conference, a widely respected colleague confessed that in her therapy outcome studies of OCD, she excludes people with hoarding problems. "They make my therapy look bad," she said. This comment reflects the clinical lore on hoarding—that it is a very difficult condition to treat and that existing treatments don't work.

This professional frustration is one of the factors that led us to develop a treatment program specifically for hoarders, based on what we have learned from our research and clinical experience. In fact, we have had some success in helping people control their acquiring and become more effective at discarding and de-cluttering their homes. In our recently completed therapy outcome study, the clients in our treatment program were significantly improved after only twelve therapy sessions compared to a control group on a waiting list. By the end of twenty-six treatment sessions, more than two-thirds had responded to treatment according to the therapists' judgments, and nearly 80 percent described themselves as much or very much improved.

Despite this success, many were only partly improved and still had cluttered homes. Further, we don't yet know how well such progress can be maintained. Some of our early success stories have struggled to maintain their homes. Irene, for example, who was able to de-clutter almost every room in her house, maintained her new life reasonably well for a number of years. Then two things happened. First, her son went away to school, leaving her alone in the house. (Our research has consistently shown that hoarders who live alone have significantly more trouble maintaining control over their clutter.) Second, Irene got a new job at the library. As she had been many years before, Irene was again in charge of "weeding" the vertical files, which meant that she was responsible for disposing of all the old newspapers and magazines. Many of them came home with her. Though not as formidable as when we first started working with her, the clutter had taken over several rooms when last I spoke with her.

Controlling one's thinking about possessions may take a lifetime of effort for people with serious hoarding problems. Paula Kotakis, who organized the hoarding tour of Berkeley, California (see chapter 4), has kept her home clutter-free for more than five years. In preparation for writing this book, I asked if I could describe her as a "former hoarder." She said no, she doesn't consider herself a former hoarder because she struggles every day with her attachments to possessions. To illustrate her plight, she sent me the following description of her recent experience in throwing away a yogurt container.

> As I tossed it into the bin, the thought crossed my mind: maybe the container would rather be dry inside instead of sitting there for a long time, humid. I resisted "rescuing" it in order to dry it out first. Although it felt very silly to have the thought about the yogurt container, it was not at all easy to resist. I felt anxious about letting the top stay on—I wanted to go back into

the bin and take the top off so as to ease my anxiety about making the yogurt container stay humid (and thus, "uncomfortable"). I also had to resist apologizing to the container, even as I was reminding myself that it was not alive and was simply a plastic container.

And yes, this all feels very crazy to me.

I remember feeling bad about not choosing "this" particular container as one that would remain at home with the others, and so I was feeling responsible for rejecting it and placing it into the recycling bin to begin its long journey to eventual destruction. I felt responsible for giving it as "comfortable" a ride as possible, seeing as how I was rejecting it, and the thought of it having to endure a humid, long journey made me very anxious. This was followed quickly by the thought of how silly this thinking was, and that I needed to resist following through on what I wanted to do to make me feel less anxious.

Paula's anthropomorphizing—ascribing feelings to an inanimate object—is not uncommon among hoarders. Clearly, hoarders can gain control over hoarding impulses, but they may have to exert considerable effort over a long period of time to do so. The next efforts in our research must involve finding ways to improve on and maintain the effects of treatment.

Fix-It-Yourself Books

As for many other human problems, there are many self-help books on the market to help people de-clutter. A quick perusal of Amazon.com produced more than ninety books promising solutions, including *Clutter's Last Stand; How to De-Junk Your Life; Outwitting Clutter; The Clutter-Busting Handbook; Clutter Control: Putting Your Home on a Diet; Help! I'm Knee-Deep in Clutter; The Clutter Cure; The Complete Clutter Solution; Love It or Lose It:*

Living Clutter-Free Forever; Good-bye Clutter; and *Clutter, Chaos and the Cure.* Many of these books were written by professional organizers who have years of experience working with a wide range of people to control their stuff. Certainly, these books are helpful in guiding people to organize their mess and get rid of things they don't and won't use anytime soon. Many provide helpful guidelines for deciding whether or not to hang on to Aunt Maude's wedding gift or clothes that are two sizes too small. The rules are sensible and work well for people who are not inordinately attached to their things. But the powerful attachment and other problems we see among hoarders makes us think that these books will not solve most of their clutter problems.

A few self-help books have been written by mental health professionals, including our own *Buried in Treasures: Help for Compulsive Acquiring, Saving, and Hoarding* and one by Dr. Fugen Neziroglu and her colleagues, *Overcoming Compulsive Hoarding.* These books provide more insight into the entrenched nature of hoarding, as well as strategies to resolve these problems. We are just beginning to test whether these books are effective for changing hoarding behavior. We suspect that some people will benefit, most likely those whose problems are less severe and less entrenched. Unfortunately, many of our patients own bookshelves full of declutter books that simply add to their clutter without fixing the problem.

Fix-It-Yourself Groups

Several self-help groups are available for people with hoarding problems. In 1981, Sandra Felton founded Messies Anonymous, the largest of these efforts. Sandra described herself as a hopeless "messie" until she made a commitment to change the way she lived.

When she regained control over her own home, she expanded her efforts to help others. Now Messies Anonymous groups are active all over the world and have large followings in the United States. Sandra also operates a Web site, which includes an interactive on-line group, a regular newsletter, and access to her writings.

"Mexico" Mike Nelson, a former "clutterer," founded Clutter-less Recovery Groups in 2000 to provide support for people with hoarding problems. Like Sandra, Mike has written several books providing useful tips on how to live a clutter-free life.

Though not associated with any one individual, a third set of groups called Clutterers Anonymous has sprung up in many places in the United States. As of yet, we know nothing about how well any of these groups help people with debilitating hoarding problems.

A more highly focused self-help group is Overcoming Hoarding Together (O-H-T). Paula Kotakis launched the group and has managed it since 1998. About a hundred people belong to the group, with another hundred on the waiting list. Those trying to join must wait more than a year for an opening. Several members who suffer or have suffered from hoarding problems serve as moderators, and the group relies on a few committed psychologists to provide backup support. O-H-T bases its program on our model and treatment methods. Group members have access to educational resources, tips on de-cluttering and organizing, professional referrals, worksheets, cognitive therapy strategies, and a real-time chatroom. Members make a commitment to work on their de-cluttering goals and are required to post their goals, action plans, and progress on the Web site at least once a month. Interaction among the members reduces isolation and loneliness, common problems among people who hoard.

The leaders of O-H-T recently asked us to find out whether membership in the group helped people with hoarding problems.

Dr. Jordana Muroff, one of our colleagues, has begun to study this question. After almost a year of data collection, it seems clear that the group is at least somewhat successful. Group members reported modest reductions in their clutter and acquiring and were able to get rid of their accumulated stuff more easily than people still on the waiting list. Still, the overall reduction in clutter was quite modest.

From our observations, Internet-based self-help for hoarding is a novel method that might be a good way to provide help for hoarders who live in locations without adequately trained treatment providers, or a good first step for those reluctant to seek treatment. We recently began experimenting with in-person facilitated self-help groups with some success. Group members enjoy interacting with one another and seem to derive motivation to work on clutter from the experience. It is too early to tell whether this approach will be truly useful.

Our first efforts at treatment began more than a decade ago, and our methods have evolved over time with the help of what we have learned in the laboratory. Nevertheless, we still have a long way to go. When we started studying hoarding, there were no other research groups working on the problem. Now at least a dozen highly sophisticated research teams from around the world are studying all aspects of this behavior, including the neurobiology, neuropsychology, genetics, comorbidity, and treatment of hoarding. Undoubtedly the next decade will produce many more advances in our understanding of this intriguing human condition.

One of the challenges for this research will be to distinguish what is positive in hoarding from what is pathological. We wonder whether the attention to the details of objects indicates a special form of creativity and an appreciation for the aesthetics of everyday things. In the same vein, empathy with the physical world expands life's horizons and can give meaning by connecting us to the world and one another. More than anything, hoarding represents a paradox of opportunity. Hoarders are gifted with the ability to see the opportunities in so many things. They are equally cursed with the inability to let go of any of these possibilities, thereby ensuring that few of the imagined options can ever be realized. Hoarding seems to be a symptom of both positive and negative capacities among those who are so blessed and afflicted. With luck, researchers will be able to sort out this paradox and to help people take advantage of the opportunities and jettison the costs.

There have been dramatic developments in the public arena as well. More than sixty cities throughout the country have formed task forces to deal with hoarding problems. These task forces are made up of officials from fire, health, housing, elder services, and mental health departments, as well as people with hoarding problems. They encounter the most severe hoarding cases and individuals who often don't recognize the threat posed by their behavior. Many members of these groups are veterans of massive and expensive cleanup operations that failed, such as Susan in chapter 9. One of the longest-running and most successful of these efforts is the San Francisco Task Force on Compulsive Hoarding, run by the city's Mental Health Association. This task force recently released a comprehensive report on hoarding in the city. The report not only estimated the financial cost of hoarding to San Francisco service providers and landlords ($6.4 million per year) but also laid out a set of recommendations for more effectively dealing with hoarding cases. Their report was a joint effort by members of the task force, which included not only agency representatives but hoarders as well. The efforts of the task force also led to the establishment of the Institute on Compulsive Hoarding and Cluttering, the first organization of its kind. It provides public education about hoarding, training for service providers, support and therapy groups for hoarders, and advocacy to prevent homelessness due to hoarding.

It also consults with other agencies and other communities about how to establish hoarding programs. We hope that this will be the wave of the future in dealing with hoarding problems.

Finding Help

If you or a loved one has a hoarding problem, here are steps you can take to get help.

- *Find a therapist with experience treating hoarding problems.* Several professional organizations provide help in locating suitable therapists in your area, including the Obsessive Compulsive Foundation, the Association for Behavioral and Cognitive Therapies, and the Anxiety Disorders Association of America. Therapists who are registered with these organizations list their areas of expertise, including the treatment of hoarding. If you are seeking help for a loved one who refuses help, these therapists can help you find ways of interacting with your loved one that increase the likelihood that he or she will seek help on his or her own.
- *Find a local hoarding task force.* Your community may have developed a hoarding task force. If you or your loved one is in trouble with the health department or other agency due to hoarding issues, a hoarding task force can sometimes help provide resources. These organizations are made up of people who are eager to find compassionate ways of solving hoarding problems, and they are less likely to make the mistake of seeking punishments or cleanouts as a first resort. The agencies involved in task forces are responsible for the health and well-being of all residents. Don't be afraid to ask for their help.

- *Find a local hoarding support group.* Many task forces have started support groups or serve as clearinghouses of information about local support groups. If no groups exist in your area, consider starting one. To find people with hoarding problems to join the group, place a small ad in a local newspaper or community newsletter. Finding other people in your situation who live in your community may be a good first step on the road to your recovery. Our initial research on self-help support groups indicates that groups that use the protocol in our book *Buried in Treasures* can have a positive effect on members.
- *Read one of the self-help books mentioned in this chapter.*
- *Read* Digging Out *by Michael Tompkins and Tamara Hartl.* This book outlines a harm-reduction approach for family members of people who hoard and is especially helpful when loved ones do not recognize that they have a problem. The authors describe how to construct a team of helpers to work with a loved one to help him or her recognize and seek/accept help for hoarding.
- *Above all, try to maintain a positive and healthy relationship with a loved one who has a hoarding problem.* Keep in mind that the person's attachment to objects is something that he or she has little control over.

REFERENCE LIST

Prologue

Alighieri, D. (1954). *The Inferno* (J. Ciardi, Trans.). New Brunswick, NJ: Rutgers University Press, pp. 73–74.

Bank and Collyers declare a truce. (August 8, 1942). *New York Times.*

Black, D. W. (2007). A review of compulsive buying disorder. *World Psychiatry, 6,* 14–18.

Collyer hermit found dead in 5th Ave. hovel. (March 21, 1947). *New York Journal American.*

Collyer home search 'nightmare' to police. (April 5, 1947). *New York Times.*

Collyer home 'unsafe': Order for its demolition will be sought on Monday. (June 26, 1947). *New York Times.*

Collyer mansion keeps its secrets. (September 30, 1942). *New York Times.*

The Collyer mystery. (March 26, 1947). *New York Times.*

Collyers get deed to home. (December 21, 1942). *New York Times.*

Court fails to act on Collyer estate. (March 28, 1947). *New York Times.*

Erskine, H. W. (1954). *Out of This World.* New York: Bodley Head, chap. 1.

Faber, H. (March 22, 1947). Homer Collyer, Harlem recluse, found dead at 70. *New York Times.*

———. (March 25, 1947). Police fail to find Collyer in house. *New York Times.*

———. (April 8, 1947). Body of Collyer is found near where brother died. *New York Times.*

Frost, R., & Gross, R. (1993). The hoarding of possessions. *Behaviour Research and Therapy, 31,* 367–382.

Frost, R. O., Steketee, G., & Williams, L. (2000). Hoarding: A community health problem. *Health and Social Care in the Community, 8,* 229–234.

Garlington, S. W. (April 12, 1947). Exposes "Collyer fire-trap." *New York Amsterdam News.*

Government gets Collyer property. (February 4, 1943). *New York Times.*

Gray, C. (June 23, 2002). Wondering whether a park should keep its name. *New York Times.*

Grisham, J. R., Frost, R. O., Steketee, G., Kim, H.-J., & Hood, S. (2006). Age of onset of compulsive hoarding. *Journal of Anxiety Disorders, 20,* 675–686.

Haberman, C. (July 19, 2002). Name game is messy, really messy. *New York Times.*

If Homer dies, I'll barricade the house so no one will ever get in — Langley. (March 22, 1947). *New York World-Telegram.*

Kerby, K. (April 12, 1947). Believe Collyer house hides gold. *New York Amsterdam News.*

Kivel, M., & Desmond, J. (March 25, 1947). Cops sift Collyer junk but fail to find hermit. *New York Daily News.*

Kivel, M., & Neal, P. (March 29, 1947). Collyers' mansion sealed; cops keep a vigil over junk. *New York Daily News.*

Kivel, M., & Patterson, N. (March 28, 1947). Find hermit arsenal; FBI in hunt. *New York Daily News.*

———. (April 1, 1947). Start to clear Collyer house; Langley is ???. *New York Daily News.*

———. (April 2, 1947). Homer Collyer buried — no Langley. *New York Daily News.*

Langley Collyer reported going to Atlantic City. (March 30, 1947). *New York Herald Tribune.*

Lewis, H. C. (August 7, 1942). Collyer brother emerges, talks, ends mystery. *New York Herald Tribune.*

Lewis, M. (March 22, 1947). Homer Collyer dies amid junk, brother Langley can't be found. *New York Herald Tribune.*

———. (March 25, 1947). No trace of Collyer is found as police chop through roof. *New York Herald Tribune.*

———. (March 26, 1947). Collyer house search shifted to top floors: Police quit basement for fear of collapse. *New York Herald Tribune.*

Lidz, F. (2003). *Ghosty men: The strange but true story of the Collyer brothers, New York's greatest hoarders.* New York: Bloomsbury.

———. (October 26, 2003). The paper chase. *New York Times.*

Merge, M. (November 19, 1942). Collyers pay off $6,700 mortgage as evictors smash way into home. *New York Times.*

Mockbridge, N. (March 21, 1947). Collyer recluse found dead: Police crash old mansion, hunt brother. *New York World-Telegram.*

———. (March 24, 1947). Fantastic junk pours out of old mansion. *New York World-Telegram.*

Mortgage on recluses' home is foreclosed, but legendary brothers still hide within. (August 5, 1942). *New York Times.*

Mueller, A., Mueller, U., Albert, P., Mertens, C., Silbermann, A., Mitchell, J. E., & de Zwaan, M. (2007). Hoarding in a compulsive buying sample. *Behaviour Research and Therapy, 45,* 2754–2763.

Newman, A. (July 5, 2006). "Collyers' Mansion" is code for firefighters' nightmare. *New York Times.*

Neziroglu, F., Bubrick, J., & Yaryura-Tobias, J. A. (2004). *Overcoming compulsive hoarding.* Oakland, CA: New Harbinger.

Nobel, A., & Patterson, N. (March 22, 1947). One Hermit Collyer dead, hunt 2nd in ghosty house. *New York Daily News.*

Order ejects Collyers: Court gives control of Fifth Ave. property to bank. (October 2, 1942). *New York Times.*

Owen, R. (March 30, 1947). Something for O. Henry: Story of the Collyers. *New York Times.*

Rent house for junk taken from Collyers. (March 30, 1947). *New York Daily News.*

Samuels, J. F., Bienvenu, O. J., Grados, M. A., et al. (2008). Prevalence and correlates of hoarding behavior in a community-based sample. *Behaviour Research and Therapy, 46,* 836–844.

Steketee, G., & Frost, R. (2003). Compulsive hoarding: Current status of the research. *Clinical Psychology Review, 23,* 905–927.

Subpoena flushes Harlem recluse; Collyer in court to press charge. (July 24, 1946). *New York Times.*

The Talk of the Town. (April 5, 1947). *The New Yorker,* pp. 24–25.

3rd search starts at Collyer house. (April 1, 1947). *New York Times.*

Thousands gape at Collyer house. (March 24, 1947). *New York Times.*

200 bid spiritedly for Collyer items. (June 19, 1947). *New York Times.*

Where's Collyer? $1,500 reward. (March 30, 1947). *New York Daily News.*

1. Piles upon Piles

Fromm, E. (1947). *Man for himself: An inquiry into the psychology of ethics.* New York: Rinehart.

Frost, R. O., & Hartl, T. L. (1996). A cognitive-behavioral model of compulsive hoarding. *Behaviour Research and Therapy, 34,* 341–350.

Frost, R. O., Steketee, G., Tolin, D. F., & Brown, T. A. (March 2006). *Comorbidity and diagnostic issues in compulsive hoarding.* Paper presented at the annual meeting of the Anxiety Disorders Association of America, Miami, FL.

Tallis, F. (1996). Compulsive washing in the absence of phobic and illness anxiety. *Behaviour Research and Therapy, 34,* 361–362.

2. We Are What We Own

American Psychiatric Association. (2000). *Diagnostic and statistical manual of mental disorders—text revision* (4th ed.). Arlington, VA: American Psychiatric Association.

Apartment floor collapses from weight of old magazines. (February 8, 2005). *Mainichi Shimbun* (Japan).

Arndt, J., Solomon, S., Kasser, T., & Sheldon, K. M. (2004). The urge to splurge: A Terror Management account of materialism and consumer behavior. *Journal of Consumer Psychology, 14,* 198–212.

Associated Press. (May 24, 2007). The rise of the "McMansions." *Daily Hampshire Gazette.*

Beaglehole, E. (1932). *Property: A study in social psychology.* New York: Academic Press.

Belk, R. W. (1988). Possessions and the extended self. *Journal of Consumer Research, 15,* 139–168.

———. (1991). The ineluctable mysteries of possessions. *Journal of Social Behavior and Personality, 6,* 17–55.

———. (1995). Collecting as luxury consumption: Effects on individuals and households. *Journal of Economic Psychology, 16,* 477–490.

Bloom, L. (1991). People and property: A psychoanalytic view. *Journal of Social Behavior and Personality, 6,* 427–443.

Csikszentmihályi, M. (1990). *Flow: The psychology of optimal experience.* New York: Harper and Row.

Dickens, C. (2002). *Bleak House* (New ed.). New York: Modern Library. (Original work published 1852–1853)

Doyle, A. C. (1986). *Sherlock Holmes: The complete novels and serials* (Vol. 1). New York: Random House.

Frazer, J. G. (1940). *The golden bough: A study in magic and religion.* New York: Macmillan.

Fromm, E. (1947). *Man for himself: An inquiry into the psychology of ethics.* New York: Rinehart.

Furby, L. (1978). Possessions: Toward a theory of their meaning and function throughout the life cycle. In P. B. Bates (Ed.), *Life span development and behavior* (Vol. 1, pp. 297–331). New York: Academic Press.

Gannon, S. (March 8, 2007). "Hooked on storage." *New York Times.*

Gogol, N. V. (1961). *Dead Souls.* New York: Penguin Books.

Greenberg, J., Pyszczynski, T., & Solomon, S. (1986). The causes and consequences of a need for self-esteem: A terror management theory. In R. F. Baumeister (Ed.), *Public self and private self* (pp. 189–212). New York: Springer-Verlag.

Harlow, H. F., & Zimmermann, R. R. (1958). The development of affectional responses in infant monkeys. *Proceedings of the American Philosophical Society, 102,* 501–509.

Hay, D. F. (2006). Yours and mine: Toddlers' talk about possessions with familiar peers. *British Journal of Developmental Psychology, 24,* 39–52.

Hood, B. M., & Bloom, P. (2007). Children prefer certain individuals over perfect duplicates. *Cognition, 106,* 455–462.

Jacobs, K. (2005). Warhol's time machine. http://www.metropolismag.com.

James, W. (1890). *Principles of Psychology.* New York: Dover, p. 291.

Kellett, S. (2007). Compulsive hoarding: A site-security model and associated psychological treatment strategies. *Clinical Psychology and Psychotherapy, 14,* 413–427.

McIntosh, W. D., & Schmeichel, B. (2004). Collectors and collecting: A social psychological perspective. *Leisure Sciences, 26,* 85–97.

Milly, Jenna (2000). Rummaging through Andy Warhol's "junk." CNN.comNewsNet.

Muensterberger, W. (1994). *Collecting: An unruly passion.* New York: Harcourt Brace.

O'Brien, G. (April 26, 1981). Living with collections (Part 2). *New York Times Magazine,* pp. 25–42.

Olmsted, A. D. (1991). Collecting: Leisure, investment or obsession? *Journal of Social Behavior and Personality, 6,* 287–306.

Papi, S., Rhodes, A., Allara, P., Arnes, K., Brandt, F., Chermayeff, S., et al. (2002). *Possession obsession: Andy Warhol and collecting.* Pittsburgh: Andy Warhol Museum.

Pierce, J. L., Kostova, T., & Dirks, K. T. (2003). The state of psychological ownership: Integrating and extending a century of research. *Review of General Psychology, 7,* 84–107.

Pipes, R. (1999). *Property and freedom.* New York: Vintage Books.

Pivar, S. (1987). Shopping with Andy. http://www.warholstars.org.

Rudmin, F. W. (1991). "To own is to be perceived to own": A social cognitive look at the ownership of property. *Journal of Social Behavior and Personality, 6,* 85–104.

Schiffer, M. B., Downing, T. E., & McCarthy, M. (1981). Waste not, want not: Anthroarchaeological study of refuse in Tucson, Arizona. In M. Gould & M. B. Schiffer (Eds.), *Modern material culture: The archaeology of us,* pp. 67–86. New York: Academic Press.

Winnicott, D. W. (1953). Transitional objects and transitional phenomena: A study of the first not-me possession. *International Journal of Psycho-Analysis, 34,* 89–97.

3. Amazing Junk

Baker, J. H. (1989). *Mary Todd Lincoln: A biography.* New York: Norton.

Csikszentmihályi, M. (1990). *Flow: The psychology of optimal experience.* New York: Harper and Row.

Frost, R. O., Kyrios, M., McCarthy, K. D., & Mathews, Y. (2007). Self-ambivalence and attachment to possessions. *Journal of Cognitive Psychotherapy, 21,* 232–242.

Frost, R. O., Meagher, B. M., & Riskind, J. H. (2001). Obsessive-compulsive features in pathological lottery and scratch ticket gamblers. *Journal of Gambling Studies, 17,* 5–19.

Frost, R. O., Tolin, D. F., Steketee, G., Fitch, K. E., & Selbo-Bruns, A. (2009). Excessive acquisition in hoarding. *Journal of Anxiety Disorders, 23,* 632–639.

Koran, L. M., Faber, R. J., Aboujaoude, E., et al. (2006). Estimated prevalence of compulsive buying in the United States. *American Journal of Psychiatry, 163,* 1806–1812.

Lemonick, M., & Park, A. (July 16, 2007). The science of addiction. *Time,* 42–48.

Tolin, D. F., Frost, R. O., & Steketee, G. (2007). An open trial of cognitive-behavioral therapy for compulsive hoarding. *Behaviour Research and Therapy, 45,* 1461–1470.

4. Bunkers and Cocoons

Cromer, K. R., Schmidt, N. B., & Murphy, D. L. (2007). Do traumatic events influence the clinical expression of compulsive hoarding? *Behaviour Research and Therapy, 45,* 2581–2592.

Frost, R., & Gross, R. (1993). The hoarding of possessions. *Behaviour Research and Therapy, 31,* 367–382.

Frost, R. O., & Hartl, T. L. (1996). A cognitive-behavioral model of compulsive hoarding. *Behaviour Research and Therapy, 34,* 341–350.

Frost, R. O., Kyrios, M., McCarthy, K. D., & Mathews, Y. (2007). Self-ambivalence and attachment to possessions. *Journal of Cognitive Psychotherapy, 21,* 232–242.

Frost, R. O., Steketee, G., Tolin, D. F., & Brown, T. A. (March 2006). *Comorbidity and diagnostic issues in compulsive hoarding.* Paper presented at the annual meeting of the Anxiety Disorders Association of America, Miami, FL.

Frost, R. O., Steketee, G., & Williams, L. (2000). Hoarding: A community health problem. *Health and Social Care in the Community, 8,* 229–234.

Grisham, J. R., Frost, R. O., Steketee, G., Kim, H.-J., & Hood, S. (2006). Age of onset of compulsive hoarding. *Journal of Anxiety Disorders, 20,* 675–686.

Hartl, T. L., Duffany, S. R., Allen, G. J., Steketee, G., & Frost, R. O. (2005). Relationships among compulsive hoarding, trauma, and attention-deficit/hyperactivity disorder. *Behaviour Research and Therapy, 43,* 269–276.

Ripley, A. (2008). *The unthinkable: Who survives when disaster strikes—and why.* New York: Crown.

5. A Fragment of Me

American Psychiatric Association. (2000). *Diagnostic and statistical manual of mental disorders—text revision* (4th ed.). Arlington, VA: American Psychiatric Association.

Coles, M. E., Frost, R. O., Heimberg, R. G., & Rhéaume, J. (2003). "Not just right experiences": Perfectionism, obsessive-compulsive features and general psychopathology. *Behaviour Research and Therapy, 41,* 681–700.

Coles, M. E., Heimberg, R. G., Frost, R. O., & Steketee, G. (2005). Not just right experiences and obsessive-compulsive features: Experimental and self-monitoring perspectives. *Behaviour Research and Therapy, 43,* 153–167.

Storch, E. A., Lack, C. W., Merlo, L. J., Geffken, G. R., Jacob, M. L., Murphy, T. K., et al. (2007). Clinical features of children and adolescents with obsessive-compulsive disorder and hoarding symptoms. *Comprehensive Psychiatry, 48,* 313–318.

Summerfeldt, L. J. (2007). Treating incompleteness, ordering, and arranging concerns. In M. M. Antony, C. Purdon, & L. J. Summerfeldt (Eds.), *Psychological treatment of obsessive-compulsive disorder: Fundamentals and beyond,* pp. 187–208. Washington, DC: American Psychological Association.

Tolin, D. F., Kiehl, K. A., Worhunsky, P., Book, G. A., & Maltby, N. (2009). An exploratory study of the neural mechanisms of decision-making in compulsive hoarding. *Psychological Medicine, 39,* 313–323.

6. Rescue

Arluke, A., Frost, R., Steketee, G., Patronek, G., Luke, C., Messner, E., et al. (2002). Press reports of animal hoarding. *Society and Animals, 10,* 113–135.

Frost, R. O., Steketee, G., & Williams, L. (2000). Hoarding: A community health problem. *Health and Social Care in the Community, 8,* 229–234.

Hoarding of Animals Research Consortium. (May–June 2001). "Collectors"—the problem of animal hoarding. *Municipal Lawyer,* pp. 6–9, 19.

Hoarding of Animals Research Consortium. (2002). Public health implications of animal hoarding. *Health and Social Work,* 27, 125–136.

Patronek, G. J., Loar, L., & Nathanson, J. N. (2006). *Animal hoarding: Structuring interdisciplinary responses to help people, animals and communities at risk.* Boston: Hoarding of Animals Research Consortium.

Steketee, G., Gibson, A., Frost, R. O., Hoarding of Animals Research Consortium (HARC), & Alabisco, J. (2008). *Characteristics and antecedents of animal hoarding: A comparative interview study.* Unpublished manuscript.

7. A River of Opportunities

Brace, P. B. (November 21, 2007). Hoarding becomes a health, safety issue. *Nantucket Independent.*

8. Avoiding the Agony

Clark, D. M. (1999). Anxiety disorders: Why they persist and how to treat them. *Behaviour Research and Therapy,* 37, S5–S27.

Coles, M. E., Frost, R. O., Heimberg, R. G., & Steketee, G. (2003). Hoarding behaviors in a large college sample. *Behaviour Research and Therapy,* 41, 179–194.

Deacon, B., & Maack, D. J. (2008). The effects of safety behaviors on the fear of contamination: An experimental investigation. *Behaviour Research and Therapy,* 46, 537–547.

Eelen, P., & Vervliet, B. (2006). Fear conditioning and clinical implications: What can we learn from the past? In M. G. Craske, D. Hermans, & D. Vansteenwegen (Eds.), *Fear and learning: From basic processes to clinical implications,* pp. 17–35. Washington, DC: American Psychological Association.

Salkovskis, P. M., Clark, D. M., Hackmann, A., Wells, A., & Gelder, M. G. (1999). An experimental investigation of the role of safety behaviors in the maintenance of panic disorder with agoraphobia. *Behaviour Research and Therapy,* 37, 559–574.

9. You Haven't Got a Clue

Clark, A. N., Mankikar, G. D., & Gray, I. (1975). Diogenes syndrome: A clinical study of gross self-neglect in old age. *Lancet,* 1, 366–368.

Cybulska, E., & Rucinski, J. (1986). Gross self-neglect in old age. *British Journal of Hospital Medicine,* 36, 21–25.

Damecour, C. L., & Charron, M. (1998). Hoarding: A symptom, not a syndrome. *Journal of Clinical Psychiatry,* 59, 267–272.

Drummond, L. M., Turner, J., & Reid, S. (1997). Diogenes' syndrome—A load of old rubbish. *Irish Journal of Psychiatric Medicine,* 14, 99–102.

Halliday, G., Banerjee, S., Philpot, M., & MacDonald, A. (2000). Community study of people who live in squalor. *Lancet, 335,* 882–886.

MacMillan, D., & Shaw, P. (1966). Senile breakdown in standards of personal and environmental cleanliness. *British Medical Journal, 2,* 1032–1037.

Rosenthal, M., Stelian, J., & Berkman, P. (1999). Diogenes syndrome and hoarding in the elderly: Case reports. *Israel Journal of Psychiatry and Related Sciences, 36,* 29–34.

Snowdon, J., Shah, A., & Halliday, G. (2007). Severe domestic squalor: A review. *International Psychogeriatrics, 19,* 37–51.

10. A Tree with Too Many Branches

Anderson, S. W., Damasio, H., & Damasio, A. R. (2005). A neural basis for collecting behaviour in humans. *Brain, 128,* 201–212.

Burkhardt, R. W. (2005). *Patterns of behavior: Konrad Lorenz, Niko Tinbergen, and the founding of ethology.* Chicago: University of Chicago Press.

Frost, R., & Gross, R. (1993). The hoarding of possessions. *Behaviour Research and Therapy, 31,* 367–382.

Harlow, J. M. (1868). Recovery from the passage of an iron bar through the head. *Publication of the Massachusetts Medical Society, 2,* 329–347.

Hartl, T. L., Duffany, S. R., Allen, G. J., Steketee, G., & Frost, R. O. (2005). Relationships among compulsive hoarding, trauma, and attention-deficit/hyperactivity disorder. *Behaviour Research and Therapy, 43,* 269–276.

Samuels, J., Shugart, Y. Y., Grados, M. A., et al. (2007). Significant linkage to compulsive hoarding on chromosome 14 in families with obsessive-compulsive disorder: Results from the OCD collaborative genetics study. *American Journal of Psychiatry, 164,* 493–499.

Saxena, S., Brody, A. L., Maidment, K. M., Smith, E., Zohrabi, N., Katz, E., et al. (2004). Cerebral glucose metabolism in obsessive-compulsive hoarding. *American Journal of Psychiatry, 161,* 1038–1048.

Smith, J. P. (1990). *Mammalian behavior: The theory and the science.* Tuckahoe, NY: Bench Mark Books.

Tolin, D. F., Kiehl, K. A., Worhunsky, P., Book, G. A., & Maltby, N. (2009). An exploratory study of the neural mechanisms of decision-making in compulsive hoarding. *Psychological Medicine, 39,* 313–323.

Zhang, H., Leckman, J. F., Pauls, D. L., Tsai, C. P., Kidd, K. K., Campos, M. R., et al. (2002). Genomewide scan of hoarding in sib pairs in which both sibs have Gilles de la Tourette syndrome. *American Journal of Human Genetics, 70,* 896–904.

11. A Pack Rat in the Family

Children of Hoarders (COH). http://www.childrenofhoarders.com.

Fromm, E. (1947). *Man for himself: An inquiry into the psychology of ethics.* New York: Rinehart.

Frost, R., & Gross, R. (1993). The hoarding of possessions. *Behaviour Research and Therapy, 31,* 367–382.

Grisham, J. R., Steketee, G., & Frost, R. O. (2008). Interpersonal problems and emotional intelligence in compulsive hoarding. *Depression and Anxiety, 25,* E63.

Overcoming Hoarding Together (O-H-T). http://health.groups.yahoo.com/group/O-H-T/.

Pollard, C. A. (2007). Treatment readiness. In M. M. Antony, C. Purdon, & L. J. Summerfeldt (Eds.), *Psychological treatment of obsessive-compulsive disorder: Fundamentals and beyond,* pp. 61–77. Washington, DC: American Psychological Association.

Tolin, D. F., Frost, R. O., Steketee, G., & Fitch, K. E. (2008). Family burden of compulsive hoarding: Results of an Internet survey. *Behaviour Research and Therapy, 46,* 334–344.

Steketee, G., Frost, R. O., & Kim, H.-J. (2001). Hoarding by elderly people. *Health and Social Work, 26,* 176–184.

12. But It's Mine!

Clarke, D. J., Boer, H., Whittington, J., Holland, A., Butler, J., & Webb, T. (2002). Prader-Willi syndrome, compulsive and ritualistic behaviours: The first population-based survey. *British Journal of Psychiatry, 189,* 358–362.

Mataix-Cols, D., Nakatani, E., Micali, N., & Heyman, I. (2008). The structure of obsessive-compulsive symptoms in pediatric OCD. *Journal of Affective Disorders, 109,* 117–126.

Olmstead, A. D. (1991). Collecting: Leisure, investment or obsession? *Journal of Social Behavior and Personality, 6,* 287–306.

Plimpton, E. H., Frost, R. O., Abbey, B. C., & Dorer, W. (2009). Compulsive hoarding in children: 6 case studies. *International Journal of Cognitive Therapy, 2,* 88–104.

Rufer, M., Grothusen, A., MaB, R., Peter, H., & Hand, I. (2005). Temporal stability of symptom dimensions in adult patients with obsessive-compulsive disorder. *Journal of Affective Disorders, 88,* 99–102.

Russell, A. J., Mataix-Cols, D., Anson, M., & Murphy, D.G.M. (2005). Obsessions and compulsions in Asperger syndrome and high-functioning autism. *British Journal of Psychiatry, 186,* 525–528.

Storch, E. A., Lack, C. W., Merlo, L. J., Geffken, G. R., Jacob, M. L., Murphy, T. K., et al. (2007). Clinical features of children and adolescents with obsessive-compulsive disorder and hoarding symptoms. *Comprehensive Psychiatry, 48,* 313–318.

Tolin, D. F., Frost, R. O., & Steketee, G. (2009). *The course of compulsive hoarding and its relationship to life events.* Unpublished manuscript.

Wagner, A. P. (2004). *Up and down the worry hill: A children's book about obsessive-compulsive disorder and its treatment.* Deerfield Beach, FL: Lighthouse Press.

13. Having, Being, and Hoarding

Abrahamson, E., & Freedman, D. H. (2007). *A perfect mess: The hidden benefits of disorder.* Boston: Little, Brown.

Anxiety Disorders Association of America. http://www.adaa.org.

Association for Behavioral and Cognitive Therapies. http://www.abct.org.

Clutterers Anonymous. http://sites.google.com/site/clutterersanonymous/Home.

Clutterless Recovery Groups. http://www.clutterless.org.

De Graaf, J., Wann, D., & Naylor, T. H. (2005). *Affluenza: The all-consuming epidemic* (2nd ed.). San Francisco: Berrett-Koehler.

Freecycle Network. http://www.freecycle.org.

Fromm, E. (1947). *Man for himself: An inquiry into the psychology of ethics.* New York: Rinehart.

————. (1976). *To have or to be?* New York: Continuum.

Frost, R. O., Kyrios, M., McCarthy, K. D., & Matthews, Y. (2007). Self-ambivalence and attachment to possessions. *Journal of Cognitive Psychotherapy, 21,* 232–242.

Gannon, Suzanne. (March 8, 2007). Hooked on storage. *New York Times.*

Messies Anonymous. http://www.messies.com.

Muroff, J., Steketee, G., Himle, J., & Frost, R. (forthcoming). Delivery of Internet treatment for compulsive hoarding (D.I.T.C.H.). *Behaviour Research and Therapy.*

National Association of Professional Organizers. http://www.napo.net.

National Study Group on Chronic Disorganization. http://www.nsgcd.org.

Neziroglu, F., Bubrick, J., & Yaryura-Tobias, J. A. (2004). *Overcoming compulsive hoarding.* Oakland, CA: New Harbinger.

Obsessive Compulsive Foundation. http://www.ocfoundation.org.

Overcoming Hoarding Together (O-H-T). http://health.groups.yahoo.com/group/O-H-T/.

Steketee, G., & Frost, R. (2007). *Compulsive hoarding and acquiring: Therapist guide and workbook.* New York: Oxford University Press.

Steketee, G., Frost, R. O., Tolin, D. F., Rasmussen, J., & Brown, T. (manuscript in preparation). Cognitive behavior therapy for compulsive hoarding: Results from a waitlist-controlled trial.

Tolin, D. F., Frost, R. O., & Steketee, G. (2007). *Buried in treasures: Help for compulsive acquiring, saving, and hoarding.* New York: Oxford University Press.

Tompkins, M. A., & Hartl, T. L. (2009). *Digging out: Helping your loved one manage clutter, hoarding, and compulsive acquiring.* Oakland, CA: New Harbinger.

Van Boven, L. (2005). Experientialism, materialism, and the pursuit of happiness. *Review of General Psychology, 9,* 132–142.

ACKNOWLEDGMENTS

A number of people helped us throughout the process of this work. The feedback and encouragement of our agent, Taryn Fagerness, was invaluable. Without her, we would have been lost. Several others provided editorial assistance along the way, including Andrea Schulz, Ellen Garrison, Cassandra Phillips, Lindsey Smith, and Erica Frost. We thank them for their helpful commentary.

Randy thanks his wife, Sue, for her support throughout the writing of this book, and his children, Erica and Olivia, whose interest and enthusiasm for this work keep it going.

Gail gives thanks and much credit to her husband, Brian, who patiently tolerated the endless hours she spent closeted away in her study writing. She also thanks her family and friends, who help keep her sane and focused on what matters in this world.